PSYCHOLOGICAL PERSPECTIVES IN EDUCATION

Mark Fox

CASSELL

Cassell Educational Limited
Villiers House   387 Park Avenue South
41/47 Strand   New York
London WC2N 5JE   NY 10016-8810

First published 1993

British Library Cataloguing in Publication Data
A catalogue record for this book is available from the British Library.

ISBN   0-304-32467-1 (hardback)
       0-304-32470-1 (paperback)

Typeset by Coltype Pte. Ltd., Singapore
Printed and bound in Great Britain by
Biddles Ltd, Guildford and King's Lynn

This book is dedicated to Sheila, without whom nothing would have been possible.

CONTENTS

Part 3 Perspectives on the classroom

FOREWORD

The 1980s and 1990s have witnessed unprecedented changes to the education system. These have had a dramatic impact, particularly in relation to:

- schools' relationships with parents and the community;
- the funding and management of schools;
- the curriculum;
- the assessment of children's learning.

It can be an extremely daunting task for student teachers to unravel the details and implications of these initiatives. This Introduction to Education series therefore offers a comprehensive analysis and evaluation of educational theory and practice in the light of recent developments.

The series examines topics and issues of concern to those entering the teaching profession. Major themes representing a spectrum of educational opinion are presented in a clear, balanced and analytic manner.

The authors in the series are authorities in their field. They emphasize the need to have a well-informed and critical teaching profession and present a positive and optimistic view of the teacher's role. They endorse the view that teachers have a significant influence over the extent to which any legislation or ideology is translated into effective classroom practice.

Each author addresses similar issues, which can be summarized as:

- presenting and debating theoretical perspectives within appropriate social, political, and educational contexts;
- identifying key arguments;

- identifying individuals who have made significant contributions to the field under review;
- discussing and evaluating key legislation;
- critically evaluating research and highlighting implications for classroom practice;
- providing an overview of the current state of debate within each field;
- describing the features of good practice.

The books are written primarily for student teachers. However, they will be of interest and value to all those involved in education.

Jonathan Solity
Series Editor

ACKNOWLEDGEMENTS

I would like to thank my educational psychology colleagues in Essex Local Educational Authority and my teaching colleagues in the Departments of Psychology and Educational Management at the University of East London for their support and advice over the last five years. It was working in these three situations that broadened my perspectives on psychology and education and fed directly and indirectly into the contents of this book.

INTRODUCTION

This book aims to empower teachers by giving them a wide range of psychological perspectives that facilitate their understanding of the process of education. Psychological perspectives, or theories, give diverse frames of reference from which teachers can view education. The interaction between pupils and teachers can be seen in a variety of ways, and psychological theories give insights into the complexity of the teaching and learning processes.

It is helpful to recognize that psychology is not a pure science – there are no hard facts that can be definitely proved. This is of fundamental importance if psychology is to be useful to teachers. Any situation can be seen and explained from a number of perspectives: for example the pupil has a very different perspective from the teacher's on what is happening in the classroom, and a newly qualified teacher has a very different perspective from the headteacher's on a disruptive pupil. Psychological theory can be considered as providing frames of reference, or orientations, that are useful in understanding people. We each find different perspectives the most useful.

THE IMPORTANCE OF PSYCHOLOGICAL THEORY

What is the value of psychological theories if no perspective can be validated and proved to be true? The answer to this is based on the fact that we already all hold theories in our heads to help us to understand the world – without them it would be completely incomprehensible. We would be unable to act, as we would have to start from first principles in every situation with which we were confronted. Our actions in any situation depend on the theories that we hold.

Of specific concern to this book is the theories teachers have about the way development and learning occur. Every time teachers teach we can see their theories in action. These theories may be unspoken and teachers may not even be able to articulate them. Nevertheless, for all of us, any action will be based on a theory that we have.

These theories in action, or theories in use, as they are called, can be contrasted with 'espoused' theories (Argyris, 1989; Schon, 1987). Espoused theories are those that we claim to follow; theories in use are those that can be inferred from our actions. Understanding the distinction between espoused theory and theory in use is critical, as there is often a large gap between the two. For example, there is within teaching a generally espoused theory about the importance of teaching the pupil at the appropriate level. The theory in use, though, means that pupils are mostly taught as a homogeneous group. Another example is the espoused theory of equal opportunities: for most of education there is a theory in use that ignores equal opportunities. Recognizing this gap between espoused theory and theory in use is a key concern for educationists.

Argyris (1989) and Schon (1987) suggest that the means for narrowing this gap is to work as a reflective practitioner. Although we are by definition aware of our espoused theories, we are often unaware of our theories in use, and unable to articulate them. But theories in use are consistent with what we do. By having a range of psychological perspectives, teachers may find it easier to recognize their theories in use and to be able to turn these into espoused theories.

THE RANGE OF FACTORS

Psychological perspectives can help teachers develop a logical and unified theory of action that will inform their teaching practice. This does not mean that there is one best psychological perspective that is the basis for effective education – there is not.

In any situation there are a large number of factors that influence what happens. For instance, a pupil's progress in mathematics is affected by a wide range of elements. These can be internal, such as the pupil's self-esteem; factors in the classroom, such as the teacher's motivation; factors in the school, such as whether the school can afford the latest textbooks; and family factors, such as the parents' concern about mathematics. These factors can be helpfully represented as a 'fishbone' (see Figure 1), where the forces can be seen acting on the specific issue. Within each of the 'bones' there is a range of forces operating, each of which will affect the pupil's progress at mathematics.

Most theoretical psychological perspectives attempt to account for the educational process by focusing on one of these factors, such as the

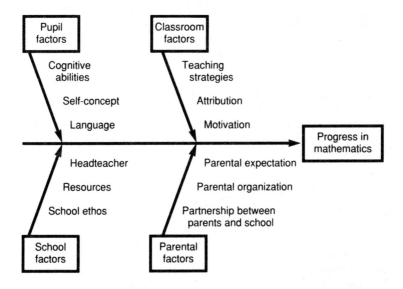

Figure 1   Fishbone of factors.

pupil's motivation. These perspectives are helpful in explaining one particular factor. But because of the intermeshed complexity of the educational process, such single-eyed perspectives are unlikely to provide answers to the question of how pupils can be taught most effectively. Because of this complexity, in recent years some practising educational psychologists prefer to think in terms of a contingency theory, which emphasizes that the most effective way of teaching is contingent upon a wide range of factors. We need to have a broad perspective so that we can spell out factors relating to the teacher, the pupils and the situation itself before we can begin to form hypotheses about how we can make education more effective. By focusing on one factor, be that curriculum, teaching methods, or the pupil's ability, we distort our view of the real complexity of the educational process. The danger is that we do this in order to simplify it so that it makes sense to us, and in a way that reinforces our present perception.

This is particularly dangerous because people are not passive receptors of the factors that affect them; people actively create their own world. A teacher is not like a video camera responding to what it sees in the environment. Teachers who are concerned about the curriculum actively make that the key factor that affects learning in their classrooms, just as pupils who are particularly concerned about peer relationships turn this into a significant factor in their learning environment. We actively create our own factors within our own learning environment. If we fail to recognize that other

3

people see the world differently and have equally strong beliefs about the importance of other perspectives, we are unlikely to understand them.

THE STRUCTURE OF THE BOOK

The book is structured to examine some of these key factors from different perspectives. The three parts focus on three different aspects of education:

- perspectives on the pupil;
- perspectives on the teacher;
- perspectives on the classroom.

Part 1 focuses on psychological perspectives on the pupil. Two main areas are addressed: pupils' behaviour and pupils' thinking. Chapter 1 provides frameworks for understanding pupils' actions and behaviour, a fundamental area of interest to teachers. Chapter 2 provides models for understanding pupils' thinking, and explores the development of new models for understanding intelligence and their relationship with cognitive processing models. One of psychology's key contributions is understanding both how and why pupils develop and change. Chapters 3 and 4 build on the preceding two chapters to examine teachers' influence on both the cognitive and personal development of pupils.

Part 2 focuses on psychological perspectives that help teachers' understanding of themselves. In particular, Chapter 5 examines the basis for stereotypes and prejudice in education. Chapter 6 is concerned with motivation and addresses the question of why teachers are energized only in certain circumstances. Finally, Chapter 7 looks at how teachers explain, or attribute, success and failure in the classroom. Though Part 2 focuses on teachers, the psychological perspectives also apply to pupils' attitudes, motivation and attribution.

Part 3 knits together these perspectives, focusing on classroom life as an interactive process between teachers and pupils. Chapter 8 deals with psychological theories that underpin effective classroom management, particularly the importance of the pupil–teacher relationship. Chapter 9 is concerned with the psychology of groups and how pupils dynamically affect each other. The final two chapters pull together this interactive perspective: Chapter 10 is concerned with the teaching strategies that teachers use for particular tasks, and Chapter 11 is the reciprocal of this, dealing with the learning strategies that pupils use in order to learn effectively.

To aid clarity, throughout the book teachers are referred to as female and pupils as male. This raises a fundamental issue as it might seem to imply that there are no differences between male and female pupils and teachers. This is not so. There is increasing evidence that psychological research may not be generalizable across gender. However, this new research is fragmented, and most research that has been done in the past does not account for differences in gender. It will take a second edition of this book to pull this perspective on gender into a coherent framework.

Another word of caution needs to be applied particularly to Part 2. Much of the original research here was not carried out on teachers specifically. I have made it explicit when teachers were the subject of the research, but when the theories stem from a more general perspective than that of education, teachers will have to decide whether this applies to them.

Psychology offers a variety of vital perspectives at every level within education. This book provides frameworks that allow teachers to understand themselves and how important their actions are to pupils' development. It is essential that teachers in the 1990s feel empowered by psychology and use it in a creative way to develop as reflective practitioners.

REFERENCES

Argyris, C. (1989) *Reasoning, Learning and Action – Individual and Organizational.* San Francisco: Jossey-Bass.

Schon, D. (1987) *Educating the Reflective Practitioner.* London: Jossey-Bass.

PART 1

PERSPECTIVES ON THE PUPIL

CHAPTER 1

Understanding pupils

OVERVIEW

Classrooms are busy places and understanding what is happening in them is difficult for teachers. Some pupils are quiet, others talk to their peers, some work hard, while others look out of the window. Every now and then an incident happens that interrupts the whole class; someone loses his temper, or just moves out of his seat. Teachers need to understand the factors that are influencing pupils' actions, in order to be better able to teach particular pupils. Different psychological theories emphasize the importance of different factors. Pupils are complex, however, and no one theory gives a complete understanding. In fact, the first step in understanding pupils is to realize just how complex they are.

This chapter focuses on:

- external factors - the situation the pupil is in;
- internal factors - pupils' thoughts and beliefs;
- the relationship of thoughts to feelings;
- an interactive perspective - reciprocal determinism.

EXTERNAL FACTORS: THE SITUATION THE PUPIL IS IN

Understanding pupil behaviour

The central position of behavioural psychology is that the mind cannot be studied scientifically and therefore cannot be the focus of psychology. The focus in behavioural psychology is on pupils 'behaviour': that is, everything pupils do – their actions. Behaviour is a neutral term. It is not used in the sense of 'good' or 'bad' behaviour. Behavioural psychology starts from the premise that to understand pupils one must observe them and their situation closely. So if a pupil is having a temper tantrum in class, the focus is on exactly what he does and what the external circumstances are – the situation that he is in. Behavioural psychologists do not focus on internal factors such as what pupils are thinking or how they are feeling.

To understand the behaviour, the teacher needs to understand the circumstances that surround it: in particular, what happens before the behaviour – the antecedents – and what happens after the behaviour – the consequences (see Figure 1.1).

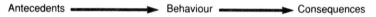

Antecedents ⟶ Behaviour ⟶ Consequences

Figure 1.1 Understanding behaviour.

The antecedents are ordinary classroom events – what the teacher and other pupils say and do. Antecedents can be seen as the triggers for the behaviour. The consequences are the way the teacher and the other pupils react to the behaviour. Consequences can be seen in terms of whether the pupil's behaviour has been reinforced – whether he has been encouraged or discouraged to behave in this way.

Understanding behaviour

Pupils' behaviour does not occur in a vacuum but depends on the situation they are in, and in particular on the antecedents and consequences. The antecedents are what happen before, and trigger the behaviour. The consequences are what happen after, and reinforce the behaviour. By closely observing the antecedents and consequences, teachers can understand pupils' behaviour in the classroom; by altering the antecedents and consequences, teachers can change this behaviour.

Understanding how the antecedents and consequences affect behaviour is the main focus of behavioural psychology. To understand pupils, teachers have to understand the situation they are in. The world acts on them, not the other way around. Behaviourists believe that the situation determines the pupils' actions.

Antecedents

Antecedents can be any number of things going on in the classroom around the pupil. The most obvious are what the teacher or another pupil says. If the teacher says, 'Get out your books', this triggers the pupils taking out their books. The teacher's request is a clear trigger (or antecedent) for the pupils' behaviour.

Antecedents can, however, be much more subtle than a direct request. They can be the actual situation; for example, where the pupil is sitting. Pupils sitting on a particular side of the room may be more likely to have a full view of the teacher and as result may talk more. Or antecedents may be the behaviour of another pupil; for example, if a pupil is sitting beside another pupil who keeps interrupting him, he may eventually become angry. Or antecedents can be the time of the day; the pupil may be particularly excited just before home time and therefore overreact to the teacher's request to start work again.

The first step in understanding pupils is to look at the antecedents for the behaviour in the classroom. For example, if the teacher wants the pupil to work quietly, she needs to identify what antecedents normally precede his doing so. These may include where the pupil is sitting, the work he is given to do, and the instructions he is given, as well as other factors.

Antecedents can be seen as cues that pupils have learnt for particular behaviour. For example, the antecedents can be the headteacher's footsteps along the corridor (see Figure 1.2). The pupils have learnt to recognize the cue; the footsteps coming down the corridor alert them to what will happen next. The sound reminds them of previous times when the head has come in and told them off for not working. The headteacher, of course, may also be well aware of the effectiveness of walking along the corridors. Headteachers have been known to wear shoes that make a particularly loud noise so that their presence triggers off the desired behaviour!

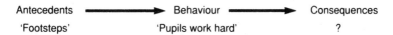

Figure 1.2   Cues for behaviour.

The importance of antecedents becomes even more apparent when considering effective classroom management. Effective teachers recognize and control the key antecedents, the triggers, within the classroom.* Kounin (1970) has shown that, contrary to popular belief, effective teachers are not those who deal better with misbehaviour after it occurs. Rather, effective teachers are those who organize the antecedents to ensure appropriate behaviour in the first place.* The

which teachers can control in class and which affect
ar are:

apings of pupils;
room and lesson organization;
ching strategies;
matching tasks to the pupils' learning strategies.

These factors are dealt with in the final part of this book, 'Perspectives
on the classroom'.

There are therefore two important reasons for understanding antecedents. They give cues to what is triggering off individual pupil
behaviour, and by close observation teachers can analyse the antecedents which lead to a pupil's behaviour. More importantly,
antecedents underpin all successful teaching; by effectively managing
them the teacher creates a positive learning environment.

The importance of consequences

The simple proposition that all behaviour is learnt is the starting point
for much of behavioural psychology and has immediate implications
for teachers.

Behaviour is learnt

A fundamental tenet of behavioural psychology is that all
behaviour is learnt. Pupils are not born to act in an aggressive,
talkative or cooperative way, but, as they grow up, they learn
how to act from the consequences of their behaviour. If a
pupil's behaviour is followed by a pleasant consequence then
he is likely to repeat that behaviour when he is in the same
situation again; conversely, if a behaviour is followed by an
unpleasant consequence then the pupil is less likely to repeat
that behaviour in a similar situation.

Consider a teacher with a class of pupils who have never been to
school before. The teacher wants the pupils to learn that they are to
sit quietly on the floor when she claps her hands. The teacher claps her
hands; the pupils may look at her, but as they have not learnt how else
to behave they go on playing and talking. The teacher now claps again
and tells the pupils what to do. She accompanies this by reinforcing the
pupils through praise, and giving them a chance to play with some
special activities – a pleasant consequence for them – when they sit
on the floor. The pupils who do not respond by sitting on the floor are
told off – an unpleasant consequence. They will quickly learn

Figure 1.3 The importance of consequences.

to sit quietly on the floor when the teacher claps her hands – the antecedent. The appropriate behaviour is reinforced, or encouraged, by the teacher (see Figure 1.3).

Consequences are often known as reinforcers, as they reinforce or strengthen learning. In a series of experiments, conducted over a 30-year period, B. F. Skinner (see box) developed the whole concept of reinforcement theory, which is at the centre of behavioural psychology.

Burrhus Frederic Skinner (1904–90)

B. F. Skinner is one of the most influential figures in the development of psychology. He was born in Pennsylvania and received a PhD from Harvard in 1931. His aim was to provide a totally objective and scientific approach to psychology, and he constructed a complete learning theory on the principles of reinforcement. He founded this theory on work with rats and pigeons – which is where the image of rat-obsessed psychologists originated! In his most controversial book, *Beyond Freedom and Dignity* (1971), he applied behaviourism to basic humanitarian concepts such as freedom, values and dignity.

Rewards and punishments

Rewards are positive reinforcers; they are anything a teacher can do to encourage pupils to behave in a certain way. Rewards lead to an increase in desired behaviour. They might include letting the pupils out at lunchtime early, or praising them, or letting them colour a picture. Similarly, pupils can be discouraged from behaving in certain ways by being punished. Punishments can be being made to sit in a particular seat, or to complete their work before they go out to play. Punishment is any undesirable consequence for the pupil that leads to a decrease in the unwanted behaviour.

Rewards and punishments can be defined only by whether they strengthen or weaken a particular piece of behaviour. In other words, they are operationally defined by their consequence. A teacher may believe that praising a pupil for quickly finishing a piece of work is a

13

...t if the pupil completes the next piece of work more slowly,
/ seen that praise actually acts as a punishment.

ɛ are significant differences between what pupils and teachers
.der are effective rewards (Burns, 1978). In his research Burns
.ıd that pupils preferred:

- favourable home report;
- to do well in a test;
- to be given a prize;
- to receive good marks for written work.

Teachers thought the most effective rewards for pupils were:

- to be praised in the presence of others;
- good marks for written work;
- to be elected to leadership by fellow pupils;
- the teacher expressing quiet appreciation.

Pupils and teachers are two global groups and clearly individual pupils
will value different specific rewards. Pupils' preferences for different
rewards change as they get older, and so the above list simply gives
examples of differences in the two groups' views rather than any hard
and fast guidelines on how to reward individual pupils.

A range of rewards is in fact used in schools with pupils (Forness,
1973). Some of these are concrete 'goodies' but many are based on social
interaction – particularly praise:

- **Edibles.** Food is used successfully as a reward for pupils with
  severe learning difficulties. For example, small drinks are given to
  pupils after they have completed difficult tasks. Parents often use
  edibles, such as sweets, as a reward for their children.
- **Exchangeables.** These usually take the form of tokens that the
  pupil receives from the teacher. They can be exchanged for something which is of value to the pupil. Points, stars and stickers are
  all examples of tokens that are used successfully in schools. Many
  schools have a well-developed point system that is used to
  encourage appropriate behaviour.
- **Activities.** These pair a desired behaviour with an activity which
  the pupil likes to do. The system is based on 'Gran's adage': 'When
  you've finished your vegetables then you can go out to play.' In
  school, the teacher may allow pupils to draw a picture when they
  have finished their writing.
- **Social rewards.** Social rewards such as praise and attention are frequently used and particularly effective in the classroom. Wheldall
  (1987) in *The Behaviourist in the Classroom* describes just how
  important positive praise is to pupils.

This 'reward menu' illustrates the fact that the rewards teachers have
available in the classroom are not complex or unnatural – they are

simple natural responses that reinforce pupils' appropriate actions. It is interesting that praise, probably the simplest to administer, is also the most powerful. Teachers often underestimate the positive effect that simple praise can have on pupils in the classroom. Rewards are easily at hand for the teacher, but they require organization if they are to have a positive effect in the classroom.

To encourage appropriate behaviour

A teacher can encourage pupils to behave in an appropriate way, such as completing a page of work, by rewarding them. It must be remembered that 'appropriate' and 'inappropriate' are defined in this context by the teacher. Rewarding is actively encouraging the pupil by repeatedly following the appropriate behaviour with something that the pupil likes. So if a pupil likes praise, then praising him following the completion of a page of writing is reinforcing.

To eliminate inappropriate behaviour

A teacher can eliminate inappropriate behaviour by withholding rewards or by using punishment. Repeatedly withholding rewards when inappropriate behaviour occurs is passive discouragement – for example, the teacher not praising a pupil while he is wandering around the class. Punishment is actively discouraging inappropriate behaviour by repeatedly following it with something the pupil dislikes. So if a pupil does not like to be told off, then being told off when he is wandering around the class is a punishment.

The difficulties of using punishment to change behaviour

Behaviourists do not advocate using punishment to change behaviour. Skinner (1971) describes a number of reasons why punishment does not work. If a teacher uses punishment the pupil may learn how to behave appropriately in order not to be punished, but the process has a number of other possible effects:

- It teaches pupils not to be caught. Pupils who are punished for bullying may learn not to be seen bullying by the teacher. They may learn not to bully at school – and bully instead on the bus going home.
- It does not teach the pupil an alternative way to act. Telling the pupil off every time he talks does not help the pupil to complete the school work which he is talking about.
- It creates feelings of bitterness, tension and stress between the pupils and the teacher. The pupil who is constantly punished by the teacher will simply grow to dislike her.

15

- It may have no effect because the pupil is also being rewarded for the behaviour by his peers. The pupil who acts 'tough' may receive peer approval, which may be more reinforcing than the teacher's punishment.

Because of these difficulties with using punishments, rewards are the most effective way of affecting pupils' behaviour. The teacher can teach pupils ways of behaving by rewarding them to encourage desired behaviour, and by withholding rewards to eliminate undesired behaviour. The secret is in choosing the right reward and applying it consistently. If teachers are fair and consistent with their use of reinforcers, pupils will learn what is appropriate and inappropriate behaviour in the classroom.

Implications of the behavioural perspective for teachers

Behavioural psychology grew in popularity because of its immediate practical application. It offers a way for teachers to understand how the situation affects pupils' behaviour. As all behaviour is learnt, the teacher can teach new ways of behaving through the appropriate use of rewards and the management of the antecedents. This means that what happens around the pupils is vital to their development. Teachers' management of the classroom is the major determinant of pupils' actions. The early success of behavioural approaches, however, produced a backlash at the end of the 1970s and in the 1980s. One promise it could not keep was that all behaviour could be changed through the appropriate use of reinforcements. Teachers still found that they had aggressive, noisy and disruptive pupils in their classes.

Behavioural psychology seems simple to apply. The problem is that it is often misapplied and teachers fail to understand either what is maintaining the pupil's behaviour or the best ways of changing the situation the pupil is in. The close observation of pupils' behaviour which is required to understand the antecedents and consequences is time-consuming and far from as straightforward as might be thought. Teachers also resist the idea that they should reward 'naughty' pupils. It is only in the last few years that changing the antecedents has been recognized as being just as important as the use of rewards. Finally, behavioural psychology, with its emphasis on external factors, does not fit easily with many teachers' beliefs about the importance of internal factors such as thoughts and feelings in understanding pupils.

It is important to recognize that behavioural psychologists' emphasis on the situation is one perspective that helps in understanding pupils. It is a perspective that can be complemented by others, and in particular by emphasizing the importance of internal factors – pupils' thoughts and beliefs.

INTERNAL FACTORS: PUPILS' THOUGHTS AND BELIEFS

The difficulties in focusing simply on the situation and obser behaviour emphasize the importance of thoughts and beliefs (inte.nal factors) when understanding pupils. Thoughts and beliefs can be seen as mediating between the situation and the pupil's actions. The situation is one key to understanding the pupil, but a pupil brings to any situation what has happened to him in the past. His reaction depends on his memory of what has happened before in similar situations. To understand a pupil's actions the present situation must be analysed, but so must the pupil's thoughts about it. Listening to what pupils say about the way they are thinking helps teachers understand their actions.

Personal construct psychology

The most useful approach to understanding pupils' thoughts and beliefs is personal construct psychology, developed by George Kelly (1955). Personal construct psychology is known as a cognitive theory, as it emphasizes the importance of internal factors – pupils' thoughts and beliefs – in explaining their actions.

George Kelly (1905–67)

George Kelly was born in a small farming community in the American Midwest. He operated a travelling schools' psychological service in Kansas. His theory grew out of this practice and was essentially a means of helping pupils with difficulties. Kelly's personal construct theory approach to understanding pupils pioneered the break with behavioural psychology's emphasis on the environment and with the Freudian psychoanalytic concern with the unconscious (see Chapter 4).

Instead of seeing pupils' actions as determined by the situation which they are in, Kelly believed that pupils are active participants in deciding how to act. Pupils are like scientists and their behaviour is an experiment; they analyse the situation that they are in and then decide what to do. They have theories about what to do and they test out these theories in the real world through their actions. Different pupils act in different ways because they have different theories

17

to explain events. So one pupil will work hard in class because he has a belief that if he does so he will please his parents (a reinforcer in behavioural terms); another will not work hard because he believes that there is no point in pleasing his parents (or in trying to, because he will not succeed). Pupils are seen as constructing their own meaning for the situations they are in.

Understanding pupils' constructs

Pupils are like scientists and their behaviour is an experiment. Pupils make choices about how they will act or behave. A pupil's choice will be made in terms of how he constructs the situation – what meaning he gives it. He makes the choice after observing the present situation (a belief shared by the behavioural perspective). But he observes that situation in the light of his previous experiences, which allow him to anticipate the result of various courses of actions. On the basis of the way he constructs the situation, the pupil will then make a choice about how to act. Pupils' actions therefore depend on their ability to 'read' situations and to anticipate what is likely to happen on the basis of their past experiences.

The construct is the central concept of personal construct theory. On the basis of the events in their own personal lives, pupils build up their own particular meaning for the world – their constructs. Pupils construct their meaning for a situation by recognizing the similarities with previous situations; so a pupil will recognize the similarities between a new teacher and the previous teachers he has had. Every situation therefore allows a progressive refinement and definition of the pupil's constructs – the more new teachers the pupil has the more refined his construct for teachers becomes.

Each construct has two poles, or opposite ends. 'Old' and 'young' is a construct, and so are 'man' and 'woman', and 'firm' and 'lax'. Pupils will see the classroom and the teacher in terms of the constructs that they have. So one pupil may see the teacher as a young man who is fair and with a sense of humour; another pupil, in the same class with the same teacher, may see him as a football supporter who dresses well and always sets homework. The two pupils have different constructs for the teacher. For the first pupil what is important, based on past experiences, are the constructs:

- old/young;
- fair/unfair;
- humour/humourless.

For the second pupil the constructs which are important are:

- football supporter/uninterested in football;
- well dressed/untidy;
- sets homework/does not set homework.

The different pupils have different constructs. The situation is the same, they are both in the same class, but the two pupils focus on different aspects of the teacher. These aspects are the factors which they think are important in judging how to act, based on their previous experiences.

Constructs are in many ways similar to attitudes (see Chapter 5). Unlike attitudes, however, they may not have an evaluative emotional component. So the pupil may have a construct for teachers of 'well dressed/untidy', but does not necessarily evaluate one pole as positive and the other as negative. The style of dress is simply something he looks for with new teachers.

Implications for teachers

Kelly's personal construct theory of course applies to teachers as well as to pupils. Teachers have their own constructs – what they look for when they are confronted with a class for the first time. These are based on their past experiences of pupils.

If teachers want to understand the pupils in their class, then they need first to recognize and understand their own constructs. For example, the teacher's constructs for clever pupils may have the poles quiet/noisy, passive/aggressive, fast worker/slow worker, and makes decisions/indecisive. She may look for pupils who are quiet, are passive, are fast workers and make decisions. On the basis of her past experiences, she may think that these are the characteristics of clever pupils. These constructs may be very important to her and have a major effect on how she relates to pupils. Only when the teacher is clear about how she is seeing things can she go on to the next step of understanding the pupils' constructs.

The second implication for the teacher is the need to find out how the pupil is constructing the world. How does the pupil see the classroom – is it a place to work, a place to play, a place to be humiliated, ignored or teased? What meaning does the classroom have for him? To find this out, the teacher needs to listen to the pupil and to try to see the world through his eyes. She has to understand and 'accept' the way the pupil is seeing the world. Kelly refers to this as the 'credulous approach', in which the teacher listens to and explores in detail what the pupil is saying – not necessarily to agree with him but to understand him. The difficulty for teachers is not of being taken in by pupils, but of being left out by them. If the teacher is left out there is no way of understanding their thoughts and beliefs.

Pupils often learn to give the answers that teachers want to hear. The teacher therefore needs to listen to what pupils say, but she also needs to question them to get to the real meaning underneath. The teacher needs 'sceptical credulity' to understand the pupils' world. Constructs are not fixed and pupils can change the way they see situations if the teacher gives them the chance to talk – for example, a pupil who believes that he is no good at drawing can be helped to change this construct by a sensitive teacher who gives him another perspective.

Personal construct theory explains how difficulties arise for pupils in the classroom in a number of different ways. They occur if the pupil cannot construct a way to make sense of changing events – that is, if he responds to new events in old and no longer relevant ways. So if a pupil used to informal teaching is taught in a formal way by a new teacher, he has to adapt to this; if he is unable to make sense of this new way of teaching, he will have problems.

Difficulties also occur if pupils have limited constructs. Pupils whose only constructs are of being tough and a bully will find it very hard to act in other ways, because they have no other meaning for their social role. So a pupil placed in any social situation with other pupils can only make sense of it from his limited past constructs.

There can also be difficulties with roles. A pupil who sees himself differently from the way he is seen by the teacher will have problems. For example, the teacher may see the pupil as weak and quiet, but he may see himself as quiet and strong; the teacher will treat the 'weak, quiet' pupil in a way which he finds unsatisfactory.

The relationship between two people, whether between a pupil and a teacher or between two pupils, depends upon them understanding each other's meaning for the world. Even if they have different roles – for example, a teacher and a pupil – if they share the same beliefs about each other's roles they will understand each other. If, however, they have different beliefs, then there are likely to be problems – for example, if the teacher thinks it is her job to keep order and this belief is not shared by the pupils.

Personal construct theory allows teachers to understand how their pupils are seeing the world. Many teachers find this internal, cognitive perspective a valuable framework to use in conjunction with a behavioural perspective which emphasizes the situation. Personal construct theory explains how pupils' thoughts affect their actions, and underlines the fact that pupils are active decision-makers in their own worlds.

THE RELATIONSHIP OF THOUGHTS TO FEELINGS

In the last few years psychologists have begun to combine the behavioural and cognitive perspectives, utilizing the strengths of both approaches. The cognitive–behavioural approach focuses, in particular, on understanding the pupil's feelings, or emotional response to different situations. One of the difficulties in understanding emotions and feelings is that they are so subjective. Because of this subjectivity, questions are asked such as, 'Are worry and anxiety the same emotions, or different?', or 'Do children feel worried, but not depressed?'

Emotions

Emotions are closely associated with feelings and are connected to changes in physiological arousal. Pupils become 'worked up' when angry and excited, and 'down' when depressed. Emotions are connected to the central nervous system and produce involuntary expressive reactions in the face, voice and gesture. Children are born 'pre-wired' with such basic emotions as anger, joy, fear and disgust. These feelings combine and synthesize, and by the time children reach school age they have developed a range of higher-order emotions that include guilt, anxiety and depression.

Cognitive–behavioural psychologists emphasize that pupils are processors of information and decision-makers in their own lives. The two most influential cognitive–behavioural psychologists are Ellis (Ellis and Harper, 1975) and Beck (1976). They, like Kelly, see pupils as scientists trying to make sense of the world. What is particularly significant to them, however, is the way that the different meanings pupils give to an event lead to different emotional reactions. Consider, for example, the reactions of other pupils to Michelle, a clever pupil who does poorly in a class test. When the teacher announces Michelle's test results her peers have a number of reactions. One thinks that this shows her cleverer than Michelle, so she is happy; Michelle's friend realizes she will be upset, and feels sorry for her; another thinks that the teacher has marked the tests unfairly, and feels annoyed; and a pupil visiting the class does not have any emotional reaction, because the event has no meaning for him. The pupils have different thoughts about the situation and these lead to different emotional reactions. Their interpretations of the situation lead to specific emotional reactions. What is important is the recognition that pupils' emotional reactions to situations can be predicted from their interpretation of them.

The cognitive–behavioural perspective can be represented by a modification of the ABC (antecedent–behaviour–consequence) sequence. A second B (for beliefs) is inserted into the analysis – ABBC

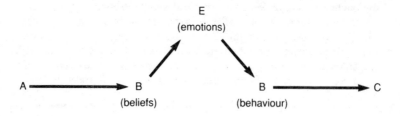

Figure 1.4   The effect of beliefs on emotions.

(see Figure 1.4). The pupil's belief about the situation gives rise to the specific emotion which leads to his behaviour.

Understanding emotions

The fundamental assumption of the cognitive–behavioural perspective is that the meaning that pupils give to their experiences determines how they will feel. A famous quotation from Epictetus is often used to exemplify the cognitive-behavioural position: 'People are not moved by things but the view they take of them.' It is the pupils' beliefs in any situation that produce their emotional response, and it is their emotional response that underpins their behaviour. Not every situation leads to an emotional response in the pupil, but certain beliefs are likely to trigger particular emotional responses.

Different beliefs lead to different emotional responses. So a feeling of sadness is usually associated with the belief that something of value has been lost or is about to be lost. A feeling of anxiety is associated with the pupil's believing that he is not safe, a belief that may be connected with illness, physical harm or social rejection. A third common emotion in the classroom is anger; common beliefs that lead to anger include those that the pupil is being humiliated ('being treated as a baby') or treated unfairly. So the pupil will have different emotional responses depending on his beliefs in a situation. In the Michelle example above, for instance, the same situation produces anger in one pupil while another has no emotional response at all. What can also happen is that similar situations may produce different reactions in the same pupil at different times. So if a pupil fails a spelling test and is told off he may feel indifference if he has not tried, anger if he feels some of the words were unfair, or depressed if he thinks that it shows him as stupid. The way the pupil feels is determined by the meaning he gives the situation.

The cognitive–behavioural approach developed as a way of understanding and helping people with emotional difficulties, particularly anxiety and depression. Pupils with emotional difficulties, those who easily get angry, or anxious and tearful, are seen as poorly functioning scientists – they interpret situations in inappropriate ways, because they have 'faulty' beliefs. For example, angry pupils are seen as having a systematic negative bias in their thinking, which means that they believe that teachers are unfair, malicious, unreasonable or putting them down. Consider a pupil who is sensitive to criticism from one teacher. Because he has a predisposition to see any comments from the teacher as criticism, he increasingly labels any neutral comments as criticism and reacts in a negative way to them. The pupil then begins to generalize from this particular teacher, and to see comments by his other teachers and peers as also critical. He starts to watch for perceived slights and becomes increasingly sensitive to any comments. The beliefs that 'people don't like me' and 'people are always trying to put me down' are constantly at the forefront of his thoughts. He ruminates about them, and becomes increasingly sensitive and out of touch with his peers and teachers. The pupil becomes locked into a self-perpetuating cycle of negative beliefs that lead to emotional difficulties at school.

Implications for teachers

The cognitive–behavioural perspective helps teachers understand pupils who are having emotional difficulties in school. There are some straightforward ways teachers can help such pupils to take positive actions to counter their distorted beliefs. The teacher needs to identify the factors in the situation – the antecedents – which are triggering off the emotional reaction. Does the pupil become upset or angry on Monday mornings, or when he is sitting with a particular group of pupils? The teacher cannot change Monday mornings, but she can identify the time the pupil becomes upset and alert the pupil to the situational factors which are triggering off the emotional reaction. She can find out what the pupil's thoughts and beliefs are – his constructs about the situation. How is the pupil seeing Monday morning? Why is it making him so upset? Is it that no one phoned over the weekend? Is it that his peers are putting him down?

The teacher does not have to be a skilled counsellor to make a difference to a pupil. What is important is that the teacher feels empowered to help the pupil and that the pupil begins to understand that his emotional reaction has a cause. If the pupil can see that it is his beliefs about the situation that are making him upset, rather than emotions just springing out of the blue, then he can gain some control over his life. The teacher is an active agent in the classroom. Not only can she help alert the pupil to what is triggering off the emotions, but she can also help change the situation. She can rearrange groupings in the classroom, devise joint activities, and socially reinforce more appropriate ways for the pupil to respond.

In the same way that the cognitive–behavioural perspective can help explain pupils' emotional responses to situations, it can also help explain teachers' reactions. A teacher can have a variety of emotional responses when confronted with a noisy class. If she believes that she is losing control, she may feel anxious and afraid; if she believes that the pupils are deliberately trying to make her appear a poor teacher, she may feel anger; if she believes that she is helpless, and can never gain control, she may feel depressed. The situation is constant but, depending on what meaning the teacher gives it, she will have different emotional reactions.

Cognitive–behavioural psychology is a helpful framework for the teacher. By understanding what meaning the situation has for the pupil, the teacher can understand the particular emotional reaction, and so can help break the chain of events in which certain situations lead to particular beliefs and then to emotional reactions in the pupil.

In fact, not only is there a chain of events, in which the situation leads to the beliefs, which lead in turn to the emotions, but this chain is cyclical in nature. This cyclical interactive process is explained by the concept of 'reciprocal determinism' which is dealt with next.

AN INTERACTIVE PERSPECTIVE: RECIPROCAL DETERMINISM

Behavioural psychology emphasizes the importance of understanding external factors – the situation the pupil is in. Cognitive psychology emphasizes the importance of understanding internal factors – the pupil's thoughts and beliefs. Cognitive–behavioural psychology combines these two approaches and emphasizes the fact that it is an interaction between the situation and pupils' beliefs that determines not only their emotional reactions but also their behaviour. This interactive perspective is now widely accepted as particularly helpful in understanding pupils. There is, though, a further aspect of the interactive perspective which is particularly useful for teachers. This is what Albert Bandura referred to as 'reciprocal determinism'.

Bandura showed that pupils learned through the process of copying, or modelling their behaviour on that of other pupils (and adults). The pupil thus actively learns how to act through observing others; but he is a selective participant, actively choosing information to attend and respond to. Through this active process the pupil also affects the situation he is in – he acts in the situation but also on the situation.

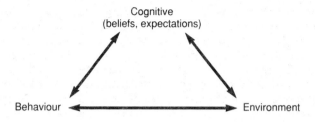

Figure 1.5   Reciprocal determinism.

Bandura synthesized these views in his classic text, *Social Learning Theory* (1977). The central concept in this work is 'reciprocal determinism', by which Bandura means that cognitive factors, environmental factors and behaviour all operate as interlocking determinants of each other (see Figure 1.5).

Albert Bandura (1925–)

Albert Bandura was born in Canada and gained a doctorate from the University of Iowa. He has lectured throughout his career at Stanford University. He is best known for his development of social learning theory, which shows how pupils learn from their social context.

All three factors affect each other: pupils' expectations affect their behaviour and the environment; the outcome of their behaviour affects their expectation and the situation that they are in; finally, the environment affects both the pupils' expectations and their behaviour. For example, a pupil becomes angry and acts aggressively because he believes that others will humiliate and act aggressively to him. And because he becomes angry and acts aggressively, other pupils do humiliate and act aggressively to him. His beliefs not only determine his own actions but influence the behaviour of other pupils; and their behaviour also determines his expectations – there is a vicious circle. In this way, angry and aggressive pupils create through their own behaviour a hostile environment. On the other hand, sociable, friendly pupils create an environment which responds to them in a sociable, friendly way. The point is that not only do pupils' beliefs and the situation which they are in determine their actions, but their actions create the situation which they are in. There is reciprocal determinism.

The interdependence of cognitive, situational and behavioural factors indicates that it is not profitable for the teacher to focus on one factor in isolation. It is the continuous reciprocal interaction between the factors which she needs to understand. Pupils play an active role in shaping their own world, and the world plays an active role in shaping them. The teacher is very much part of this world. Her importance in creating the right environment for learning cannot be overemphasized, and will be returned to throughout this book. What teachers need to recognize is that pupils' reactions and selective attention to them also change them and how they teach. The teacher needs to be aware of this reciprocal influence – not in order to counteract it, but to understand that classroom teaching is an interactive process.

SUMMARY

Psychology gives a number of perspectives on understanding pupils in the classroom. The behavioural perspective emphasizes the importance of external factors – the situation which the pupil is in. By analysing the antecedents and the consequences, it is possible to see what triggers the behaviour off and how it is being reinforced. The cognitive perspective emphasizes that pupils see situations in different ways. It stresses that pupils actively make sense of situations. It is internal factors – the way pupils construct situations through their thoughts and beliefs – that determine how they will act. The cognitive–behavioural perspective explains how the situation and the pupils' beliefs interrelate. Both need to be taken into account when understanding pupils. This perspective is especially useful in explaining how particular beliefs will lead to specific emotions. The perspective of reciprocal determinism stresses that pupils' actions are interactive and of a cyclical nature. There is an interdependence between the cognitive, situational and behavioural factors. Pupils play an active role in shaping their own world, and the world plays an active role in shaping them.

REFERENCES

Bandura, A. (1977) *Social Learning Theory*. Englewood Cliffs, NJ: Prentice-Hall.

Beck, A. (1976) *Cognitive Therapy and the Emotional Disorders*. London: Meridian.

Burns, R. (1978) The relative effectiveness of various incentives and deterrents as judged by pupils and teachers, *Educational Studies* **4**(3), pp. 229–33.

Cheeseman, P. and Watts, P. (1985) *Positive Behaviour Management*. London: Croom Helm.

Ellis, A. and Harper, R. (1975) *A New Guide to Rational Living*. London: Prentice-Hall.

Forness, S. (1973) The reinforcement hierarchy, *Psychology in Schools*, **10**, pp. 168–77.

Kelly, G. (1955) *The Psychology of Personal Constructs*. New York: Norton.

Kounin, J. (1970) *Discipline and Group Management in Classrooms*. New York: Holt, Rinehart & Winston.

Skinner, B.F. (1971) *Beyond Freedom and Dignity*. New York: Knopf.

Wheldall, K. (ed.) (1987) *The Behaviourist in the Classroom*. London: Allen & Unwin.

Wheldall, K. and Glynn, T. (1989) *Effective Classroom Learning*. Oxford: Basil Blackwell.

RECOMMENDED READING

A. Beck, *Cognitive Therapy and the Emotional Disorders* (London: Meridian, 1976), is a lively and original introduction to cognitive–behavioural psychology. Aims to help adults understand the basis of emotions.

P. Cheeseman and P. Watts, *Positive Behaviour Management* (London: Croom Helm, 1985), is a readable introduction to the use of behavioural psychology in the classroom. Provides a wealth of practical strategies that can be used by teachers.

K. Wheldall and T. Glynn, *Effective Classroom Learning* (Oxford: Basil Blackwell, 1989), introduces teachers to a behavioural interactionist approach to teaching. Has a practical series of chapters on how to make the classroom environment more conducive to pupils' learning.

CHAPTER 2

Pupils' thinking

OVERVIEW

This chapter examines frameworks for understanding pupils' thinking. Most of the time, pupils' minds are full of thoughts that can range from understanding what the teacher is saying, through how to do a mathematical problem, to what they saw on television last night. This field is known as cognitive psychology, and is about the way the mind represents and processes information. Cognition is a very large field, and this chapter covers only a number of key areas. In particular, it deals with:

- information-processing models of thinking;
- long-term memory;
- network models of memory;
- the concept of intelligence;
- information-processing models of intelligence.

It might seem that cognitive psychology should be the cornerstone of the use of psychology in the classroom – it is about the whole process of how pupils think. For many psychologists, though, cognitive psychology has had a disappointingly limited, even negative, influence on the educational world. This has been because psychologists started off by focusing on how to measure cognitive ability before they had a clear, accepted framework for what cognitive processes were. For much of the twentieth century, cognitive psychology's practical impact on education was the measurement of pupils' intelligence. Both in Britain and in the USA, the psychologist's original role in education was intelligence testing. This has been of concern to many educational psychologists, who have long recognized the limitations and biases of intelligence tests – yet often continue to use them. One of the reasons that such tests are still used is that the new cognitive perspectives, discussed below, have yet to find major recognition, let alone application, in the classroom.

INFORMATION-PROCESSING MODELS OF THINKING

Between 1960 and the early 1970s, cognitive psychology was dominated by information-processing models of thinking that mirrored the functioning of the computer. It is useful to put labels on a number of the key functions. It must be remembered, however, that these are simply labels; they do not represent an actual physical structure in the brain. The brain can be imagined as a filing cabinet kept by the school secretary. Information can be stored in and retrieved from it. However, a teacher is not actually allowed to see how the files are kept. Information may be filed alphabetically, or by date; it may be kept on microfiche, or as handwritten notes, or on a video, or by a combination of these methods. The teacher can speculate that there are four drawers to the filing cabinet, but as she cannot see into it, even this cannot be checked. She can try to find out how the filing system works by putting in information and seeing whether, and how, it is changed when it is withdrawn. In the same way, psychologists have only basic assumptions about the way the cognitive processes operate. These assumptions are working hypotheses, which are altered and developed over time.

Information-processing models of thinking

These models distinguish between the following processors in the mind:

- the sense receptors;
- the sensory stores;
- the short-term store;
- the long-term memory.

These provide a model for understanding how pupils process information. By having a model – however tentative it may be – teachers can understand how their teaching style may make it relatively easy or difficult for pupils to process new information.

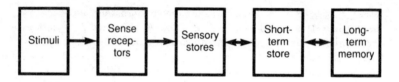

Figure 2.1   Information processes.

It is important to stress again that these processes are not separate structures in the brain. Rather, they are simply useful labels to help us begin to distinguish between different processes which occur in the brain. The processes are all interconnected and one of the major questions which psychologists address is how they are so connected. Visual representations (see Figure 2.1) may be helpful – but they must be considered speculative.

The sense receptors

The starting points for pupils processing information are the five sense receptors: sight, hearing, touch, smell and taste. In the classroom the two most important are sight and hearing, as it is through these two that pupils gain most of their information. They see the teacher and what is happening in the classroom and, most importantly, use sight to gain information through reading; and they listen to the teacher and to other pupils. The significance of these two sense receptors is also emphasized by the regular checking of vision and hearing by school medical officers.

The sensory stores

The sense receptors sense environmental stimuli. Perception, however, is more than this; it is the assignment of meaning to the incoming information. So a pupil will see a pattern of lines, but before he perceives them as his name he has to assign meaning to them. The process by which the mind temporarily holds information – the pattern of lines – in order for meaning to be assigned to them is known as the sensory store.

There appears to be one sensory store for each of the senses. The most important sensory stores are the auditory (echoic) and the visual (iconic). These stores serve as short-term holding systems for maintaining a record of the incoming stimuli. So while a pupil's eyes scan a line of writing, his iconic store holds the information while some initial meaning is assigned to the letter shapes. The sensory stores can hold information for only a very short period of time. It is estimated that the iconic store can hold information for 0.5 of a second, the hearing or echoic store for approximately 3 seconds (Rock, 1975). Because of the limited time that information is held in the sensory stores, there can only be limited processing of it.

Before a pupil can decide on the meaning of a stimulus, various cognitive processes have to be carried out. Perception is not, therefore, an instantaneous process. The pupil has to attend to the stimulus and match it to information stored (in the long-term memory: see below), and only then can a decision be made about its meaning. As stimuli often last for only a brief period, the sensory register stores the stimulus to allow the process to begin to be carried out.

Consider a pupil listening to a teacher. The pupil has to hold a number of sounds in his head for a period of time if he is to begin to recognize the spoken word. He can hold the sound for only approximately 3 seconds in this first sensory store before it begins to fade. In these first 3 seconds some assignment of meaning to the stimuli must be made in order to process the sound further.

The short-term store

The further processing of the recognized sound (or visual pattern) in the sensory store is done in the short-term store. Though there may be other short-term stores, the most important one is the a–v–l, the 'auditory–verbal–linguistic' store (Atkinson and Shiffrin, 1968). The triple term is used because of the difficulty of separating these three functions. The character of information in the short-term memory store does not necessarily depend on the sensory input. So visual information – a written word – may be encoded in the same way as a spoken auditory input. These two different sorts of information are encoded in the same way in the a–v–l store.

The short-term store holds information for a limited duration, normally estimated at about 30 seconds. This function appears to be determined by capacity rather than time. The amount of information that can be stored is as much as can be verbalized in 30 seconds. Typically this is between five and nine bits or 'chunks' of information. It was Miller (1956) who first suggested that the short-term store could hold only a limited amount of information. He suggested the magical number of 7 plus or minus 2, and it is this figure that has appeared in popular psychology as the key figure for 'chunking' information. The implication is that pupils will find it easier to learn information that is chunked into 7 (plus or minus 2) units.

Information from the short-term store can be maintained there if it is paid attention to and actively rehearsed. This is why it is so important for pupils to concentrate actively. If they do not engage with new information in this way, it will not be processed. Initially information can be very fragile; a thought can be lost completely following a brief interruption. However, once the thought is in the long-term memory, rehearsal hardly seems necessary. Pupils can remember the names of different animals, for example, even if they are not rehearsed for years on end.

It is important to recognize that the short-term store is not some fixed storage place, but rather a mechanism for processing information. The short-term store can be seen as the working memory. It is the part of the process that can be used consciously: the pupil can deliberately think about new information and manipulate it in his mind.

LONG-TERM MEMORY

The long-term memory is the process by which information and knowledge – memories – are held for relatively long periods of time. Some psychologists would say memories are held indefinitely. By knowing how the long-term memory operates, teachers can understand why pupils remember some pieces of information while others cannot be recalled. Chapter 11 describes strategies that the teacher can use to improve pupils' memory.

The long-term memory is a whole series of interlocking processes rather than a fixed storage system. For example, there are different types of memory that decay at different rates over time. A funny story is forgotten in a few days, while visual memories of a holiday from early childhood can come flooding back years after the event. The long-term memory can, again, be compared to a filing system that each pupil has within his head. An enormous amount of information is available to be placed in it. Whether pupils can use this information at a later date depends on their placing it in such a way that they have a system for knowing where the material is stored. The issues are what sort of information is stored and how it is organized so that it can be retrieved at a later date.

It is useful to distinguish between a number of different types of memory for different information and events. These differences are only hypothetical but they give a useful framework for understanding the memory processes.

Verbal and imaginal memory

The first distinction is between verbal and imaginal memory. Alan Paivio has proposed a dual coding theory (1986). This consists of two fundamentally distinct systems, one for verbal information and one for imaginal information. Words, sentences, conversations and stories are stored in the verbal information system, while pictures, sensations, sounds and smells are coded in the imaginal memory. Imaginal information, particularly visual, can be easily stored in the memory; pupils can remember particular scenes from their life experiences with little effort. Incoming information can be stored in one or both systems. If it is stored in both, it is more likely to be remembered. So if teaching about the Battle of Waterloo consists of asking the pupils to read a factual text on the subject, they are likely to store most of the information in the verbal memory; however, if the teacher can make the battle come alive, so that images can also be stored, then this lesson is much more likely to be remembered. Similarly, pupils will find difficulty remembering abstract information because it can only be stored in the verbal memory; if the information can also be presented in such a way that it can be imagined, then they will find it easier to remember.

It is important to remember that the a–v–l store means that information presented in one way can be transformed. Imaginal information does not have to be presented as pictures. It can be presented as words – as any poet will testify.

Declarative and procedural knowledge

A second distinction can be made between declarative and procedural knowledge. Declarative knowledge is knowledge about facts: knowing that something is so – for example, that Australia is an island. Procedural knowledge, on the other hand, is knowing how to do something – for example, knowing how to solve a mathematics problem, or how to read.

The importance of procedural knowledge is that it is often automatic: a pupil who knows how to write the letters of the alphabet does not have to think about it. Declarative knowledge is often not so simple to remember: pupils have to think consciously, to search their memories, before being able to remember what the capital of Bolivia is. So one of the keys for learning basic skills is turning declarative knowledge into procedural knowledge. A pupil who has to think about the correspondence between letters and the sounds that they make has some way to go before turning this into the largely automatic process of reading.

A lot of education is about declarative knowledge – knowledge of facts. But even facts are transformed before they are stored in the pupils' memories.

Propositions

Propositions are the most common way to represent declarative knowledge (Kintsch, 1988). A proposition is the smallest unit of knowledge about which it makes sense to make a judgement as to whether it is true or false. Proposition analysis can be used on chunks of information, such as sentences or paragraphs:

Cyprus, a small island in the Mediterranean, is a popular destination for British tourists, especially in the summer months.

This sentence can be broken down into idea units:

- Cyprus is a small island.
- Cyprus is in the Mediterranean.
- Cyprus is a popular destination for British tourists.
- British tourists go to Cyprus especially in the summer months.

Each of these sentences represents a unit of meaning which can be judged true or false. Propositions are not the sentences themselves; they are the meanings of the sentences. It is these meanings that are stored, not their exact forms. Consider, for example, the following sentences:

Tourists from Britain go to Cyprus for their holidays. Cyprus is especially popular with British tourists in the winter.

The second sentence here will be judged as false, even though there is no reference to winter in the original sentence above. The first sentence here is judged on the same basis as true – despite the fact that it has not been seen before. The information contained in it is recognized as true.

Propositions are linked to each other in the memory. So when pupils read a textbook or listen to the teacher giving information they have to understand the propositions and relate them to the propositions that they already carry in their memories. The more propositions there are in a piece of reading the more difficult it will prove for the pupil and the more slowly he will read it.

Propositions

The concept of propositions gives a particularly useful way of understanding how declarative knowledge – facts and information – is given meaning before it is stored. It follows that the more meaningful the information is to the pupil the better it will be remembered, as it is the meaning that is stored not the actual auditory or visual stimulus. This concept has similarities to the cognitive–behaviour perspective (see Chapter 1), which emphasizes that it is not the situation that triggers a pupil's behaviour, but the meaning that the pupil gives to the event.

Propositions represent the units of meaning. These units of meaning are organized and linked together in a way represented by the concept of schemata.

Schemata

The concept of schemata is particularly popular with cognitive psychologists in explaining how memory works (Rumelhart, 1981). A schema is the fundamental organizational element on which all information processing is seen to depend. Schemata are the complex representations of a pupil's memories, the 'slots' that store the contents of memory. They represent all the pupils' declarative and procedural knowledge, and their verbal and imaginal memories.

When a pupil is faced with a new situation or event, it has to be made meaningful. He makes sense of it through an active reconstruction, using memory. Much of this occurs at a semi-automatic level, through the use of the sensory store – a bus, for example, is recognized instantaneously as a bus. It is only if the object is unfamiliar or seen in an unfamiliar context that the pupil has actively to think about it.

Schemata are the elements which enable not only recognition of familiar objects and events, but the actual storage of unfamiliar events. Past experiences and information are organized into schemata or frames, and new information is interpreted in relation to the schemata which the pupil already holds. Either its meaning is matched to present schemata, or they are reorganized if they do not fit the new information. Perception, though generally automatic, is therefore an active process by which incoming information is matched to schemata, but will also adapt and shape them.

New information is encoded according to the schemata activated at the time of processing. The context becomes all-important if the information is to be remembered. Consider, for example, the following information:

14 March
16 April
7 November

By itself this information means nothing and will not be remembered. But if it is known that these are significant dates of the Russian Revolution in 1917, they can be encoded by the schemata in a different way, although the information is still not likely to be remembered unless the pupil has a well-established schema about the Russian Revolution. If, however, further information is added – what happened on those dates – then these further slots in the schema are triggered:

14 March: abdication of the tsar;
16 April: Lenin returns;
7 November: Bolsheviks occupy Petrograd.

Parts of the imaginal representation system are activated as well when the events are added to the dates. When asked to recall information about the Russian Revolution, the memory does not simply reproduce this information – unless it has been learnt by rote. Instead, it actively reconstructs the information from the different slots in the schema. Each slot contributes its meaningful memories to build up the picture of what happened during the Revolution.

Schema theory demonstrates that pupils' long-term memories work in a dynamic, interactive way. The memory is not simply a bucket waiting to be filled with information; instead, pupils act on and make sense of incoming information. They have to build it into a meaningful structure for themselves. Schemata are seen as the building blocks in which information is encoded, sorted and retrieved. They have to be organized, and this is done through a dynamic network of interconnected parts. This concept of a network is the final part in the picture of the pupils' cognitive processes.

NETWORK MODELS OF MEMORY

In Anderson's ACT* (to be read as 'ACT star') network model of memory (1983), knowledge is represented as a web or network. 'ACT*' stands for the 'adaptive control of thought'; the star signifies that it is the final version of the model, following 15 years of research. Its name highlights Anderson's view that thoughts can be controlled; so pupils can control and direct what they think about. They do so to adapt to the particular situation that they are in. This model of cognitive processes thus puts pupils at the centre of their own thinking. This can be contrasted with cognitive models that equate thinking with intelligence and place the pupils in a very passive role – dependent on their intelligence to deal with a situation.

John Anderson (1947–)

John Anderson went to Stanford University in 1968, where he started working on computer-simulated models of the structure of memory. He has taught at a number of universities, receiving major grants to continue his work on developing the ACT system. He is presently teaching at the Carnegie-Mellon University, Pittsburgh.

The network consists of 'nodes', schemata which are related by a series of links. The basic building blocks are propositions and images.

A basic cognitive unit consists of a unit node (a proposition or image) and a set of up to five elements (information that relates to the proposition or image). The cognitive units combine together in larger units known as 'tangled hierarchies'.

There are two types of memory structure, as described above: a declarative memory for knowledge about facts, and a procedural memory for knowledge about how to do something. The system is activated by the working memory (the short-term store), which brings together the declarative and procedural memory to tackle the task in hand.

The network model

Memory works by a cognitive unit – 'the focus unit' – being activated, either externally, for example by the teacher saying something, or internally, by the pupil thinking about his work. This focus unit then activates other, associated units. Continued attention spreads the activation to other parts of the network. Spreading is cumulative: the more units that are activated the more likely it is that information will be both stored and retrieved.

The concept of spreading activation indicates how a phrase, like 'the Russian Revolution' , can trigger off a range of memories, each of which can be followed up by giving attention to them. So the pupil can think about the tsars, Lenin, communism, and so on. Each word will trigger off a range of memories – the tangled hierarchy. Some of these memories will be propositions, some images. The more the pupil thinks about the Russian Revolution, the more the network will be activated. A teacher can prompt the pupil's recall of information about the Russian Revolution by giving hints and cues which may activate different pathways – for example, by mentioning *Dr Zhivago* or *Reds*.

Units are activated at different degrees of intensity – memories can either be strong or weak. Strong memories, such as well-learnt information, have many associations and therefore are accessed from a number of pathways. The more often particular information is accessed, the stronger the pathway. What is interesting is that the stronger the pathway, the more activation it will produce. So well-learnt information will produce, and capture, more activation than poorly learnt information. The effect is cumulative: well-learnt information is easily activated and therefore grows increasingly strong. Pupils relate new information to existing well-learnt knowledge. The more connections new information can make, the more likely it is that it will be recalled.

Anderson's network model is a particularly comprehensive way of viewing memory and the whole concept of thinking. It provides a framework which shows how pupils have an active control over their thinking processes. (See also Chapter 11.) It needs to be stressed again that this model of how the mind works will, over the course of time, develop as new research provides evidence for other ways of viewing cognitive processes.

What the above models demonstrate is that thinking is a complex process. Unfortunately, for many years the dominant theme in cognitive psychology was the concept of intelligence, which limited the use of cognitive psychology in the classroom. How does the concept of intelligence relate to cognitive psychology, and why is it still such a powerful influence within education?

THE CONCEPT OF INTELLIGENCE

Direct references to pupils' intelligence, particularly their IQ (intelligence quotient) are commonly made in education by both parents and teachers.

Intelligence

Intelligence is commonly used to refer to a pupil's capacity to think and to learn. This capacity is usually considered as both the speed at which a pupil learns and also the amount which he learns. Intelligence is not simply a descriptive word; it is also a highly evaluative word – in education, it is a term of admiration. The concept of intelligence would probably have retained the same status as other concepts such as 'motivation' if it had not been given a reality by the creation and use of intelligence tests.

Intelligence testing originated as a practical solution to an administrative difficulty. At the turn of the century, Alfred Binet was asked to devise a way of measuring which pupils would not benefit from education – which pupils were ineducable. Binet's response to the assignment was to devise with his colleague, Theodore Simon, the Binet–Simon Intelligence Test (Binet and Simon, 1905). They tried to ascertain what tasks pupils could complete at different ages; for example, at what age most pupils could complete a simple jigsaw.

Though Binet and Simon were not concerned with assigning mental ages to pupils, other psychologists were. Assigning a mental age concerns specifying what tasks a normal pupil should be able to do at certain ages. It was a short step from specifying a pupil's mental age to that of developing the concept of IQ:

$$IQ = \frac{\text{Mental age}}{\text{Chronological age}} \times 100$$

This simple mathematical formula indicates that a pupil of 9 who has a mental age of 9 (can do all the tasks on the test that a normal 9-year-old can do) has an IQ of 100. (An average pupil has by definition an IQ of 100.)

Such a mathematical formula gives a completely unfounded impression of simplicity to pupils' cognitive processes, and it is this apparent simplicity that has attracted institutions in need of a method of distinguishing between individuals. So the measurement of intelligence has found its most practical application in the armed forces for selection of officers, in industry for recruitment purposes, and in education for the classification of pupils to different types of schools. There is a fundamental assumption that a pupil's IQ is an indication of his potential to achieve success in school, if not in life.

Lumpers and splitters

There developed, in the first half of the century, a tension between psychologists who recognized separate functions of the mind, such as reasoning, memory and sensory discrimination – the splitters – and those who wished to exploit the opportunities provided by intelligence tests, considering the mind as something which was unitary and could be measured – the 'lumpers'. This tension was only partially resolved by the development of statistical methods for analysing data. In particular, the development of 'factor analysis' gave impetus to the identification of the components or factors of intelligence. Factor analysis is a fairly complicated statistical technique that allows for the simplification of information by showing the intercorrelation between variables in a set of data. Most intelligence tests consist of a series of subtests, and by factor-analysing the scores on the subtests, it is possible to see the intercorrelation between them.

The development of statistical techniques led to the division of intelligence into a number of separate factors by the 'splitters'. Theirs is the predominant view in the USA. Thurstone (1938) identified seven primary mental abilities: spatial ability, numerical ability, word fluency, verbal comprehension, inductive reasoning, perceptual ability and memory. This position was taken to its mathematically logical, if completely meaningless (in the real world), conclusion by Guildford (1982). He statistically defined no fewer than 150 factors which constituted intelligence.

Charles Spearman and Cyril Burt were among a group of psychologists associated with University College London who believed in the concept of general cognitive capacity. Burt held that this depended on the complexity and number of the interconnections between the nerve cells in the cerebral cortex. Intelligence was thus seen as having a biological basis and this led directly to the notion that it was genetically determined. Burt identified intelligence as 'innate general cognitive ability', but believed that this ability could be divided into two major group factors, verbal and non-verbal ability. This distinction is still present in many people's conception of intelligence: 'Oh, he's good verbally' , or 'She's so good with her hands.'

Statistical analysis and particular factor analysis are sufficiently complex and sophisticated mathematical techniques to give an aura of scientific credibility to intelligence tests. Statistical analysis has, however, no validity if the underlying models are inaccurate. Sufficient is now known about cognitive processes for it to be recognized that there is no such thing as chunks of ability in the brain that can be measured.

Implications of lumping and splitting

Factor analysis has not led to any clarity about which are the key components of intelligence – it appears that you can slice the statistical cake of intelligence in a number of ways. What it has done is to confirm the common-sense notion that some pupils may be able to solve mathematical problems quickly but have a poor memory for historical facts, or be good at drawing but have difficulty learning languages. This is hardly an earth-shattering conclusion, given the amount of research that has gone into trying to identify the components of intelligence.

A second issue is that, though the 'splitters' have divided intelligence into a number of factors, when it actually comes to measuring intelligence it is an overall IQ that is quoted and remembered. Common intelligence tests, such as the WISC-R, have a number of subtests that are combined to give two scales, verbal and non-verbal. When a pupil is assessed on the WISC-R, these two scales are usually added together to give an overall IQ.

This is an excellent example of the way practitioners can use the techniques which support their jobs and ignore the research which indicates that such practice has been divorced from its research validity.

The difficulties with the concept of intelligence

The simplicity and immediacy of intelligence testing has shaped teachers' perception of intelligence and, most vitally, it has directly affected decisions about the structure of education in Britain. Though the structure of primary schools is substantially homogeneous and stable, secondary pupils have, over the years, had their education moulded by the prevalent view of intelligence. The division between secondary modern and grammar schools was, and still is, largely founded on the belief that pupils have a general intelligence that can be assessed at age 11 and used to predict the best type of secondary education for them. The comprehensive system is based on a belief that all pupils can be taught in the same school, and even in the same class. The present drive is towards diversification, through grant-maintained schools specializing in key areas of the National Curriculum. It is believed that pupils have particular abilities which can be recognized and improved through the appropriate school.

Though there is a statistical correlation between pupils' scores on intelligence tests and their future academic achievement, it is not a one-to-one correspondence. This means that to make decisions about an individual pupil's educational future on the basis of an intelligence test is an abuse of psychology. Enough is known about the complexity of cognitive psychology for it to be recognized that intelligence tests are not good predictors of life outcomes for many pupils (McClelland, 1973). There are many other factors that affect the career and job prospects of pupils. It is worthwhile reflecting on what your feelings as a teacher would be if you were asked to take an IQ test as a factor in gaining promotion!

These are common criticisms of intelligence testing at the individual pupil level. More worrying are the concerns from minority ethnic groups that the tests are intrinsically unfair. Not only because test items reflect the dominant culture, but because the whole concept of test-taking is alien to many cultures. Of course, many sociologists would argue that the fact that the tests are unfair is the reason why they are so popular – the dominant culture can use intelligence tests to exclude large sections of society from social and economic opportunities.

INFORMATION-PROCESSING MODELS OF INTELLIGENCE

In the last decade there have been increasing number of attempts to develop more sophisticated models of intelligence. In particular, Sternberg (1985) has created a model which combines elements of the debate about the nature of intelligence with the present understanding

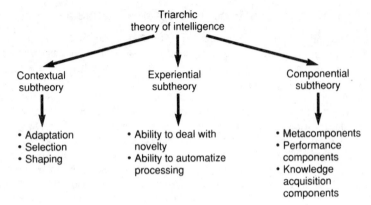

Figure 2.2 The triarchic theory of intelligence.

of cognitive processes. His model combines the concept of intelligence with the social and cultural environment in which the pupil lives.

Robert Sternberg

Robert Sternberg received his PhD from Stanford University. He is now Professor of Psychology and Director of Graduate Studies at Yale University. He has written extensively on intelligence and thinking and is best known for his triarchic theory of human intelligence.

Sternberg proposes a triarchic theory that divides intelligence into three subtheories, divided in turn into successively narrower sets of subtheories. It is the theory of intelligence that he divides in this way, not the cognitive structures (see Figure 2.2).

The contextual subtheory

The contextual subtheory highlights the fact that intelligent behaviour happens in a context. Intelligence is the ability of the pupil to solve real problems in the world rather than to function in an artificial test situation. Intelligence is the use of the cognitive processes for purposive adaptation to, selection from and shaping of the situation that the pupil is in. Within the contextual framework, part of the pupils' intelligence for the teacher is their ability to adapt to the reality of classroom life. As part of this process, pupils need to make selections about their day-to-day work – for example, a pupil has to select whether to sit at the front or the back of the class. Finally, the pupil needs to be able to shape the environment which he is in. This may mean encouraging the teacher to be more lenient about certain rules, or spending more time reading than is allowed.

The contextual subtheory emphasizes the fact that intelligence can be defined only within a context. Two pupils in the same class may show differences in their intelligence by their differing ability to adapt to the situation which they are in. Similarly, a pupil will show greater or lesser adaptation and flexibility at different times in his school career.

This subtheory also emphasizes the fact that intelligence is relative rather than fixed. The starting point for teachers looking at the contextual aspects of intelligence is to identify the important indicators of intelligence in their school. A pupil will then be seen as matching or not matching these contextual expectations. Different cultures have different expectations about what is intelligent. North Americans consider the following as signs of intelligence:

- practical problem-solving ability: the ability to reason logically and identify connections between ideas; the ability to see all aspects of a problem;
- verbal ability: the ability to speak clearly and articulately and to hold a fluent conversation; the ability to talk knowledgeably about specific issues;
- social competence: the ability to be interested in other people and the world at large; the ability to accept other people for what they are.

Teachers need to be aware of the context for intelligence in their schools. This context can be seen to be built on constructs (see Chapter 1). It may well be that some of the constructs identified by Americans for adults are what are considered intelligent in British schools. There may, however, be other constructs, such as finishing work first or answering questions.

These contextual factors highlight the distinction that Sternberg makes between explicit and implicit theories of intelligence. Explicit theories are those which are based on teachers' use of intelligence tests; on the other hand, implicit theories are the informal judgements that teachers make about pupils' intelligence. The importance of implicit theories of intelligence is that they are the basis on which most teachers assess intelligence. These assessments are made informally in the course of everyday classroom interactions rather than by using intelligence tests. Sternberg suggests that teachers are more likely to trust these implicit assessments than they are an IQ score. In fact, teachers are likely to question an IQ score if it does not match their own implicit judgements. Teachers often want formal testing to confirm what they already know. If it does not, they are likely to dismiss the assessment rather than change their judgement.

The experiential subtheory

The experiential subtheory proposes that intelligence consists of two skills: the ability to deal with novel kinds of task, and the ability to process information automatically.

The ability to deal with novel tasks is one of the traditional aspects of many of the tasks used in intelligence tests. There is a thin dividing line between a task which is novel and outside the pupil's experience, and one which is so alien that it is meaningless to him. In the past, intelligence tests often contained items that were meant to be novel to the pupil, and thus not able to be taught. There has gradually been a recognition that such items are also relatively meaningless. Present good practice on assessment, such as that for the National Curriculum, has ensured that novelty has a minor role to play in assessment.

On the other hand, the ability to make automatic the processing of information is extremely important. It stems from the fact that many tasks, such as reading, require an extraordinary number of separate operations. Tasks which are as complex as reading are possible only because a substantial proportion of the processes are automatized and require minimal mental effort. There are differences in cognitive processes between a pupil who can perform a complex mental task automatically and a pupil who can only perform the same task haltingly and under conscious control. This is the same distinction that has been made above between declarative and procedural knowledge. A pupil who reads haltingly is using very different processes from those used by a pupil who is a fluent reader. The point is worth emphasizing: it is now recognized that it is not just that one is quicker than the other. The fluent reader is not having to use his working memory actually to decode the words, and this allows him to retain much more information. The ability to process information automatically is crucial to pupils' learning. If cognitive tasks can be done automatically then this releases cognitive processing capacity to tackle other tasks.

The componential subtheory

Components are the cognitive processes which a pupil has to solve problems. Sternberg describes three types of component:

- **Performance components** are the processes which the pupil actually uses to execute the task.
- **Knowledge acquisition components** are the processes which the pupil uses in learning new information.
- **Metacomponents** are the higher-order processes which the pupil uses in planning and monitoring the task.

Sternberg also describes retention components, which allow for the retrieval of information from memory, and transfer components which allow the pupil to generalize information from one situation to another. This componential subtheory contains many elements similar to the other cognitive models, such as Anderson's, and will not be elaborated on again.

The third group of components – metacomponents – refers to 'thinking about thinking'. This is a particularly useful way of looking at the cognitive strategies which pupils bring to learning. These meta-components can be taught to pupils and are a way in which teachers can improve pupils' ability to tackle problems (see Chapter 11).

This brief description of Sternberg's triarchic framework shows how new models of cognitive psychology are realistically complex in their attempts to explain pupils' thinking. The implications for the classroom are only gradually becoming apparent. The model draws attention to three subtheories which provide a helpful bridge between cognitive processing models and the traditional concept of intelligence. The key point is that it is too simplistic to talk about a pupil's intelligence. What teachers can do is to recognize the complex and dynamic nature of pupils' thinking. This will ensure that simplistic concepts of pupils' intelligence are seen as historically interesting but outmoded representations of cognitive factors in pupils' education.

SUMMARY

Information-processing models of thinking provide a sequential framework that explains how information is taken in and remembered by pupils. Underpinning this are a number of divisions between the types of information that are processed. This information is seen to be stored in schemata – the fundamental building blocks of memory. The sequential model, though helpful in exploring the process, is now being replaced by a network model which emphasizes how the various processes are working in parallel with each other. These models are seen as describing cognitive processes more accurately than the concept of intelligence does. Nevertheless, 'intelligence' still has a pervasive influence in schools. It is hoped that recent developments, and in particular Sternberg's triarchic model, will ensure that the concept of intelligence will develop to fit the current state of knowledge.

REFERENCES

Anderson, J. (1983) *The Architecture of Cognition*. Cambridge, MA: Harvard University Press.

Anderson, J. (1985) *Cognitive Psychology and Its Implications*. New York: Freeman.

Atkinson, R. and Shiffrin, R. (1968) Human memory: a proposed system and its control processes, in Spence, K. and Spence, J. (eds), *The Psychology of Learning and Motivation*, Vol. 2. New York: Academic Press.

Binet, A. and Simon, T. (1905) New methods for diagnosis of the intellectual level of subnormals, *L'Année psychologique* **14**, pp. 1–90.

Guildford, J. (1982) Cognitive psychology's ambiguities: some suggested remedies, *Psychological Review* **89**, pp. 48–59.

Kintsch, W. (1988) The role of knowledge in discourse comprehension: a construction-integration model, *Psychology Review* **95**, pp. 163–82.

McClelland, D. (1973) Testing for competence rather than for intelligence, *American Psychologist* **28**, pp. 1–14.

Miller, G. (1956) The magical number seven plus or minus two: Some limits on our capacity for processing information, *Psychological Review* **63**, pp. 81–97.

Paivio, A. (1986) *Mental Representations: A Dual Coding Approach.* New York: Oxford University Press.

Rock, I. (1975) *An Introduction to Perception.* New York: Macmillan.

Rumelhart, D. (1981) Schemata: the building blocks of cognition, in Guthrie, J. (ed.), *Comprehension and Teaching: Research Reviews.* Newark, DE: International Reading Association.

Sternberg, R. (1985) *Beyond IQ: A Triarchic Theory of Human Intelligence.* Cambridge: Cambridge University Press.

Thurstone, L. (1938) *Primary Mental Abilities.* Psychometric Monographs, No. 1.

RECOMMENDED READING

J. Anderson, *Cognitive Psychology and Its Implications* (New York: Freeman, 1985), is a detailed and fairly complex book. It provides a well-informed analysis of the present knowledge on cognitive psychology.

J. Blum, *Pseudoscience and Mental Ability* (London: Monthly Review Press, 1978), traces the rise of intelligence testing and the political and social forces on it. A highly readable book.

R. Sternberg, *Beyond IQ: A Triarchic Theory of Human Intelligence* (Cambridge: Cambridge University Press, 1985), is a detailed account of Sternberg's triarchic theory of intelligence. This is the book that showed how cognitive psychology and intelligence could be linked together.

CHAPTER 3

Cognitive psychology: a developmental perspective

OVERVIEW

The next two chapters focus on a number of areas of developmental psychology that are particularly important for teachers. Developmental psychology offers ways of conceptualizing development rather than giving immediate solutions to educational issues. It provides a framework that underpins teachers' actions in the classroom as opposed to a set of prescriptions for teaching. This chapter follows on from Chapter 2 in describing the development of thinking. One of the most important aspects of cognitive development is the relationship between language and thought, and this area is covered in some detail. This chapter focuses on:

- a framework for developmental psychology;
- the nature/nurture debate;
- cognitive development: the influence of Piaget;
- language and thought.

A FRAMEWORK FOR DEVELOPMENTAL PSYCHOLOGY

Developmental psychology is concerned with describing and explaining the development of people from birth to old age. Within this area there is a vast body of literature on child development. Mussen (1983) takes four volumes and 4,000 pages to review the field. Psychologists have offered a variety of alternative theories to explain how development occurs. These range from Piaget's theory of the structure of the mind changing, through Freud's psychoanalytic theory of personality development, to Bronfenbrenner's ecological theory.

It is easy to be confused by the number of theories in developmental psychology. Because of the size of the field, and because different areas have been studied, no one developmental theory has satisfactorily covered both a description of development and an explanation of how development occurs. There are therefore a number of reasonable theoretical alternatives that help explain development.

Some psychologists are principally interested in studying the development of thinking (cognitive psychology) while others have been mainly interested in the study of the development of personality. Within each content area there are two principal focuses: some psychologists are interested in describing development, and some are interested in explaining it as a process.

Describing development

Developmental psychologists have spent a lot of time studying normal development and trying to ascertain the 'norms' – what is normal for development at various ages. This includes normative information both on the cognitive side – such as the normal age at which pupils can recognize letters – and also on personality – such as the age at which pupils begin to cooperate with their peers. So, for example, Binet (see Chapter 2) was a developmental psychologist in so far as he tried to establish the ages at which the normal pupil could complete certain tasks. The whole of the National Curriculum rests on the assumption that it is normal to learn things at different ages and that there is some kind of developmental sequence in the acquisition of skills. Teachers usually develop a normative view of pupils' development based on their experiences with pupils, as well as on reading the research in this area (see Sylva and Lunt, 1983, for an introduction). There is increasing recognition by developmental psychologists that descriptive studies of normal development are not as helpful as was first thought. In particular, it is recognized that there are wide variations between pupils in their acquisition of skills. It is important to recognize that this variation is normal, rather than see it as a problem.

Explaining development

The other focus has been on trying to explain the process of development, rather than simply describing it. An example of this is Bowlby's attachment theory (see Chapter 4), which explains how the process of bonding occurs between parents and children.

Recent research on the processes affecting development have concentrated on whether critical incidents in a child's life are indicators of future maladaptive behaviour. Is susceptibility to life events, such as depression following retirement, dependent on early events in a person's life? One well-researched area is how far adult criminal behaviour is dependent on the way children are brought up; another is how far alcoholism in middle age is dependent on earlier events in a person's life.

A developmental perspective is a way of looking at people in the present in the light of their earlier experiences. Development is about attempting to explain changes over time.

Developmental psychology

Contemporary developmental psychology has five particular characteristics (Tharinger and Lambert, 1990):

- acceptance of theoretical pluralism, or the fact that there may be a number of reasonable theoretical alternatives to explain development;
- a concern about the continued use of developmental norms;
- an interest in theories to explain the process of development, rather than just a description;
- an interest in understanding maladaptive development that contributes to putting pupils at risk – for example, of alcoholism;
- a transactional view of development that emphasizes a continual, reciprocal relationship between pupils and their environment.

The transactional view of development, which emphasizes the reciprocal relationship between pupils and their environment, is such an important characteristic of contemporary developmental psychology that it is worth exploring in some detail. Teachers' views on whether a pupil's development is dependent on the environment or on factors inside him are fundamental to the way they view education. This is known as the nature/nurture debate.

THE NATURE/NURTURE DEBATE

A major debate that has raged over the twentieth century concerns the relative effects of the environment (nurture) and inheritance (nature) on development. This debate often focuses on intelligence, but it includes other aspects of development, such as pupils' personality. The debate is characterized by highly emotive overtones. This is because the teacher's position on it will have a profound effect on her teaching practice.

If development is largely determined at birth by genetic characteristics, then it is seen as largely stable – education can have little effect on it, and is about fulfilling a pupil's given potential. Practical implications are, for example, the teacher believing that some pupils will inherently not be good at mathematics no matter how well they are taught. If, on the other hand, development is largely determined by the environment, then education is the key to each pupil's progress and achievements in school, and is about developing a pupil's potential. Practical implications are, for example, teachers believing that pupils' progress at mathematics depends, or at least partially depends, on their skills at teaching.

In the last few decades there have been an increasing number of attempts to show the importance of the environment on pupils' development. The best-known research is that of the Head Start programme.

Environmental influences: the Head Start programme

The Head Start programme provided compensatory education for thousands of pre-school children in the USA in the 1960s. It was a result of the recognition by educationists and politicians that a stimulating early environment would help pupils' development. Head Start comprised a number of different types of programme, but they all shared a belief that early intervention could improve the development of children's skills.

The aim of Head Start was to prevent failure at school – and it would have been sensible to have evaluated success on the basis of whether the programme actually did prevent failure at school. But because of the need to prove the programme's success, intelligence tests were, unfortunately and inappropriately, used for pragmatic reasons.

The educational programmes varied widely and there were initially many reports of short-term gains in IQ. Unfortunately, the gains in initial IQ when the children entered school usually faded out after a few years, with the pupils' IQs failing to remain higher than the control groups' (the pupils who had not taken part in the programme). Because of this, critics were quick to dismiss these compensatory education programmes as a waste of money. Long-term studies have, though, confirmed the validity of the original basis for the Head Start programme – that early education does help pupils achieve success at school (Zigler and Valentine, 1979). Pupils who had been part of Head Start were 40 per cent less likely to be placed in special education classes and 20 per cent less likely to be kept back a grade than pupils in the control groups. They were also more than four times more likely to go on to college or skilled jobs than the control group. These long-term results stand in direct contrast to the earlier results based on the IQ scores.

The critics of the effectiveness of the Head Start compensatory education programme were encouraged by Arthur Jensen's infamous article (1969), 'How much can we boost IQ and scholastic achievement?'. In this he asserted that lower-class ethnic minority children fail in school because of their genetic limitations. He reasserted the 'nature' position – that intelligence is inherited and that, therefore, compensatory education is doomed to failure. This classic argument for the genetic base for development destroyed good educational practice. From a political view it was, however, welcome, as it helped justify cutting back on the funding for pre-school compensatory education. In Britain, where the education provision for children under age 5 is among the lowest in Europe, it may still be that Jensen's work allows policy-makers to justify their position. Many educationists, however, took violent exception to Jensen's racist tone, and certainly in Britain few psychologists involved in education would accept the substance of his arguments at all.

The present position

The nature/nurture debate continues, but largely for political reasons. Research has expanded enormously in the last two decades and highlighted the inadequacies of an either/or polarization. The advent of more sophisticated models for describing developmental processes, such as the cognitive processes (see Chapter 2), means that from a psychological perspective the debate has moved on. Most psychologists now believe that both internal (hereditary) and external (environmental) factors affect development.

If teachers accept the premise that development is dependent on both environmental and internal factors acting interactively, then it seems unnecessary, on other than purely ideological grounds, to argue about the percentages of influence. What is important is how the teacher can modify the effect of the factors. The received wisdom is that environmental factors can be influenced, but internal factors cannot. So the argument is for better buildings, more resources and a higher standard of living to overcome the poverty that affects the education of many pupils in Britain today.

It is worth considering whether this is the wrong way around. Maybe what teachers can directly affect is the effects of the internal factors – the way pupils use the skills and abilities that they have – and that this should be the focus for the way teachers can affect development.

At the centre of the internal factors that the teacher may be able to affect are thinking and language. The rest of this chapter focuses on their development, starting with the work of probably the most famous developmental educational psychologist – Jean Piaget.

COGNITIVE DEVELOPMENT: THE INFLUENCE OF PIAGET

Jean Piaget is one of the most frequently mentioned and least-understood developmental psychologists. There are a number of reasons why he is so poorly understood. His writing is extensive, and both the language and the concepts that he uses are difficult to understand. In addition, there often appears a gap between the conclusion that he draws and what he actually describes. His method of research is largely based on detailed observations of his own children, and from these often apparently minor observations he draws major conclusions about the way pupils' minds develop.

Jean Piaget (1896–1980)

Jean Piaget dominated cognitive developmental psychology during the 1960s and 1970s. He was born in Switzerland and lived there most of his life. He trained as a zoologist, which give him a particularly biological perspective on development. He lectured at the University of Geneva, spending his summers in the Alps writing his remarkable series of books on child development. In all he wrote over 300 works including 30 books. His most important contribution was to show that cognitive development consists of a series of qualitative changes in cognitive structure.

The focus of Piaget's work

Piaget (1966, 1972) focused on the way pupils' cognitive structures develop through their interaction with the environment. He described his work as 'genetic epistemology' – a developmental theory about the way knowledge develops. (Reading Piaget is similar to doing a crossword – a large dictionary should be kept open for referencing key concepts!)

One extremely important Piagetian concept which is useful in education is the principle of auto-regulation or equilibrium. Cognitive development is a period of disequilibrium followed by adaption as the pupils change their present cognitive structure to the new demands of the environment. The pupil's mind adapts to the environment through two key mechanisms: assimilation and accommodation. Assimilation is concerned with the pupil's adapting and modifying information from the environment to fit with his cognitive structures; accommodation, on the other hand, consists of a pupil's adapting and modifying structures to fit the new information.

When a pupil faces an issue, he needs to assimilate the new information into his existing cognitive structures. If the information does not fit, he then needs actually to change the cognitive structures to accommodate the information. The pupil is seeking to make an equilibrium between the information from the environment and his cognitive ability to deal with it. So for the reader, assimilation is fitting Piaget's theories into your existing theories about how development occurs. Accommodation is about actually changing the structures in your mind so that you now see them from a Piagetian perspective.

There are links between this theory of changing cognitive structures and the more recent cognitive models of Anderson, described in Chapter 2. Both suggest that the mind changes to assimilate and adapt to new information. However, Piaget and Anderson come at this question from very different perspectives. Anderson sees cognitive development as continuous whereas Piaget sees it as a series of stages.

Stages of development

Cognitive development is a series of stages that are linked to the pupil's biological development. As each stage unfolds, the pupil is able to understand a more complex view of the world. There are essentially four stages, named after the dominant cognitive structure of each:

- sensori-motor (age 0–2);
- pre-operational (age 2–7);
- concrete operational (age 7–11);
- formal operations (age 11 plus).

Piaget believed that these stages are biologically determined and are more or less age-related. He recognized that cultural and environmental factors lead to variations in the rate of development.

Sensori-motor (0–2)

Children at this age structure the world through their senses and actions. Children gradually develop internal representations of well-defined sequences of physical or mental activity, such as grasping, sucking and looking at objects. These representations – similar to schemata – develop during the first few years of the child's life. The child begins to learn how to be able to represent actions and objects internally. A good example of one of these representations is 'object permanence'. The child at the sensori-motor level does not know that

53

objects exist as separate entities. Piaget describes, in the heavily edited sequence below, the way his daughter Jacqueline's thinking develops from about the age of 7 months. This is typical of the naturalistic observations on which he builds his theories:

> Jacqueline tries to grasp a celluloid duck on top of the quilt. She almost catches it, shakes herself, and the duck slides down beside her. It falls very close to her hand but behind a fold in the sheet. Jacqueline's eyes have followed the movement, she has even followed it with her outstretched hand. But as soon as the duck has disappeared – nothing more! It does not occur to her to search behind the fold in the sheet . . .

Some months later . . .

> Jacqueline watches me when I put a coin in my hand, then put my hand under a coverlet. I withdraw my hand closed; Jacqueline opens it, then searches under the coverlet until she finds the object.
>
> (Piaget, quoted by Flavell, 1963, pp. 132–4)

It is only when children are about 2 years old that they realize that an object has an existence independent of their perception of it. It is only gradually that Jacqueline becomes aware that even if the object is out of her sight, it is still there. This is the development of object permanence. Object permanence develops through children representing an object in their minds by overtly imitating it through their actions. Gradually children stop overtly imitating the object and simply have an image of it in their minds – the action becomes internalized. This thought, or image, is very limited and develops before the child has any language.

Pre-operations (2–7)

At the next pre-operations stage children's thoughts become more flexible. They can remember, imagine and pretend. Piaget differentiates between two subphases: a preconceptual phase (age 2–4), when language develops, and an intuitive phase (age 4–7). The most important feature of the intuitive phase is the development of 'mental operations', such as being able to think in terms of relationships and classes.

The term 'operation' is used by Piaget to described an 'internalized action'; that is, an action that takes place in the imagination. The characteristic of this stage, and the reason it is called pre-operations, is that the pupil performs these mental operations as isolated events rather than relating them to a system of possible operations. A good example of this is that the pre-operational child cannot think in terms of reversibility; so although 5-year-olds can understand that if ice is heated it turns to water, they do not easily (or automatically) see that this process can be reversed. Their lack of flexibility means that their logical thinking is limited. It is only through children's playing with concrete materials such as clay and water that they learn that operations can be reversed. This is why it is so important for young children to have the opportunity to play – it is through this play that they begin to think logically.

The thinking of the pre-operational child can be differentiated from the next stage by the fact that the pre-operations child finds it difficult to change viewpoints. He sees the world from his own position and finds it difficult to shift perspectives.

Concrete operational (7–11)

During this stage, children begin to realize that operations can be reversed. The importance of this realization is that it is the basis of logic. If pupils can understand that a sequence of actions can be always logically reversed – that ice that becomes water can become ice again, that $2 + 5 = 7$ and $7 - 2 = 5$ – they then can go beyond the information given in any situation. Year 4 pupils do not have to see the water being refrozen again; they know the sequence can be reversed. They are still only functioning at the concrete level, however; they can perform mental operations with concrete materials but not with abstract possibilities. Thus it is argued that arithmetic can be taught to 9-year-olds, but not algebra.

Formal operations (11+)

At this stage pupils are mentally able to solve abstract problems. They are able to think through the problem and possible solutions for it, and to test out a number of hypotheses before finding a logical solution to a problem.

The validity of Piagetian theory

Piaget's theory is descriptive – it describes how pupils think at various ages. There is considerable evidence that pupils across a range of countries go through some sort of sequence of cognitive development similar to that which Piaget describes. This is quite remarkable, given that his entire writing is based on his own three children in Switzerland. However, there are two critical issues involved with his theory.

The first is over the way Piaget explains qualitative differences in thinking. It can be argued that many of the changes that Piaget observed are basically changes in pupils' thinking due to developments in their language – as their language develops, so their ability to think about the world differently also develops. They can talk about the world differently, so it appears that they are actually thinking about it differently. Piaget believed that it is the cognitive structure that changes first and that language development stems from the changes in cognitive development, rather than vice versa. The research that has been done to clarify the issue can be used to support either view.

The second issue is over whether the four stages are an accurate reflection of pupils' cognitive development. Bruner (1959), a follower of Piaget (see Chapter 10), believes that there are other stages of development once a pupil reaches 11.

These two fundamental issues mean that many psychologists question the validity of Piaget's perspective on cognitive development. Nevertheless, his theories provide an underpinning framework for primary education in Britain.

Applying Piagetian theory

Probably the best-known systematic application of Piagetian psychology to the classroom is in Furth and Wachs's book, *Thinking Goes to School* (1975). In this book they describe their attempt to set up and run a 'thinking school' (or at least a thinking class for 5–6-year-olds) based on Piagetian theory. Activities such as logical and visual thinking games were used to develop the pupils' thinking. Furth and Wachs contrasted their attempt to run a 'thinking' school with the traditional approach – a 'reading' school. In 'reading' schools, so much time goes into the teaching of reading that the development of thinking never actually happens. Their brave attempt came to its logical end when parents of pupils in the class complained that too much time was being devoted to thinking rather than reading!

More recently a High/Scope training programme for nursery teachers that incorporates aspects of Piagetian theory into its work has been available in the UK. The High/Scope approach is based on longitudinal research in the United States, known as the Ypsilanti Perry Preschool Project, that demonstrates the benefits of pre-school education for disadvantaged children (Berruta-Clement *et al.*, 1985).

Piaget does not provide specific answers to particular pragmatic questions about how to help pupils develop in the classroom. Despite this, most teachers would find that Piagetian theory provides a framework of principles that underpins their teaching practice (Dale, 1975).

Many teachers, especially in primary schools, would recognize these principles as fundamental. It was Piaget who turned these psychological principles into taken-for-granted, common-sense principles of good teaching. He also backs up these assertions about what is good teaching practice with a developmental psychological perspective. Piaget's influence is indubitable – it lies in the complexity of the description of pupils' cognitive development and the audacity of the attempt to confine it to four stages of development (admittedly with some subdivisions). As with any theory, the importance of Piaget may be, in the end, not whether he is right or wrong but rather whether his framework helps teachers understand pupils. Using his framework helps make sense of cognitive development; it is not the only perspective but it is a starting point. In particular, it is a starting point in seeing how language affects thought.

Piagetian principles for teachers

1 New ideas and knowledge should be presented at a level consistent with the pupil's present state of thinking. Piaget showed that there are major limitations to the logical thinking skills that pupils have at different ages.

2 Teaching should be matched to the needs of individuals. Pupils should be presented with moderately novel situations. This ensures cognitive adaptation and assimilation.

3 A major source of learning is activity by the pupils. Pupils must have the opportunity to experiment actively with concrete materials in order to develop their thinking skills.

4 Pupils learn by social interaction. They need to share their learning experiences and discuss their differences in thinking and solutions to tasks.

5 Pupils should have considerable control over their own learning. They need to learn how to find out for themselves and to be able to verify what is true rather than being told how, or what, to think.

LANGUAGE AND THOUGHT

One of the major difficulties with the development of thinking is that thinking and language are so intertwined. As we have seen, one of the problems in evaluating Piagetian stages of development is the question of whether it is changes in language or in thinking that underpin development. Language is a major area of psychological research, and language development is a substantial part of this field. This section will concentrate on the development of the links between thought, language and the development of meaning, rather than reviewing all the theories of language development.

An initial distinction must be made between language and speech. Speech is the production of speech sounds – it is a tangible, physical process. Language is a system of meanings and linguistic structures in the brain. It is intangible and can only be inferred from speech (and other forms of communication, such as writing). When the pupil talks to the teacher, what the teacher hears is speech. There is an assumption that language and thought underlie this speech – though teachers would sometimes question this! On a more serious note, it can be seen that if a pupil is reciting a poem or the alphabet learnt by heart, little if any thinking may be going into the process. Speech is involved in communication between people, while language is concerned with thought. Language is not always reflected in speech. A pupil can think about what to say in answer to a teacher's question – words that may never be spoken.

The distinction between language and thought

In the first half of the century, radical behaviourists argued that there was no sense in making a distinction between language and thought. They were interested in promoting the theory that no intervening processes in the head were required in order to explain behaviour.

This was an American behavioural position; Russian psychologists saw things differently. (Though behavioural psychology is rightly associated with American psychologists, the father of behavioural psychology was the Russian, Ivan Pavlov, he of the famous salivating dogs.)

The development of language and thought

The Russian position is exemplified by Vygotsky (1962). He was interested in the social construction of the mind – the way the social environment shaped the mind mainly through the mediation of language.

Vygotsky proposed that language for the child has two functions: communicating with other people (speech), and internally for thinking. Speech, language and thought are closely linked in the young child, but a crucial feature of development is to free thought from speech. Thought develops from the internalization of action – particularly speech. By about age 3, children talk to themselves as they play. This egocentric speech is about the problems and issues that arise out of the play situations that they are in. So, for example, a young child describes how he is putting the ball through the chair legs so that it can hit the peg on the far side. The function of this egocentric speech is similar to that of thinking – to help the child consciously understand the difficulties that the task presents. It is this inner speech that is connected with the child's thinking. It is only gradually that egocentric speech directed at events in the outside world is separated from inner language and thought. The child stops speaking to himself, and thinking develops.

While Vygotsky believed that it is the gradual internalization of speech that leads to the development of thinking, Piaget took a different view. He believed that children's development of thinking depends on their acting on the environment. Language may be involved to amplify or facilitate thinking, but is not essential for thinking.

Lev Vygotsky (1896–1934)

Vygotsky was born in White Russia, in the same year as Piaget. He came to psychology from a background of literature and the theatre. He worked for only 10 years as a psychologist before his early death. He inspired many psychologists and in particular his followers Luria (1902–79) and Leontyev (1904–79). The three of them have been called the Russian troika. Vygotsky tried to develop a specifically Marxist psychology that could be tied to education. He believed that all individual functioning had a social origin and that the way to bring about development was by improving social conditions. Stalin, however, decreed that all psychology had to be based on Pavlov. It was only from the 1960s that Vygotsky's ideas were brought to the West. His work is referenced from the dates of these translations.

It is certainly possible to have language without speech – as any deaf person who uses sign language can testify. Is it possible to think without any language? There are number of mental processes that seem to be pre- or non-linguistic. The executive part of thinking – for example, decision making and the intention to act – is non-linguistic. This distinction between thought and language can be seen in the models of long-term memory mentioned in Chapter 2; in particular, Paivio's dual coding theory, which distinguishes between verbal and imaginal memory, is similar. The imaginal processes do not require words. But then imaginal processes cannot be easily manipulated in a way that conveys thinking, so the aspects of thinking that appear to be non-linguistic are limited.

In summary, speech is not required for language, and language is not required for thought; nevertheless, the development of all three is very closely interlinked. The recognition that language and thought are intimately related underpins the importance of language development in the classroom. By school age, pupils have developed a clear distinction between speech and thought. Any thought that a pupil, or adult, has, has to be transformed through language before it can be communicated to others.

> ### The communication of any thought is a developmental process
>
> Thought, unlike speech, does not consist of separate units. When I wish to communicate the thought that today I saw a barefoot boy in a blue shirt running down the street, I do not see every item separately . . . I conceive of all this in one thought, but I put it into separate words. A speaker often takes several minutes to disclose one thought. In his mind the whole thought is present at once, but in speech it has to be developed successively. A thought may be compared to a cloud shedding a shower of words.
>
> (Vygotsky, 1962; quoted Slobin, 1971, p. 101)

So the actual act of communication is a developmental process in which a thought, which may have been imaginal, is changed and transfigured through language into speech. This is not a one-way process, as the actual language feeds back on the thought and thus changes and develops it too. Language is at the very centre of the thinking processes. Not only does language transform thoughts before they are communicated, it actually shapes the thoughts themselves.

Linguistic relativity and determinism

In the first part of the century, Benjamin Lee Whorf developed a theory that language was even more fundamental to thinking than so far described. This is known as the theory of linguistic relativity and determinism.

> ### Benjamin Lee Whorf (1897–1941)
>
> Whorf studied chemistry at the Massachusetts Institute of Technology. He worked for chemical and insurance companies most of his life. He became a pupil of the great linguist and anthropologist, Edward Sapir. He eventually ended up lecturing in anthropology at Yale University in 1937.

Whorf's (1956) fundamental proposition was that people – pupils and teachers – do not live in an objective world. Instead, the world that they live in is created, unconsciously, by the particular language which they use. Language is not merely a way of expressing the pupils' thoughts and therefore reflecting the world; it is the foundation of the real world. The language that pupils use predisposes them to look at the world in a particular way. Thus what they experience is very largely determined by their language.

An example of this is pupils' perceptions of careers. Consider a pupil who lives in a culture where higher education is talked about. In this culture, words such as 'degree' and 'higher degree' are commonly used. This pupil actually lives in a career world very different from that of a pupil whose conception of a career is to work in the local supermarket. This is more than a difference in economic aspirations: the two pupils see a career as two very different things. This is not to say that both pupils' worlds could not be developed through language. The second pupil, whose aspirations are to the local supermarket, if given the language could understand the world of higher education. What is interesting is that the first pupil might find it more difficult to change his understanding of the world. Once a pupil has the wider language, he will have difficulty conceiving the world that the supermarket aspirant lives in. (The same failure of comprehension can often be observed in politicians.) People with wide horizons can find it difficult to comprehend a more limited world. For example, there is often difficulty in understanding how limited opportunity and deprivation can lead to violence.

Linguistic relativity and determinism

Language does not simply represent the 'real world' – instead, it actually determines the pupil's world. This is known as linguistic determinism. It is language that determines the world pupils live in. Exactly what is determined is relative to the language spoke – this is linguistic relativity. Linguistic relativity and determinism can be summed up by the phrase, 'The limits of my language stand for the limits of my world.'

A multicultural perspective

Much of the work on linguistic relativity and determinism stems from cross-cultural phenomena – comparing the similarities and differences of languages in different societies. Such comparisons are particularly important in multicultural Britain in the 1990s. Pupils who come to school with a linguistic background that is not English will have different ways of seeing the world as compared with those whose first language is English. For example, English promotes a view of the world in which individual identity is all-important. Other cultures stress, through their language, that it is the individual's role within a family, and the family's role within the larger community, that are important.

The same phenomenon of linguistic determinism applies within a single culture. Bernstein (1971) showed that there are considerable differences between working- and middle-class pupils in both the content and structure of their language. The working-class pupils' 'restricted code' or language is a distinct disadvantage when trying to progress in an educational system that is operating a middle-class linguistic code. The pupils' world is dominated, if not completely determined, by their language.

Linguistic determinism and education

Linguistic relativity and determinism highlight the importance of language as a key process for education. The language pupils use influences their thinking and the way they see the world. Teachers have a primary function of expanding and developing pupils' language, whatever age and whatever subject they teach. Without this development of language, education cannot take place. This primary function comes with its own particular responsibilities.

There is a danger that the teacher's values, meanings and perceptions may override those of the pupil (Shipman, 1985). This is particularly apparent if one thinks of the fact that pupils from different social and cultural groups have different language structures and therefore different meanings for events. It is less apparent when considering how teachers develop the reality for every child. For example, King (1978) showed how teachers define the meanings of concepts such as 'play' for infant pupils. Pupils are told what activities are considered 'work' and what are considered 'play'. In the same way pupils are told what constitutes a 'proper picture'. Teachers need to recognize that their language and meaning for events may be unfamiliar to the pupils. So, for example, teachers' use of abstract words may be meaningless to the pupils. At another level, their insistence on the one right answer to a question may prevent rather than help the development of pupils' thinking.

As teachers develop the pupils' breadth and depth of understanding of the world, they are, at the same time, limiting the pupils' world by imposing their own constructions on it.

SUMMARY

Developmental psychology underpins a teacher's work in the classroom. A cognitive developmental perspective is a way of understanding how pupils' thinking develops. Teachers' beliefs about the hereditary and environmental factors that influence cognitive development fundamentally affect their beliefs about the effectiveness of their own teaching. Piagetian theory on how thinking develops has permeated primary teaching in Britain. In particular, the importance of matching tasks to stages of development and of pupils' active involvement with real material have been established as fundamental to cognitive development.

The other key to cognitive development is the development of language. The relationship of language to thought is a complex, dynamic process, and it is helpful to think of both an imaginal and a verbal aspect to thinking. The development of the pupils' language is at the very heart of the development of thinking. The importance of language is less obvious, but equally important for teachers. It is all too easy to use limited language to describe complex aspects of the educational process. Teachers need to talk about education and to understand different ways of thinking about pupils' development. For both teachers and pupils, the limits of their language are also the limits of their worlds.

REFERENCES

Bernstein, B. (1971) *Class, Codes and Control*. Vol. 1: *Theoretical Studies towards a Sociology of Language*. London: Routledge & Kegan Paul.

Berruta-Clement, J., Schweinhart, L., Barnett, W., Epstein, A. and Weikart, D. (1985) *Changed Lives: The Effects of the Perry Preschool Programme on Youth through Age 19*. London: High/Scope Publications.

Bruner, J. (1959) Inhelder and Piaget's *The Growth of Logical Thinking*, *British Journal of Psychology* **50**, pp. 363–70.

Dale, J. (1975) Some implications from the work of Jean Piaget, in Gardener, P. (ed.), *The Structure of Science Education*. Melbourne: Longman Australia.

Flavell, J. (1963) *The Developmental Psychology of Jean Piaget*. Princeton, NJ: Van Nostrand.

Furth, H. and Wachs, H. (1975) *Thinking Goes to School: Piaget's Theory in Practice*. London: Oxford University Press.

Jensen, A. (1969) How much can we boost IQ and scholastic achievement?, *Harvard Educational Review* **39**, pp. 1–123.

King, R. (1978) *All Things Bright and Beautiful*. Chichester: Wiley.

Mussen, P. (ed.) (1983) *Handbook of Child Psychology*, Vols 1-4. New York: Wiley.

Piaget, J. (1966) *The Origins of Intelligence in Children*. New York: International Universities Press.

Piaget, J. (1972) *The Principles of Genetic Epistemology*. New York: Basic Books.

Shipman, M. (1985) *The Management of Learning in the Classroom*. London: Hodder & Stoughton.

Slobin, D. (1971) *Psycholinguistics*. London: Scott, Foresman.

Sylva, K. and Lunt, I. (1983) *Child Development: A First Course*. Oxford: Basil Blackwell.

Tharinger, D. and Lambert, N. (1990) The contributions of developmental psychology to school psychology, in Gutkin, T. and Reynolds, C. (eds), *The Handbook of School Psychology*. Chichester: Wiley.

Vygotsky, L. (1962) *Thought and Language*. Cambridge, MA: MIT Press.

Whorf, B. (1956) *Language, Thought and Reality* (edited with an introduction by J. Carroll). New York: Wiley.

Zigler, E. and Valentine, J. (eds) (1979) *Project Head Start: A Legacy of the War on Poverty*. New York: Free Press.

RECOMMENDED READING

H. Furth and H. Wachs, *Thinking Goes to School: Piaget's Theory in Practice* (London: Oxford University Press, 1975), describes an attempt to turn Piaget's theory into practical classroom activities. This classic book contains ideas for numerous games to stimulate thinking.

K. Sylva and I. Lunt, *Child Development: A First Course* (Oxford: Basil Blackwell, 1983), is a practical and readable introduction to child development.

R. Vasta (ed.), *Six Theories of Child Development* (London: Jessica Kingsley Publishers, 1992), has each chapter written by an authority on a particular theory of child development. Each gives an intelligent analysis of the present state of the theory and contains a wealth of information. This book is highly recommended as it covers theories dealt with throughout this first part.

CHAPTER 4

Personality development

OVERVIEW

Personality means the individual characteristics of a pupil – who he is.
It is sometimes assumed that the personality is inherited: 'He's got a
temper just like his father's.' On the other hand, sometimes personality
is seen as dependent on upbringing: 'He's had an unsettled home life –
that is why he is moody.' Personality is also used as a label to describe
the positive features of a pupil: 'He's such a personality.' This carries
overtones of the pupil being bright and socially engaging. So a 'personality' is something to be coveted – even if all pupils have one!

Chapter 1 examined psychological theories for explaining pupils'
actions at a particular time – now. All these theories depend upon a
developmental perspective, in so far as they consider the way a pupil's
present actions relate to how he has acted in the past. There are a
number of other psychological perspectives that focus on personality
development. In particular, this chapter covers:

- the development of the self-concept;
- personality traits;
- early experiences: psychoanalytic theory;
- the importance of significant adults;
- the ecological perspective;
- the development of competence.

THE DEVELOPMENT OF THE SELF-CONCEPT

At the centre of personality development is a belief in the importance
of the self. The self consists of all the beliefs, values and attitudes that

a pupil has about himself. It is the 'I', the 'me'. These beliefs are collectively called the self-concept. Carl Rogers proposed that self-knowledge – knowledge about one's self-concept – is the basis for all personal development.

Carl Rogers (1902–87)

Carl Rogers was brought up on a farm and went to college in Wisconsin. He started to study agriculture and then switched to theology. While still in college, he went to China as part of an international World Student Christian Federation Conference. His experiences there made him break with the religious beliefs of his parents. He moved from theology to psychology and worked as a child psychologist for the Society for the Prevention of Cruelty to Children for twelve years. There he developed the principles of 'non-directive, client-centred therapy'. From there he moved to a series of academic positions before ending at the University of Wisconsin. The emphasis in non-directive, client-centred therapy is on facilitating the natural growth of the child, or adult. This can be contrasted with most other psychotherapeutic approaches, which take a more directive line, with clients being told how to resolve their difficulties.

The origin of the self is in social interaction. A pupil's self-concept develops from the reactions of other people to his behaviour. Parents, teachers and peers can be seen as mirrors in which a pupil comes to see himself. They give the pupil feedback about what is acceptable and what is not, what is clever and what is not. Gradually the pupil builds up a picture of who he is. This is the 'self' – the core of the pupil's personality. Interaction with other people is crucial to the development of the pupil's self-concept.

Rogers (1983) suggests that parents and teachers can develop high self-esteem in their child by ensuring the love they give is not conditional on success or obedience. This is called by Rogers 'unconditional positive regard' – the need to feel loved just for being yourself. The pupils' need for unconditional positive regard overshadows all other needs. It is the need to be thought well of. If a pupil does not believe that he is thought well of by others, he will find it difficult to think well of himself.

The relationship between self-concept and the way the pupil is treated has been supported by the frequently quoted research by Coopersmith (1967). He investigated the relationship between child-rearing practices and self-esteem in 1,700 10–12-year-old boys. Both intelligence and school performance had the expected positive effect on self-esteem. Nevertheless, 90 per cent of the variation in self-esteem was unaccounted for by these two measures. He found the most significant factor was the difference in the child-rearing practices of the boys' parents. He found that the boys with high self-esteem had parents who set firm, fair, high standards, used rewards rather than punishments as incentives, and showed their sons interest and warmth. On the other hand, boys with low self-esteem had parents who were permissive, who showed little interest and were punitive and unfair to them. Boys with high self-esteem were brought up to see the world as a stable place where they were accepted and valued for their attainments. Most importantly, it was a world that they could have some control over. (The importance of these particular beliefs is returned to in Chapter 7.)

Though it is helpful to see the self-concept as developing through the direct feedback that others give to the pupil, it is more complex than this. The pupil's self-concept does not directly reflect the feedback he receives; instead, it is influenced by the pupil's perception of that feedback. This is known as a phenomenological perspective.

The self-concept

A pupil's self-concept is not stable – it changes through his interaction with others. The pupil will become more self-confident through success and praise. He will become more secure in himself from consistent feedback from important adults. On the other hand, if the pupil receives inconsistent or limited interaction he may become confused about how to see himself.

The phenomenological approach to the self

Aspects of the phenomenological approach have already been introduced. George Kelly's personal construct theory (see Chapter 1) is essentially phenomenological, as it emphasizes that each pupil has his own constructs. Linguistic relativity and determinism (see Chapter 3) also showed how pupils see the world through their own language. Phenomenological approaches are concerned with the way pupils perceive themselves and their own personal experiences. For example, assume two pupils sitting in class are asked by the teacher to complete an exercise. One of the pupils may interpret the request in one way: 'It's an easy piece of work and I'm bored.' The other pupil may interpret the same request in a different way: 'She's trying to show me up – I can't do that.' The two pupils interpret the same event in different ways and therefore it has different effects on their self-concepts. This is the heart of the phenomenological perspective – that everyone is different and pupils have different meanings and interpretations for the same event.

This phenomenological approach is also known as 'constructive alternatism'. By this is meant that any event can be seen in different ways – any event is always open to 'reconstruction' . This reconstruction is not arbitrary, as a pupil interprets the world so that it makes coherent sense to himself. In the example above, the second pupil can reconstruct the teacher's request to complete the exercise by deciding that she is not trying to show him up.

The phenomenological perspective

The phenomenological approach is 'humanistic', as it emphasizes the human aspects (as opposed to the biological aspects) of development. Development is a self-directing, self-actualizing phenomenon. Pupils are active interpreters of the world around them – at the centre of the development of their own self-concept. They are not dependent on the feedback that they get from others but can create their own selves.

Teachers have a key role in the development of pupils' self-concepts. The classroom is one of the major challenges in pupils' lives, so, the feedback that teachers give them will shape their whole conception of themselves. This is not to deny the phenomenological perspective – in the end, it is each pupil who decides how to interpret the teacher's comments. But this process is interactive, and the starting point is the interactions the teacher has with each pupil.

The strength of the phenomenological perspective is that it recognizes the uniqueness of individual pupils. This open-endedness can be contrasted with the trait approach to personality, described below.

PERSONALITY TRAITS

Raymond Cattell was one of the main exponents of this concept. He believed that a pupil's personality is made up of a number of traits, defined as a disposition to act in a particular way in particular circumstances. Traits have similarities with Kelly's personal constructs (see Chapter 1), but whereas Kelly emphasizes the importance of the

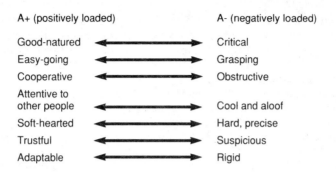

Figure 4.1 Personality factors.

unique constructs each individual has, Cattell tried to reduce the constructs to a number of key or 'source' traits. The way he did this was through our old statistical friend, factor analysis.

Raymond Cattell (1905-)

Raymond Cattell was born in Staffordshire and educated at King's College London. He was one of the pupils of Charles Spearman, and the London school. The members of this 'school' based their work on the tenet, 'Whatever exists, exists in some quantity and can in principle be measured.' He went to the United States in 1937 and lectured at a number of universities before settling in Illinois in 1944. Cattell is most famous for his work on personality testing, popularized in his book *The Scientific Analysis of Personality* (1965).

Through questionnaires, Cattell identified 16 factors that he believed to be the basic underlying personality traits. Each factor has two dimensions and each pupil's personality is loaded somewhere along the dimension from positive $(+)$ to negative $(-)$. The positive–negative dimension is purely statistical – there is no implication that it is best to be positive. The factors are identified by the letters of the alphabet and the most fundamental is concerned with temperament – Factor A (see Figure 4.1). Factor B is one of intelligence, Factor C is of emotional strength, and so on.

The development of traits depends on both environmental and genetic influences. So a quiet pupil has some of this characteristic determined genetically, but the rest is shaped by being reinforced for being quiet. Gradually, over time, this pupil's characteristic reaction in situations is to be quiet. Cattell believes that much of the basic formation of personality occurs in the first six or seven years. However, adolescence gives new fuel to personality development that can continue all through life.

Any experience produces personality development in more than one trait. A key concept is 'chiasms' or dynamic crossroads, which are choice points where the pupil decides how to act in specific situations. When the pupil is at a dynamic crossroad, there are a number of conflicting forces prompting him to act in different ways. It is his self-concept that influences his decision on how to act and therefore the development of the traits.

Implications for teachers

Cattell believes that teachers have two responsibilities. The first is to develop the most appropriate personality traits in the pupil to help him learn effectively. On the basis of statistical analysis, Cattell (1965) showed that pupils will make more progress in school if they:

- are outgoing and adaptable and relate warmly to teachers;
- are emotionally balanced and not easily upset;
- are conscientious.

By reinforcing these traits, teachers can help develop pupils who learn effectively.

Teachers' second responsibility is to help pupils develop as useful citizens. This has recently been given increased political prominence. As personality is at least partially determined by the environment, schooling is about the development of pupils' personalities as well as academic skills. Pupils' personalities can be measured by questionnaires to give a personality profile – a sketch of the pupil's personality measured along the 16 factors. From this profile, teachers can select those personality characteristics that useful citizens have!

Personality testing is used extensively in industry, in selection procedures to predict how suitable a person is for a particular post. It is not common in the education world, though it is sometimes used in the selection of local education authority officers. The attraction of the trait approach to personality is similar to that of the psychometric approach to intelligence: it appears that through a pen-and-paper test that is relatively easy to administrate, a pupil's personality can be assessed.

There are a number of problems with this approach. At a theoretical level, there is no unifying perspective that integrates the studies of personality traits. This means there is no agreement about what the underlying traits are. Cattell suggests that there are 16 traits, but other psychologists have identified 5 or 20. The problem relates, once again, to the use of factor analysis: there is no agreement on the best way to use this technique. Different methods of analysis lead to different factors and different explanations about what the key personality traits are.

Another problem, this time at the practical level, is that pupils' actions are affected by the situation that they are in. A pupil may be trusting with his peers but extremely suspicious of adults. Not only are traits unstable across situations, but their value changes over time. As a pupil develops, the influence of the trait changes. Cattell has shown that on trait A, temperament, the educationally successful pupil up to the age of 12 is at the + end; that is, good-natured. At university age, however, the successful student is at the − end; that is, critical and aloof. The usefulness of identifying personality traits is therefore limited.

The trait approach focuses on taking a snapshot of a pupil's personality characteristics. Many psychologists are more interested in the dynamic aspects of personality development – how it changes over time. The foundation for present thinking on this development is the work of Sigmund Freud.

EARLY EXPERIENCES: PSYCHOANALYTIC THEORY

Sigmund Freud believed that personality depends on critical stages of development that the child goes through (see Stafford-Clark, 1969). Personality develops because of emotional changes and disturbances within the child. The source of these disturbances can be external frustrations or internal conflicts.

The child is born with instinctive forces – psychological energy. In this sense, Freud's theory is 'dynamic' – pupils are driven by these sources of energy. Pupils' personalities develop as a result of these instinctive inner forces and the way they are dealt with and controlled by adults.

Freud divides the pupils' self, the psyche, into three processes:

- **The id**. This is everything that is present at birth – primitive energy. By definition, it is inherited.
- **The ego**. This is the intermediary between the id and the external world. It is the self-concept and self-control – the executive part of personality. It is determined by the pupils' experiences.
- **The superego**. This is the influence of parents and the wider environment. It can be considered as a pupil's conscience.

A baby is completely controlled by the id; that is, the primitive, instinctual force. For example, babies have an instinctive need for food, which demands instant gratification. As the baby develops into an infant and begins to become aware of the environment, the ego begins to develop, and to mediate between the environment and the demands of the id. So the baby learns to mediate its need for instant gratification – it learns to wait. Between the ages of 4 and 6, the superego develops. This is a realization by the pupil that there are cultural and societal rules, in the narrow sense of the word, that must be taken into consideration. The infant learns that the situation affects what is appropriate. As the pupil develops, the ego's role is to strike a balance between the primitive desires of the id and the societal boundaries of the superego. If the pupil cannot maintain this balance, the result is emotional conflict or anxiety.

Sigmund Freud (1856–1939)

Sigmund Freud was born into a Jewish family in a small town in Moravia. He studied medicine in Vienna. Following a period in Paris, where he studied hypnosis, he began to work with hysterical patients. From the turn of the century, Freud began to develop his theory of psychoanalysis which has had a profound effect on the development of psychological treatment. He acquired a following of eminent people including Carl Jung, Alfred Adler and Otto Rank – though it is notable that most split with him after a period of time. Freud was a prolific writer and his theory has had an enormous impact on not only psychology but also art and literature. His writings are, once again, widely quoted but seldom read.

The stages of psychosexual development

A pupil's personality develops through a number of psychosexual stages. Freud called these stages 'psychosexual' to emphasize the importance of the instinctive sexual drive – the 'libido'. At each stage, a different part of the body is primarily concerned with libidinal satisfaction. These stages have become part of our culture in terms of jokes and artistic references to them.

The first year of life is dominated by the mouth and the child obtains sexual satisfaction by sucking things – the oral stage. In the second year, it is the anal region that dominates as the child focuses on toilet training and the expelling and retention of faeces – the anal stage. At about age 4, the child focuses on his genitalia – the phallic phase. This period is followed by one of relative stability and is known as the latency period. Finally, adolescents renew their interest in the genitalia and the development of sexual relationships – the genital period.

Children who are not able to resolve the problems and frustrations associated with each stage become fixated at this stage. This has major implications for the development of their personality. The pupil fixated at the oral stage will have an oral personality, characterized by competitiveness and impulsiveness. Fixation at the anal stage in the second year, resulting from difficulties with toilet training, leads to an anal personality. This is characterized by being compulsively neat and stubborn if the toilet training was too strict; on the other hand, if toilet training was too loose, the personality is careless and generous. Finally, fixation at the phallic stage leads to adult neurosis.

So Freud believed that pupils' personality development is dynamic and depends on their upbringing.

Implications of Freudian theory for teachers

Early development

The key aspect of the Freudian view of personality development is that early experiences are critical to later development. Pupils develop particular personality traits if they have difficulties at a particular psychosexual stage, and their personalities are affected by the way their parents and other significant adults handle them in those first pre-school years.

Though thinking has moved on from Freud's description of stages, it is recognized that development is crucially affected by the child-rearing practices of the significant adults (see Bowlby below). It is Freud who opened up the whole debate on how the way children are treated in early life affects the development of their personality.

The unconscious

The second key aspect of Freudian theory is that pupils (as well as adults) are unconscious of the basis for their actions. Pupils are largely unaware of the primitive energy from the id that drives their actions, and so are unaware of the reasons for their actions; for example, losing their temper or feeling afraid. This is not to say that these actions are haphazard or random; they have determinable causes but pupils are unaware of what they are.

Many other psychological perspectives share this view that pupils are unaware of the forces acting on them, but couch it in rather different language. Behavioural psychologists, for example, would acknowledge that pupils are often unaware of the factors, both antecedents and consequences, within the environment that are influencing their behaviour. Cognitive behaviourists also believe that pupils are unaware of the thoughts that trigger particular emotional responses. The difference between these and a psychoanalytic perspective is that Freud emphasized that the ego does not allow the pupils to be aware of some of the baser, more primitive motives that drive their behaviour. The behaviourist and cognitive behaviourist argue that it is simply that the pupil is not reading the environmental cues sensitively or accurately enough. They would not presume that there were any 'deeper' mechanisms. The pupil can be taught to recognize the cues in the environment and the beliefs that trigger the actions.

Defence mechanisms

A third key aspect of Freudian theory is the concept of defence mechanisms. As pupils develop, they establish processes for dealing with the conflicting demands which are placed on them, and which create anxiety and other emotional reactions in the pupil. A mature personality will deal with conflicting demands directly, in so far as it will acknowledge that there are conflicts, and attempt to resolve them. A less mature personality will use defence mechanisms to deal with conflicts.

The most common defence mechanism is repression – an attempt to push the conflict into the unconscious. Though the emotional conflict is repressed, the teacher can see symptoms of it in pupils' aggressive, anxious, obsessional or ritualistic behaviour. The pupil who wants to hurt his brother but who knows that he should not represses this feeling. This emotional conflict may not be resolved and the pupil may show other symptoms instead – for example, being aggressive to his peers.

Repression is another of the Freudian concepts that have entered into Western culture; when someone forgets to carry out an unpleasant task we talk about his repressing it. Many psychologists would question the concept of repression, particularly of its leading to other symptoms. Teachers need to recognize that emotional conflict often dissipates if kept under control rather than resurfacing as another problem.

Transference

Transference occurs when pupils transfer feelings and relationships they have had for and with significant adults in the past to adults in their present environment. So a pupil may transfer the way he related to his grandmother to the way he relates to his new class teacher. Understanding the concept of transference thus helps teachers understand their relationships with pupils.

The present status of Freudian theory

Though Freud emphasized that it is experiences in childhood that are crucial to the development of personality, he did not work with children in any extensive way. The adults he worked with were all clinical patients with psychological difficulties. They can hardly be considered a normal group on which to develop a universal theory for explaining the development of personality. So, while psychologists recognize the originality of Freud's thinking and the breadth of his vision, many question the validity of the conclusions that he came to.

Psychology has developed substantially since the beginning of the century, both in terms of the way theories are built on research and in the importance of focusing on a specific field of study. It can be argued that contemporary psychologists' breadth of vision is limited, and even that there is a failure of nerve in the attempts to explain personality development. It is fairer to say that the rapid expansion in the field of psychology has enabled a more detailed contribution to specific issues concerned with the development of the personality.

One of these more specific issues is the way pupils' attachments to significant adults affect their development.

THE IMPORTANCE OF SIGNIFICANT ADULTS

The importance to children's development of their attachment to significant adults was first highlighted by John Bowlby. Bowlby (1979) was concerned with needs of refugees after the Second World War. At that time the primary concern was for the physical needs of the child: health, food and a decent place to live. Bowlby suggested that children's emotional needs were also critical and depended upon their attachment to significant adults. The need for this attachment is a fundamental innate characteristic that promotes the survival of the human race. For Bowlby, there is a clear progression from the relationship children have with their parents to the relationships they will have in later life.

John Bowlby (1907–)

John Bowlby was born in London and studied medicine and psychology at Cambridge. He specialized in child psychiatry and psychoanalysis. For most of his life he worked at the Tavistock Clinic and the Tavistock Institute of Human Relations. Bowlby was interested in how children's experiences with their parents shaped their personality. He was particularly concerned about how separation from their mother affected their development. Bowlby has had an immense influence on child-rearing practices in Britain.

All children become attached to significant others, but these attachments can be secure or insecure. It is vital that children are given a secure attachment – the parents, or other significant adults such as grandparents, need to give children a secure base from which they can explore the world. When threats are encountered, the child feels safe through his attachment to the significant adult. Pupils who learn that there are adults around them who will protect and comfort them in times of uncertainty become more confident and self-reliant. They also grow up willing to cooperate and trust others. On the other hand, pupils who have an insecure or anxious attachment to their parents grow up having difficulties with relationships. These insecure attachments may result in an overdependence on adults. Relationships may be characterized by emotional over-reactions, tears or anger, due to the pupils' lack of self-confidence.

Insecure or anxious attachments may occur for a number of reasons. The most obvious is any prolonged or irregular separation from the parents. Bowlby, however, stresses that it is not simply the actual physical separation but rather the adults' relationship to the child that causes insecure attachments. Insecure attachments occur if parents are unresponsive to children's needs even if they are physically present.

There are two consequences of insecure attachments in childhood:

- They make children more vulnerable to later difficult circumstances, thus increasing their insecurity.
- They make it more likely that the child will have similar insecure relationships as an adult.

The whole process is cyclical. If children have insecure attachments, then they are likely to have insecure relationships as adults, because they do not trust their relationships with people. Such insecure adults are likely to have anxious attachments with their own children, who, when they grow up, will have anxious attachments with their children, and so on. This cycle is compounded by the fact that insecure adults may also believe that their own problems, such as illness, depression and anxiety, are their children's fault. This further damages their relationship with the child and creates more difficulties.

This is a fairly pessimistic view of pupils' development, locked into a cycle of insecure relationships. How much validity is there to this view, and is it inevitable that a pupil's early experiences lead to these later difficulties?

The present status of attachment theory

Bowlby's theory and the subsequent body of work on attachment have caused fierce controversy because of the implications they have for society as well as for individuals. The benefits of secure relationships with significant adults are not in dispute; there is evidence that pupils who experience secure attachments as infants become more competent cognitively, emotionally and socially than children who have insecure attachment relationships (Campos *et al.*, 1983) and children who have secure attachment relationships when they are a year old, in a pre-school setting, are more popular, have higher self-esteem and are less aggressive than their peers (Sroufe, 1983). What has caused the controversy is the question of whether it can only be mothers who can be significant adults.

Bowlby's position was that healthy psychological development depends on a warm, continuous relationship between children and their mothers. It follows, therefore, that children deprived of this relationship with their mothers will be insecure. The belief that mothers cause their children damage by being separated from them has enormous implications for women's child-rearing role. It means that mothers of young children should not work, as this would mean separation for substantial lengths of time. This view is unacceptable in modern Britain, where many mothers wish to work. Bowlby is seen as holding a male-oriented, reactionary view on mothers' rights.

It is more helpful to acknowledge that children do need to develop secure attachments with significant adults. These may be the children's mothers, but they can be other people – fathers, grandparents and non-related adults. The significant adult is one who is constant and who is responsive to the child's needs.

The long-term effect of early experiences

There is considerable evidence that pupils' personality development is not solely dependent on early experiences. The link between insecure attachments and later difficulties is not inevitable (Clarke and Clarke, 1960). Pupils who have unsatisfactory relationships in early childhood do not inevitably have later problems. Pupils can be considered to be differentially vulnerable or differentially resilient to such experiences.

Teachers as significant adults

One way that pupils can develop resilience is through having secure attachments in later childhood and adolescence (Rutter, 1983), so the relationships that teachers have with pupils can be an important factor in their development.

Parents are obviously significant adults, but so also are teachers.

This is not to say that a teacher is automatically significant in every pupil's life – teachers can think back on their own school days and recognize teachers who were significant for them, and others who were not. But teachers can be a powerful factor in a pupil's life, particularly for one who has few other relationships. Such pupils are likely to have difficulties with their emotional development and especially their social ability to make and retain friends. In these circumstances, a significant teacher, who forms a secure attachment with such pupils, can mitigate their emotional vulnerability. As well as being a positive, secure, significant force in the vulnerable pupil's life, the teacher can also do a lot to promote positive peer relationships. By building good relationships between vulnerable pupils and their peers, the teacher can significantly affect pupils' development.

Attachment theory stresses the importance of significant adults in pupils' development. Though secure relationships with significant adults may be one key factor, there are many other factors that also play a part. An ecological perspective takes into account the complexity of the interrelationships in the world and helps explain how pupils can be differentially vulnerable or differentially resilient to life's difficulties.

THE ECOLOGICAL PERSPECTIVE

Freudian and attachment theory emphasize the importance of significant adults to the development of the pupil's personality. Adults' influence on pupils is part of a set of wider influences. Bronfenbrenner (1979) provides a framework for viewing the other factors that affect pupils' development. This ecological theory integrates biological, psychological and social factors in the development of the pupil.

Bronfenbrenner describes development as a series of nested structures (see Figure 4.2). At the centre is the pupil. The innermost level is the microsystem, which contains the pupil's most important relationships: significant adults, siblings and peers. The next level – the mesosystem – contains the interrelations among major settings containing the pupil; for example, the relationship between parents and teachers that will have an influence on the pupil's development. The third level – the ecosystem – is an extension of the mesosystem, consisting of the situations that do not in themselves contain the pupil but influence the situation in which he is found. Examples of the ecosystem are the teacher's home life and staff meetings. For example, if staff meetings are in turmoil following the resignations of members of staff, this will have an effect on the pupil.

Finally there is the macrosystem. This is the whole culture of the society that the pupil is in, including the economic climate, the political system, and of course the educational culture. For example, in times of recession, pupils will be affected by the closure of the local

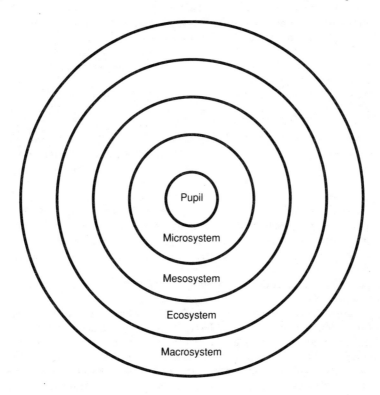

Figure 4.2 Ecological factors.

factory. The changes in educational funding brought in by the 1988 Education Reform Act are part of the macrosystem and were explicitly introduced to affect pupils' educational development.

The strength of an ecological model is that it emphasizes the variety of forces that affect pupils' development – not only the immediate environment but also the wider factors inherent in the school, the teacher's home life, the government and the whole fabric of society. This helps explain how one factor, such as insecure attachments in early childhood, can be mitigated by events in the wider system.

Pupils have to develop dynamically and progressively to accommodate themselves to the microsystem that they are in. For example, they have to develop in order to respond appropriately to the new class teacher. This development is influenced by the meso- and macrosystems that are outside the classroom. Pupils' development depends on what is happening in their parents' lives, as well as what is happening to the teacher in her life outside the school.

Bronfenbrenner's theory of development is one of environmental interconnectedness. No event happens in isolation; all have implications and are mediated by other forces up and down the chain. His theory accounts for the many different factors outside pupils that affect their development. It does not account for the internal – organismic – factors.

An organismic view

Bronfenbrenner's ecological perspective can be tied to an organismic view of the pupil. These two perspectives give a frame of reference that begins to account for the complexity of pupils' development.

An organismic approach views pupils' development as influenced by numerous variables coming from different, yet interconnected systems: genetic, neurobiological, biochemical, behavioural, psychological, environmental and sociological. Development is a series of qualitative reorganizations among and between these different systems, which can be conceived of as being in dynamic transaction with one another all the time. Development takes place when pupils mesh the demands of the changing environment with their resources to adapt.

Pupils' development depends on their being able to use both internal and external resources in order to adapt to the changing demands the environment makes of them. Internal resources include specific cognitive skills (for example, skills such as reading and language) as well as the pupil's self-concept and self-esteem. External resources include the environmental factors that help the pupil to adapt, such as secure relationships with significant others, appropriate role models, and teachers able to teach the key skills.

It is a combination of internal and external resources that ensures that the pupil adapts to new demands in the environment. So a pupil with limited reading skills may still be able to take an exam course in secondary school if he has other resources, whether internal, such as determination, or external, such as a skilled teacher willing to help with difficult tasks.

THE DEVELOPMENT OF COMPETENCE

Waters and Sroufe (1983), among others, have used the concept of 'competence' to describe a pupil who is able to adapt to the demands of the situation. This is the resilient pupil who is able to overcome life's challenges. They suggest that there are many different successful mechanisms by which the pupil can develop competence, rather than one particular way. The pupil can use a combination of internal and external resources.

There is a complex relationship between early competence and later development. Early competence exerts a positive influence towards ensuring competence at a later stage. So talking early will have a positive influence on learning to read, which not only is particularly important in infant school, but also will have an influence on the rest of a pupil's education, and his adult life. The failure to achieve competence in one area makes competence in another area more difficult: the failure to learn to read, for example, has implications for the entire self-concept of the pupil.

Competence

A pupil's competence – the ability to adapt to the demands of a situation – is cumulative. Later competence is built on earlier competence, and pupils' competent adaptation to earlier situations allows them to adapt successfully to later situations. This explains the significance of early experiences and the concept of differential vulnerability. If pupils do not adapt competently to early demands, whether developing language or dealing with the absence of significant adults, then they may not be able to adjust competently to later demands.

There are, however, many forces that mediate between early competence or failure and later development. So by bringing other factors into play a teacher can overcome early incompetence and ensure the pupil develops. There are many ways that early developmental problems can be countered by the resourceful teacher (Cicchetti and Schneider-Rosen, 1986).

There is still a tendency in psychology to separate the influences on pupils' development into internal forces – the pupil's self-concept – and external ones – the whole macrosystem. It is a mistake to view pupils' development independently of the situation that they are in; but it is equally misleading to view the situation independently of the pupils. The relationship between the pupil and the situation is one of mutual creation (see Chapter 1) – the environment and the pupil are reciprocally influencing each other. So pupils' personalities will reflect at any time not only their past experiences, as emphasized, for example, by Freud and by Bowlby, but also their interpretation of these past experiences (the phenomenological approach of Rogers). Pupils' personalities will, too, be influenced by the situation that they are in, which in turn is influenced by the macro-environment outside it. But these environments are not independent of the pupil: they are reciprocally determined.

So it is possible to view a pupil's sullen personality as stemming from the way that he was handled in his early years, mediated by the way he resolved the conflict in tensions, mediated by his present experience of the teacher handling his sullenness, mediated by the way the teacher is being dealt with by her headteacher, mediated by the school's falling rolls and so on. And the influence is not only one way, from the wider environment to the pupil. The influence goes the other way too. So the pupil who has temper tantrums in class affects the way the teacher relates to him which affects the relationship between the teacher and the pupil's parents and the teacher's ecosystem – her relationships outside the classroom. Not only does the environment shape the pupil's development, but also the pupil shapes his own environment.

The competence every pupil, teacher and parent brings to the situation is based on their previous competence. If there are sufficient resources, then the pupil will be able to adapt to the new challenge, whether that is learning to control his temper or learning to read. If there are not sufficient resources, the pupil will fail to develop, making it increasingly difficult for him to be able to meet the next challenge that he faces. This is why it is so important for teachers to be resourceful. They really can make a difference to pupils' development. The challenge that faces teachers is feeling sufficiently empowered and in control to be significant adults in pupils' lives.

SUMMARY

This chapter describes the factors that influence pupils' personality development. At the core of every pupil is his self-concept – who he is. The development of pupils' self-concept depends on how people interact with them. Significant adults are particularly important, but the entire environment that the pupil lives in influences his development. The pupil faces many challenges as he develops, and the effects of these challenges are cumulative. If pupils develop competence to overcome the first challenges, then they are likely to become competent at dealing with the new challenge. Teachers can help pupils develop by giving them resources, ranging from internal resources, such as boosting their self-confidence, to teaching them specific skills. Teachers need to use their resources to help pupils' development.

REFERENCES

Bowlby, J. (1979) *The Making and Breaking of Affectional Bonds.* London: Tavistock Publications.

Bronfenbrenner, U. (1979) *The Ecology of Human Development: Experiments by Nature and Design*. Cambridge, MA: Harvard University Press.

Campos, J., Barrett, K., Lamb, M., Boldsmith, H. and Stenberg, C. (1983) Socioemotional development, in Mussen, P. (ed.), *Handbook of Child Psychology*, Vol. 2: *Infancy and Developmental Psychobiology*. New York: Wiley.

Cattell, R. (1965) *The Scientific Analysis of Personality*. Harmondsworth: Penguin.

Cicchetti, D. and Schneider-Rosen, K. (1986) An organizational approach to childhood depression, in Rutter, M., Izard, C. and Read, P. (eds), *Depression in Young People: Clinical and Developmental Perspectives*. New York: Guilford Press.

Clarke, A. and Clarke, A. (1960) Some recent advances in the study of early deprivation, *Journal of Child Psychology and Psychiatry* 27(6), pp. 719–59.

Coopersmith, S. (1967) *The Antecedents of Self Esteem*. San Francisco: Freeman.

Rogers, C. (1983) *Freedom to Learn for the '80s*. New York: Macmillan.

Rutter, M. (1983) Stress, coping and development: some issues and some questions, in Garmezy, N. and Rutter, M. (eds) *Stress, Coping and Development in Children*. New York: McGraw-Hill.

Sroufe, R. (1983) Individual patterns of adaptation from infancy to preschool, in Permutter, M. (ed.), *Minnesota Symposium on Child Psychology*, Vol. 16. Hillsdale, NJ: Erlbaum.

Stafford-Clark, D. (1969) *What Freud Really Said*. Harmondsworth: Penguin.

Waters, G. and Sroufe, L. (1983) Competence as a developmental construct, *Developmental Review* 3, pp. 79–97.

RECOMMENDED READING

S. Apter, *Troubled Children/Troubled Systems* (Oxford: Pergamon Press, 1982), expands on the ecological perspective on children's development. Particular focus on children with special educational needs and how the system can be changed to help them.

L. Pervin, *Personality*, 5th edition (Chichester: Wiley, 1989), provides a helpful, readable introduction to all the major personality theorists.

M. Richards and P. Light (eds), *Children of Social Worlds* (Oxford: Basil Blackwell, 1986), is a difficult and challenging book that shows how child development can happen only in a social context. Explores the relationship between the child, family and society.

PART 2

PERSPECTIVES ON THE TEACHER

CHAPTER 5

From attitudes to prejudice

OVERVIEW

Attitudes have been extensively studied by psychologists and underpin most areas of educational concern. In the last few years, people's attitudes to key educational issues have been highlighted, including parents' attitudes to the teaching of reading, the government's attitude to the funding of education, and teachers' attitudes to assessment and appraisal. Attitudes are part of a whole categorization process that enables teachers to organize and make sense of the world. This process leads to stereotypes – oversimplified, fixed perceptions of a group of people. 'Attitude' is an evaluative but neutral term – a teacher has both positive and negative attitudes. Attitudes, are, however, the basis of prejudice, a negative categorization process which is of major concern to teachers.

Understanding teachers' attitudes is crucial to understanding their actual teaching practice. There is not, though, a direct link between attitudes and behaviour. For example, a teacher's attitude to the teaching of reading may be that using real books is the most appropriate; despite this, she may use phonics rather than real books in the classroom. To take another example, a teacher may strongly believe in the importance of equal opportunities; whether she is actually prepared to act to combat racial prejudice in her school is affected by other factors as well as her attitude.

This chapter focuses on:

- what attitudes are;
- the categorization process and attitudes;
- the danger of stereotypes;
- the step from stereotypes to prejudice;
- changing attitudes;
- the relationship between attitudes and behaviour.

WHAT ARE ATTITUDES?

One of the difficulties with attitudes is the different meanings there are for the word. Teachers' attitudes are interlinked with their thoughts and beliefs. A teacher's attitude to a situation, or person, has three components.

Attitudes

An attitude has three components: knowledge, feelings and behaviour. Though all three are interconnected, it is the feelings that distinguish an attitude from simply knowledge or behaviour.

Consider, for example, teachers' attitudes to the teaching of reading. First, teachers have some knowledge or information about the teaching of reading, which is likely to be based on their own experiences – how they were taught to read, how they have seen reading taught, and any research or theory that they are familiar with. Second, teachers make judgements on an evaluative, positive–negative dimension. So they decide whether the teaching that that they have seen is good or bad teaching, and whether the theory makes sense to them or not. Finally, these beliefs and feelings may affect the teacher's behaviour – she may decide to teach reading in line with her evaluation of the information that she has. Whether teachers' attitudes actually affect their behaviour is a key point that will be returned to later in the chapter.

Though these three components are interlinked, there is not a simple cause–effect relationship between them. A teacher can have knowledge about a certain area, but if there is no evaluation and therefore no feelings she does not have an attitude to it. A definition of attitudes that encapsulates the subjective and evaluative component is a 'subjective experience involving an evaluation of something or somebody' (Eiser, 1986, p. 13). Teachers have knowledge about numerous things without necessarily having an attitude to them. For example, a teacher knows that there are three core subjects in the National Curriculum. If she has evaluated the choice of these three and has feelings about their relative importance, then she can be said to have an attitude about this matter. People outside education may also know that there are three core subjects; but if they do not have any feelings about this, then they do not have an attitude to the choice.

Everyone has attitudes. They form automatically as part of a categorization process that helps make sense of the world.

THE CATEGORIZATION PROCESS AND ATTITUDES

The complexity of interactions in the classroom means that teachers are constantly bombarded by information coming at them from all directions. To make sense of the information, the teacher establishes schemata to help organize and 'categorize' it (see Chapter 2). This categorization process goes on all the time and has a necessary function, in that it simplifies the world so that it can be made sense of. When a teacher meets a class for the first time, she begins to categorize the pupils. She may distinguish boys from girls, noisy from quiet pupils, quick workers from slow workers, those who sit at the back from those who sit at the front, and so on. This categorization simplifies teaching, as it allows the teacher to make predictions about a particular pupil. For instance, if a pupil reads well the teacher may make the assumption that he can also spell well. On the basis of the first piece of information the teacher begins to make assumptions about the pupil.

This process is normal – everybody does it. It does, though, cause difficulties. Categorizing simplifies, and in simplifying information is lost. For example, if a good reader is labelled as bright, the teacher may overlook particular difficulties that he is having with mathematics. For this pupil the worst that may happen is that his difficulties may take a little longer to uncover. Consider, however, a poor reader who is categorized by the teacher as having limited ability in all areas. The categorization process in this instance may effectively distort the entire education that this pupil receives.

The ideal pupil

The teacher's attitude to a particular pupil depends on this categorization process. She selects particular information on the pupil to pay attention to. This selection process depends on what is important to the teacher and need not be done consciously. MacIntyre *et al.* (1966) investigated teachers' attitudes to male pupils in Scotland. They identified differences between teachers in working- and middle-class areas. The teachers of working-class pupils focused their attention on pupils who were hard-working and paid attention to the teacher; those in middle-class areas focused on pupils who were 'pleasant' – nice to get on with.

The information teachers select is for their 'ideal type' of pupil (Hargreaves, 1977). Teachers have beliefs about what constitutes the ideal pupil and each pupil is viewed to see whether he matches this ideal type. If 'hard work' is particularly important to a teacher, she will be cued to see how much work the pupil completes; if cleanliness is an important characteristic of the ideal pupil, then the teacher will be looking at the pupil's clothes, hair and appearance to pick up cues.

This ideal type can lead to the 'halo' effect, which occurs when one particular feature of a pupil dominates the teacher's perception of him. A teacher notices that a particular pupil speaks well; this feature, whether it is the pupil's accent, fluency or range of vocabulary, becomes so dominant that the teacher generalizes from this to other aspects of his skills. She sees him as bright, intelligent, responsible and alert – just because he speaks well.

The ideal pupil and physical attractiveness

One particularly interesting cue in terms of 'ideal type is physical attractiveness. Though logically there is no link between intelligence, hard work or pleasantness and physical attractiveness, nevertheless it is well documented that these are all associated with it by teachers (Clifford and Walster, 1973). Teachers believe that physically attractive pupils have greater ability and greater levels of parental interest, and will achieve more in life than their less attractive peers. There is a good deal of research in this area that shows that pupils' physical attractiveness plays a role in determining the teacher's attitude to them and consequently how they are treated.

Physical attractiveness is not just a cue that is applied to pupils. Adults, too, can be affected. Otherwise identical women with identical performances in their job are evaluated differently depending upon their attractiveness (Heilman and Stopeck, 1985). If they are in a subordinate position to the evaluator, attractiveness improves their evaluation; if, on the other hand, they are in management positions, attractiveness reduces their ratings. In the same study men's attractiveness made no difference to their evaluation.

The implication of these studies is that teachers need to be aware that their own evaluation of pupils as well as their own professional appraisal may be influenced by the attractiveness of the evaluatee. Recognizing this categorization process means that the teacher can take steps to increase objectivity when involved in assessments.

Categorizing the ideal pupil

Teachers cannot attend to and process all of the information that they have about pupils, so they focus on particular characteristics that are important to them. These reflect the 'ideal' pupil for the teacher. Each pupil is judged as having or not having these ideal characteristics. The teacher's attitude to pupils is not based on how they really are but on these assumptions about their characteristics.

Teachers are no different from everyone else: they form their attitudes to make sense of the pupil. If these attitudes help the teacher understand the pupils, then they are useful. Unfortunately, only too often the categories limit the teacher's perception and lead to the formation of stereotypes.

THE DANGER OF STEREOTYPES

Stereotypes are simple clusters of attitudes that do not contain contradictions. Everyone has stereotypes, pupils as well as teachers. The issue is not about having stereotypes – it is about recognizing them and counteracting their influence.

People can be stereotyped in a number of ways; for example by race, age, gender and class. Racial stereotypes are very common – typical ones are that Irish people are talkative, English people are emotionally cold, and Asians work hard. People are racially stereotyped by simplifying the complexity of their culture. Britain in the 1990s is a multicultural society and pupils' culture clearly has an effect on their behaviour, beliefs and attitudes. Teachers need to be sensitive to pupils' cultural background. There is, however, a thin and difficult line to draw between cultural sensitivity and cultural stereotyping.

Stereotypes

A stereotype is a widely shared, oversimplified, fixed perception of a group of people. Stereotypes can be based on a whole range of characteristics: 'pupils who wear glasses are swots', 'PE teachers are insensitive', and so on.

An example of socioeconomic stereotyping by teachers is described by Darley and Gross (1983). Teachers were informed that a pupil had either a high or a low socioeconomic background, and were asked to rate her academic ability. They all maintained that her background had no influence on her ability. They then watched a video tape of the girl taking an academic ability test. Those who had been told they had been watching a girl from a well-off background rated her ability above average, and those who had been told she was from a poor background judged her as performing below the average. Darley and Gross suggest that teachers have stereotypes about pupils' ability based on their socioeconomic class. Teachers selectively remembered information from the video that supported their expectations. This research is another example of the difficulties of objectively assessing pupils' progress in the National Curriculum. It is also a reminder about how difficult teacher appraisal can be, given how unaware people are of their stereotypes.

At an even more fundamental level, all pupils can be stereotyped by teachers in the same way as managers stereotype workers (McGregor, 1960). McGregor made a fundamental distinction between how managers see workers – according to either Theory X or Theory Y. This classic distinction can, with slight modifications, be applied to teachers' stereotypes of pupils.

- **Theory X:** pupils are by nature lazy and therefore must be motivated by outside rewards. Pupils' natural goals run counter to the classroom's, hence they must be controlled by the teacher to ensure that they work. Because of their irrational feelings, pupils are basically incapable of self-discipline and self-control. They do not want challenge, they want security.
- **Theory Y:** pupils do not inherently dislike work. It can be a source of satisfaction and will be voluntarily performed. Pupils do not work best under external threats. They are motivated by fulfilling self-actualization needs. They are capable of exercising autonomy and independence.

Such a division is simplistic; nevertheless, it dramatically focuses attention on teachers' stereotypes about pupils. McGregor believes that many problems in organizations occur because managers assume Theory X about workers – that people are inherently lazy and have to be forced to work. He suggests that as Theory Y is a more accurate perception of what people are really like, managers need to change their attitudes.

Is McGregor's distinction valid for teachers? What stereotypes do teachers have about pupils? What stereotypes do headteachers have of teachers – Theory X or Theory Y? Unless teachers recognize their own stereotypes they will have difficulties recognizing the individuality of not only pupils but their own colleagues. Stereotypes are simplifications of the complexity of people. When they become really dangerous is when they lead to prejudice.

FROM STEREOTYPES TO PREJUDICE

Stereotypes are the basis for prejudice. Prejudice occurs when teachers make negative judgements about pupils on the basis of their stereotypes. Prejudice is apparent in school when teachers see pupils in a negative way simply because they belong to a particular group. Prejudice is seen in teachers' attitudes to racial groups – 'What do you expect from him, he's black'; to gender – 'Boys can't cook'; to class – 'With that background you can't expect A levels'; and to more subtle groups like age – 'Old teachers never change'. In each case the prejudice is expressed by the negative attitude towards members of a group – simply because they are members of that group.

In the last few years there have been an increasing number of efforts to recognize and address prejudiced behaviour in both schools and society at large. The main focus has been on gender and cultural (or racial) prejudice, though there are many other areas where prejudice also occurs.

Psychological theories of prejudice

Over the years there have been a number of psychological perspectives on prejudice. Each has tried to explain why prejudice occurs and, leading on from that, how it can be prevented.

The earliest theories on prejudice stem from a Freudian psychodynamic perspective (see Chapter 4). At the end of the Second World War, there was a need to understand the prejudice against gypsies, homosexuals and particularly Jews in Germany. Adorno *et al.* (1950) explained anti-semitism in psychodynamic developmental terms as the result of parents, anxious about their own status, strictly enforcing rules on their children. This enforcement of discipline made the children hostile, anxious and fearful of failure. These feelings were repressed, only to reappear as an 'authoritarian personality' in adult life. Such personalities need to dominate and feel superior to others, and are attracted to social movements such as anti-semitism that repress other groups. Prejudice was believed to be tied to a certain sort of personality.

This developmental aspect is also emphasized by social learning theory (see Chapter 1), which holds that it is their upbringing that makes children prejudiced. Pupils model their behaviour and attitudes on the people around them, particularly the significant adults. The pupils' socializing process predisposes them to see other cultures negatively, in comparison with their own. Messages from their parents, peers, teachers and the media teach the pupil that their own culture is the best.

A third perspective, based on cognitive consistency theories, is the principle of congruity (Osgood and Tannenbaum, 1955). People look for maximal simplicity in their attitudes. It is easier, for example, to believe that all Irish people are stupid than to try to distinguish between individuals. Extreme views are also simpler than complex differential evaluations. There is continued pressure towards polarization, which makes people's attitudes always change towards more extreme positions.

A fourth perspective is that prejudice is based on ignorance. If prejudice is a simplified view of the characteristics of a particular group, then widening the person's knowledge of that group should make them less prejudiced – if a teacher thinks that Irish people are stupid, then widening her knowledge of Irish people should change her attitude. These attempts to change prejudice by giving the person more information have largely been unsuccessful. There is a belief that the group as a whole still has these characteristics, even if the prejudiced person accepts that a particular individual may not have the characteristics of the group. For the teacher who believes that pupils from low socioeconomic class are not intelligent, the progress of an intelligent working-class pupil is seen as the exception that proves the rule, rather than destroying the prejudice.

In the 1970s and the 1980s, a different view of prejudice developed, which recognizes its functional importance to the individual. This fifth perspective emphasizes that prejudice stems from protecting the self-concept (Lynch, 1987). It also explains how economic and political factors lead to prejudice. To take self-concept first: people ascribe positive traits to the members of the group to which they belong; so men ascribe positive characteristics to being a man, women ascribe positive characteristics to being a woman, black people ascribe them to being black, and white people ascribe them to being white. Prejudice is the positive comparison teachers make between their own characteristics – male/female, black/white, homo-/heterosexual – and the characteristics of other groups. Recognizing that prejudice is a rational attempt to build self-esteem and self-worth is more useful than seeing it as an illogical and negative process. The racist football supporter is not the mindless, irrational animal the media sometimes portray, but a logical, rational person who believes that he can bolster his own self-concept by degrading other nationalities.

Prejudice

Prejudice occurs when teachers make negative judgements about pupils on the basis of their stereotypes. Prejudice is a functional and logical way for people to protect their own self-concept and identity. It is not irrational, based on limited information about other people, or an authoritarian personality trait.

This is not to condone prejudice, but rather to explain that the roots of it lie in a person's self-concept rather than in authoritarian personality characteristics. This need to protect the self-concept also explains how prejudice is affected by the political and economic relationship between groups at any point in time. For instance, unemployed people have a particular need to protect their self-concept. One way of doing this is to look at members of other cultural or economic groups as responsible for their unemployment. As they feel powerless both politically and economically, the development of prejudice is a means of protecting their self-concept.

This protection of the self-concept explains a number of common psychological phenomena that have been identified with prejudice.

Projection

Teachers 'project' their own attitudes on to others. This is done unconsciously, but stems from the way the teacher has categorized and stereotyped people. The attitudes that are projected are often negative and act as a defence mechanism. This allows teachers to suggest that someone else has the attitudes that they are embarrassed or ashamed to have. For example, the teacher who says parents are hostile and negative towards the headteacher may actually have a hostile and negative attitude to the headteacher herself.

As the basis of prejudice is power, there is a tendency for teachers to blame their own difficulties or hardships on to other groups. This projection of prejudice on to others is a key aspect of scapegoating.

Scapegoating

Scapegoating occurs when another group is held to be the cause of a teacher's problems. It often relates directly to the economic situation that the teacher is in. When there are difficulties with employment or career development and teachers lose their self-esteem, they need to project the cause of this on to another group. If a teacher has a secure job and feels comfortably superior to other people, then it is easy not to be prejudiced; if, on the other hand, life is not going well, it becomes psychologically necessary to find someone to blame – a scapegoat.

Self-fulfilling prophecy

It is easy to see how the self-fulfilling prophecy works in terms of racial prejudice. Through categorization and stereotyping, teachers have expectations about other groups; these expectations affect the teachers' behaviour which in turn affects the behaviour of the person in the other group, whose response will confirm the expectations. This is very similar to Bandura's reciprocal determinism (described in Chapter 1). So if a white teacher believes that black youths are hostile and lazy, she will act in a way that triggers this response – being aggressive and threatening. When the black youths react to this, it confirms the teacher's expectation and thus the prejudice. So the self-fulfilling prophecy locks both the teacher and the pupil into a cycle of destructive racial stereotyping.

These are all common mechanisms by which teachers form attitudes to protect their own self-concept. The problem is how to change the attitudes that are locked into this protection. This is not easy, despite the money poured into this area of research.

CHANGING ATTITUDES

People's prejudices can be changed; the attitudes on which they are based are not immutable and fixed. But such attitudes do have a functional purpose for the individual – protecting his or her self-concept – and they are therefore difficult to change. There are two main approaches: the peripheral approach and the central (cognitive) approach (Petty and Cacioppo, 1981).

The peripheral approach

The peripheral approach suggests that, on issues where teachers do not have strong feelings, they process information only at a peripheral level. The peripheral approach concerns factors that focus on the unthoughtful way this happens. Teachers will use the peripheral route when they are not engaged by the subject – for example, if they find the information hard to comprehend or if it has a limited emotional component for them. So teachers' attitude to the Children Act may be processed only at the peripheral level. Prejudice, which has a powerful emotional component, will not be changed at this level.

At the peripheral level, the credibility of the source of information becomes all-important in changing attitudes. If the teachers believe the source, they will accept its perspective on the information. There are many issues where teachers do not weigh up the arguments but simply accept what an expert, such as a significant colleague, tells them.

Attitudes are often changed through the peripheral approach, particularly ones that are not at the core of a teacher's self-concept. For example, teachers change their attitudes to children with special educational needs when they have positive interactions with them, according to Hannah and Pliner (1983). The researchers did not attempt to change teachers' attitudes by giving them information about special needs pupils or having them think about the pupils. Instead, by simply being exposed to these pupils, the teachers' attitudes changed.

Change through the peripheral route has less stability than change through the central cognitive approach. In the example above, the teachers' attitudes might quickly change again if they were exposed to negative experiences with special needs pupils. Though the peripheral approach will not change teachers' core attitudes, it is the process by which teachers gain most of their educational attitudes. Effective headteachers who create a positive attitude to educational innovation in their schools recognize it is largely based on creating the right climate. Teachers do not have the energy to think through every change, but will take their lead from people that they can trust.

The central approach

The central approach focuses on the cognitive processes that go on when information is received. On certain issues, teachers have strong, well-developed groups of interconnected attitudes. To change these through the cognitive approach involves the active processing of new information. The teacher has to:

- pay attention to the source of the information;
- understand its contents;
- reflect on what is said.

Imagine a teacher being given new information about the examination success of black pupils, which connects with the teacher's attitude on this issue. The precise attitudes that are aroused depend on the teacher's understanding of the incoming information. The information will be processed if it meshes with schemata favourable to it. It is the teacher's active involvement that largely determines whether the information is taken on – not the information itself. It is not a question of remembering the information; rather it is the active processing of any evaluative information to achieve consistency with the self-concept.

The teacher's active involvement in this process is crucial. She must think about the new information if it is to be accepted. If she is not involved, she will not think about the issue.

This is the reason that the distinction between 'consociate' and 'contemporary' relationships between teacher and pupil is so useful (Sharp and Green, 1975). 'Consociate' describes the relationship when the teacher and the pupil are in direct, face-to-face contact with each other, as when they are in the classroom together. It implies that the teacher may change her attitudes to the pupil in the light of her active involvement on a day-to-day basis. On the other hand, a 'contemporary' relationship occurs when the pupil and the teacher are not in direct, face-to-face contact. The teacher's attitude to the pupil is based on her remembered impressions and is therefore relatively fixed. She is unlikely to change her attitude to the pupil, as it is based on remembered impressions, not on day-to-day interactions. The importance of the distinction between consociate and contemporary relationships is in understanding how teachers' attitudes will change. If teachers do not have a direct consociate relationship – direct in terms not only of being in the classroom with the pupil but also of actually viewing the pupil's action without prejudgement – they will never change their attitudes to a pupil. If the teacher's view is purely a contemporary one based on her remembered impressions, she will see the pupil in a stereotyped, fixed way. It is extremely difficult for a pupil to shift a teacher's negative contemporary perspective on him.

The importance of cognitive involvement has been supported by a number of studies (Petty and Cacioppo, 1981). These confirm the importance of teachers' active, conscious involvement in changing and developing new attitudes. Attitude change is difficult to bring about through the cognitive approach because teachers muster their existing attitudes to defend their self-concept. It follows, therefore, that when change occurs through the cognitive active progress it is relatively stable. To shift the attitude again, the teacher would have to readjust her whole attitude structure. So a teacher who understands and has thought about the importance of inclusive education and its value, in terms of equal opportunities for pupils with disabilities, is likely to have a stronger and more stable attitude on this issue than a teacher whose attitude has been formed by the peripheral approach. Whether teachers' behaviour to pupils with disability is congruent with their attitudes is another, and more complex, issue.

THE RELATIONSHIP BETWEEN ATTITUDES AND BEHAVIOUR

One of the major issues in the whole field of attitudes is the relationship between attitudes and behaviour. The interest in this relationship stems from the classic study of prejudice by LaPiere (1934). In the course of this, he travelled around the USA with a Chinese couple, booking into over two hundred and fifty hotels and restaurants. They were only once turned away. Nevertheless, when LaPiere subsequently wrote to the same hotels and restaurants over 90 per cent said that they would turn away a Chinese couple. The study tells us a lot about racial prejudice in the USA in the 1930s; what it also shows is the vast discrepancy between people's attitudes – what they say they would do – and people's behaviour – what they actually do.

Nearly thirty-five years later, Wicker (1969) reviewed over thirty studies on the relationship between attitudes and behaviour, and confirmed that there is not a simple link. Nevertheless, there is a general belief that by changing attitudes you can change behaviour. The amount that is spent on advertising is an obvious indicator, not only for commercial concerns but also public service campaigns – for example, on drugs and AIDS. There is evidence that the recent British

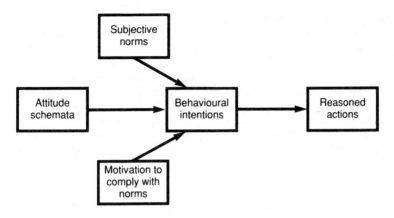

Figure 5.1 The relationship between attitude and behaviour.

government campaign on AIDS altered young people's attitude to sex; whether it also changed sexual behaviour is not so clear.

The relationship between attitudes and behaviour

In education, there is a belief that if you change pupils' attitude to school you will also change their behaviour in school. The relationship between attitude and behaviour is not as clear as this. There is no direct link between pupils' or teachers' attitudes and their behaviour. The link can be conceptualized as one of 'reasoned action'.

Fishbein and Ajzen (1974, 1975) have developed a model of 'reasoned action' that is particularly useful in explaining the complex link between attitude and behaviour (see Figure 5.1). Teachers act in a reasoned and logical way – they have reasoned actions. The connection between teachers' attitude schemata – their set of attitudes – and their reasoned actions is mediated by 'behavioural intentions'; that is, an intention to act in a particular way. These are dependent upon two forces:

- the subjective norms – what the teacher thinks her colleagues and other significant people expect her to do;
- the teacher's motivation to comply with these norms.

The reasoned action model highlights the fact that there are a number of forces influencing a teacher's actions, not just her attitude.

For example, a teacher may feel very strongly about the importance of homework – she has a consistent and strong attitude schema on this issue. This would lead to a behavioural intention to set homework regularly. Whether she does set homework or not will depend upon the two other forces, namely, the subjective norms (her colleagues' view of homework) and how motivated she feels to comply with them. By taking these two forces into account it is easier to see the link between attitudes and behaviour. It is still not possible to predict a teacher's actions accurately, even if her attitudes are known. Once the social context is understood, the forces that are influencing the gap between the teacher's attitudes and her behaviour can be identified.

One of the reasons for this gap is that actions can be linked to very specific attitudes. For example, a teacher may appear to have a positive attitude to topic work and wish to teach in this way; but she may actually have a positive attitude only to a specific type of topic work or in a particular school – change the type of topic work or the school, and her behaviour may change. It is thus difficult to generalize from a teacher's attitude in one situation to predict her actions in another.

The reasoned action model highlights the distinction between prejudice and prejudiced behaviour. A teacher may feel prejudice towards another group; whether this is turned into action is reasoned, depending on subjective norms – what the teacher thinks other people expect of her – and on her motivation to comply with these norms. This underlines the importance of tackling prejudice within a school as a whole staff working together. It is only if the school recognizes the untenability of a system built on prejudice that individual teachers will change their behaviour.

The mutual effect of behaviour and attitudes

Not only do attitudes affect behaviour, behaviour also affects attitudes. This perspective of cognitive dissonance ties together the importance of the cognitive approach to changing attitudes and reasoned action.

Cognitive dissonance (Festinger, 1957) is an extremely popular theory in social psychology and has generated well over a thousand research studies. The fundamental tenet is that teachers feel uncomfortable when there is dissonance – an imbalance – between their behaviour and their attitudes. In many situations teachers have choices about what they do. For example, after school a teacher might have a choice between taking work home for marking or talking in the staffroom to her colleagues. If she knows that she should go home and mark the papers but instead stays talking, it causes dissonance. Cognitive dissonance theory suggests that she will try to reduce the dissonance between her action and their attitudes; so she will reduce her worry about not getting the work done by telling herself that she can do the marking the next day. She changes her attitude to the importance of the marking in order for it to be consistent with the action – she needs to think that she has done the right thing.

Teachers will take action to reduce dissonance. A teacher who has a group of noisy black pupils in class but who believes that a good teacher has a quiet class will feel some dissonance. How can she believe that she is a good teacher if she has a noisy group? She can reduce this dissonance in a number of ways:

- She can take action and reduce the level of noise from this group.
- If she is unable to reduce the level of noise in the class, she can change her perception – 'Maybe it is not such a noisy class after all.'
- If she is unable to change her perception (because her colleagues are telling her what a noisy group it is), she can change her attitude – 'Maybe black pupils are different from white pupils.'

The need to reduce dissonance can directly affect the teacher's attitude – in this case, her beliefs about black pupils.

Cognitive dissonance often happens after making an important decision. Having decided to accept a new job, often after a good deal of heart-searching, the teacher is left with a feeling of dissonance. Was it the right move? Was the head really that friendly? The teacher cannot reverse the action, so she is left with a number of cognitive strategies for reducing dissonance. These are largely based on re-evaluating the factors that caused the dissonance in the first place (Eiser, 1986).

- **Seeking selective information:** the teacher, having accepted a new job, will seek out positive information about the position that supports her decision.
- **Selective recall:** the teacher will remember only the positive aspects of the chosen job and the negative aspects of the old job.
- **Denying freedom of choice:** the teacher will say to herself that she did not really have any choice over accepting the new job – for example, that she had to accept it as it fitted in with her partner's work.
- **Denying foreseeability:** if the new job does not work out too well, then she can deny to herself that she could have foreseen the difficulties. This confirms, therefore, that she did not really have a choice.

The teacher will use a selection of these cognitive strategies to reduce dissonance. The cognitive strategies outlined above highlight the fact that dissonance is greatest when the teacher's self-concept is threatened. Through these self-talk strategies, teachers change their attitudes and confirm to themselves the actions that they have taken. It can be seen that teachers placed in a situation where their belief in equal opportunities cannot be put into practice will change their attitude to equal opportunities, in order to reduce their dissonance and protect their own self-concept. So action affects attitudes, just as attitudes affect actions.

Reactance to others

Dissonance theory shows how teachers internally maintain consistency between their attitudes and behaviour. Reactance theory explains how teachers react against attempts to change their attitude or behaviour (Brehm, 1976). This is a particularly useful perspective for helping understand teachers' reactions to attempts to reduce prejudice and introduce equal opportunities in education.

Reactance is especially powerful if the teacher believes that another person's desire for change is in pursuit of a selfish interest. So if she believes that religious teaching should focus on Christianity and a colleague tries to force her to change her beliefs by introducing a new scheme, she is especially likely to react against this if she believes that her colleague's real aim is to get promotion rather than to enhance the pupils' religious knowledge or understanding.

Reactance theory

Teachers naturally resist attempts to change their attitudes and behaviour. If a teacher believes that someone is trying to limit her free expression in an area that is important to her there is 'reactance' against this. The teacher will try harder to assert her own idea or action, which she believes is being threatened.

Reactance is not a negative childish attitude but stems from the need of teachers to feel in control of their own lives. It may be that people want to appear to be independent rather than that they actually seek freedom of choice. Reactance theory predicts that attempts to force teachers to change their attitudes to issues such as equal opportunities will cause a reaction and rejection. This can be avoided by asking teachers to choose freely between alternatives and by making public their commitment. So colleagues are more likely to change their attitude to the introduction of a new religious curriculum if they are given a chance to discuss the proposal and if they make a public commitment through their own choice. Reactance theory emphasizes that attitudes are organized to protect the self-concept.

Attitudes do not change easily, and changing stereotypes and prejudice is extremely difficult. Because prejudice is such a complex inter-locked schema of attitudes, it is changed only through the cognitive approach, when teachers think about the issues. Stereotypes and prejudice have functional purposes for the individual: stereotypes simplify the world and prejudice protects the self-concept. Recog-nizing their functional value is the first step in understanding and changing them.

SUMMARY

Psychology has a number of perspectives that help to make sense of attitudes and prejudice. It is normal for people to categorize the world and this is the basis for the formation of attitudes – what people like and dislike. Stereotypes are a widely shared, oversimplified schema of attitudes about a group of people. Prejudice stems from stereotypes and is a negative attitude to members of a group, based solely on their membership of that group.

Attitudes are organized and maintained to enhance the teacher's self-concept. Teachers maintain consistency between their attitudes and their own positive self-image. Recognizing the political and economic relationship between two groups is a starting point from which the teacher can address the logical and cyclical nature of categorization, stereotyping and prejudice in schools.

One way for people to feel good about themselves is to look down on members of other groups. This is the basis for all forms of prejudice: social, sexual and particularly racial. The first step in tackling racial prejudice in Britain is to shift the core attitude that underlies much racial prejudice in this country; the Eurocentric, Western perspec-tive that people originating from parts of the world other than Britain are by definition inferior. In the end, it is as simple and difficult as that.

REFERENCES

Adorno, T., Frenkel-Brunswick, E., Levinson, D. and Sanford, R. (1950) *The Authoritarian Personality*. New York: Harper & Row.
Brehm, S. (1976) *The Application of Social Psychology to Clinical Practice*. New York: Wiley.
Clifford, M. and Walster, E. (1973) The effects of physical attraction on teacher expectation, *Sociology of Education* **46**, pp. 248-58.
Darley, B. and Gross, P. (1983) A hypothesis-confirming bias in label-ling effects, *Journal of Personality and Social Psychology* **44**, pp. 20-33.

Eiser, R. (1986) *Social Psychology: Attitudes, Cognition and Social Behaviour*. Cambridge: Cambridge University Press.

Festinger, L. (1957) *A Theory of Cognitive Dissonance*. Stanford, CA: Stanford University Press.

Fishbein, M. and Ajzen, I. (1974) Attitudes towards objects as predictors of single and multiple behavioural criteria, *Psychological Review* **81**, pp. 59–74.

Fishbein, M. and Ajzen, I. (1975) *Belief, Attitude, Intervention and Behaviour: An Introduction to Theory and Research*. Reading, MA: Addison-Wesley.

Gill, D., Mayor, B. and Blair, M. (eds), (1992) *Racism and Education: Structure and Strategies*. Milton Keynes: Sage, in association with the Open University.

Hannah, M. and Pliner, S. (1983) Teacher attitudes toward handicapped children: a review and synthesis, *School Psychology Review* **12**, pp. 12–25.

Hargreaves, D. (1977) The process of typification in classroom interaction: models and methods, *British Journal of Educational Psychology* **47**, pp. 274–84.

Heilman, M. and Stopeck, M. (1985) Being attractive, advantage or disadvantage? Performance evaluations and recommended personnel actions as a function of appearance, sex, and job type, *Organizational Behavior and Human Decision Processes* **35**, pp. 202–15.

LaPiere, R. (1934) Attitudes v. actions, *Social Forces* **13**, pp. 230–7.

Lynch, J. (1987) *Prejudice Reduction and the Schools*. London: Cassell.

McGregor, D. (1960) *The Human Side of Enterprise*. New York: McGraw-Hill.

MacIntyre, D., Morrison, A. and Sutherland, J. (1966) Social and educational variables relating to teachers' assessments of primary school pupils, *British Journal of Educational Psychology* **65**, pp. 238–43.

Osgood, C. and Tannenbaum, P. (1955) The principle of congruity in the prediction of attitude change, *Psychological Review* **62**, pp. 42–55.

Petty, R. E. and Cacioppo, J. T. (1981) *Attitudes and Persuasion: Classic and Contemporary Approaches*. Dubuque, IA: Brown.

Sharp, R. and Green, A. (1975) *Education and Social Control*. London: Routledge & Kegan Paul.

Wicker, A. (1969) Attitudes versus actions: the relationship of verbal and overt behavioural responses to attitude objects, *Journal of Social Issues* **25**, pp. 41–78.

RECOMMENDED READING

R. Eiser, *Social Psychology: Attitudes, Cognition and Social Behaviour* (Cambridge: Cambridge University Press, 1986), is a detailed and comprehensive overview of the psychology of attitudes. Not an easy read.

D. Gill, B. Mayor and M. Blair (eds), *Racism and Education: Structure and Strategies* (Milton Keynes: Sage, in association with the Open University, 1992), is a series of papers showing how racism functions in British schools. Describes the various methods that have been adopted, often unsuccessfully, to deal with racism.

J. Lynch, *Prejudice Reduction and the Schools* (London: Cassell, 1987), is an excellent practical and theoretical text on understanding and dealing with prejudice in schools.

CHAPTER 6

Motivation

OVERVIEW

Teachers often complain that pupils do not work hard enough at school. 'More effort required' is the proverbial remark on many pupils' reports. This is a common complaint, too, about adult workers, who are often portrayed by the media as lazy and unmotivated. What are teachers' attitude to work? Are they full of energy and enthusiasm or bored and uninterested? The simple answer is, 'it depends'. But what it depends on is motivation – the reason why one teacher will enthusiastically spend hours preparing lessons while her colleague in the staffroom is reluctant to expend any energy.

Psychologists originally considered that motivation depended on internal factors – factors inside teachers, such as their need to be successful. The focus then shifted to external factors – factors outside teachers, such as being paid a good salary. Recently, more sophisticated theories show how the internal and external factors interconnect. These give teachers a helpful framework for understanding their own motivation.

This chapter looks at a number of different theories that are used by psychologists to explain motivation. In particular it covers:

- the concept of motivation;
- internal factors: need theory;
- external factors: reward theory;
- social factors: equity theory;
- a combined approach: expectancy theory;
- systems for motivation in schools.

THE CONCEPT OF MOTIVATION

Motivation is a hypothetical concept, as it cannot be directly observed. All that can be observed are teachers' actions, and then assumptions are made about their motivation. One can only speculate whether the assumptions are true. A teacher may work very hard at a task – a curriculum project, say. She appears highly motivated by the project. It may be, though, that what is motivating her, energizing her and keeping her focused on the project is her attraction to another member of the project group. The teacher appears highly motivated, and is so – but not by the project, which in reality has little interest for her.

The word 'motivation' is used in a number of different ways. *Chambers English Dictionary* defines motivation as 'motivating force, incentive'. 'Motivating force' could be something inside teachers, such as needs they have, or something outside them, such as the fear of being made redundant. 'Incentive' seems to imply something outside a teacher – a reward or reinforcement, the term used in behavioural psychology.

Is motivation a force that drives teachers from inside; for example, the desire to do well? Or is it an incentive that draws teachers on from outside – the lure of success? Do teachers look for motivators in themselves or in the world around them? Motivation is given both meanings in normal conversation, and different theories emphasize the internal or the external aspects.

Motivation

Motivation is the set of processes that energize a person's behaviour and direct it towards obtaining some goal (Baron, 1986, p. 73).

Baron's definition covers a number of the key aspects of motivation. By emphasizing that it is 'the set of processes', he highlights the fact that it can be a combination of internal and external forces. He also emphasizes that motivation must 'energize' the person, to produce the effort that the teacher puts into an activity. Thirdly, he highlights the importance of the goal or the focus of this energy. A teacher may have a lot of energy, but it need not necessarily be focused on teaching – she may be highly motivated to go sailing, but not to plan lessons. It is important to specify the goal of the energy rather than make bland statements, such as, 'She's not motivated.'

Baron's definition is a useful starting point for examining the different psychological theories that have been used to explain motivation. These theories offer different perspectives that help teachers to understand the effort, or lack of effort, that they put into various teaching tasks. By understanding the various theories and how they interrelate, teachers can rearrange their lives so that they feel greater motivation for teaching. By understanding their own motivation teachers can also understand how to motivate pupils.

There is, however, one fundamental difference between pupils' and teachers' motivation. When considering teachers' motivation the normal focus is on the effort that they put into teaching – a task that they can already do. However, with pupils the issue is often how to motivate them to engage in a task that they cannot do – learning new skills. Pupils' motivation has often been confused with pupils' learning, and the lack of learning has been seen as a lack of motivation or effort. Clearly this is a confusion of two interrelated processes. Pupils' learning, as described in Part 3, is influenced by a large number of factors, including their motivation. A pupil can be strongly motivated and still have difficulty with a particular task.

INTERNAL FACTORS: NEED THEORY

There developed in the 1920s theories of motivation that were based on the concept of 'drives'. Teachers' drives came from a biological need, for food, water or sex, that left them in an aroused state and led to a drive in that particular area. Teachers were motivated or 'driven' to fulfil these basic physiological desires. By satisfying their need they reduce their basic drive in this area. This is drive reduction theory. Drive theory is very clearly based on a physiological, mechanical model of people, and the research in this area was usually done on animals. The model uses machine-based metaphors such as overflowing energy and drainage from containers of fixed capacity. Motivation is seen to stem from an internal need. Drive reduction theory is no longer seen as particularly helpful in explaining motivation, as it does not take into account the other needs that people have. (Nevertheless, if you have been on holiday in an area populated by young male British holidaymakers, drive reduction theory, with its emphasis on the search for food, drink and sex, suddenly makes an awful lot of sense!)

Psychological needs

In the 1930s and 1940s, Abraham Maslow developed a popular framework for these other needs that teachers have. As well as the basic physiological needs for food, drink and sex, as identified by the drive theorists, he outlined other, higher-order needs.

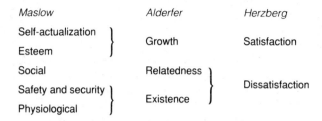

Figure 6.1 Need theories.

Abraham Maslow (1908-70)

Abraham Maslow was born in New York City and received a PhD from the University of Wisconsin. He was one of the founders, with Carl Rogers, of the American Association of Humanistic Psychology. Maslow felt that psychology had concentrated too much on people's difficulties – their failings – and not enough on their strengths. He looked for a more positive side to people. He is best remembered for his need theory of motivation.

Teachers have a series of physiological needs, psychological needs and social needs that they are motivated to try to satisfy. Maslow divides needs into a hierarchy of five levels (see Figure 6.1). It is a hierarchy in so far as teachers are only motivated by their higher-level needs if their lower-order ones are met. The bottom three levels of needs – physiological, security and social – are known in Maslow's theory as 'deficiency' needs. A deficiency in these means that a teacher is not able to live a healthy life. On the other hand, the top two needs, esteem and self-actualization, are seen as 'growth' needs – they are necessary for the teacher to grow and develop as an individual. Without these, teachers may exist physiologically, but psychologically they will not really live.

The most basic needs are physiological: the need for food, water and sex. It is only when these needs are fulfilled that teachers are motivated by the next level of need, security – a desire for safety and protection. For teachers, this translates most directly as the need for job security through having secure contracts. If a teacher is on a short-term contract, she is likely to be motivated to resolve this need before being motivated by the higher-order ones.

The third level, social, is also referred to as belongingness and love. This emphasizes the importance of the social aspects of work – and of life outside work. Teachers need affectionate relationships. Teachers, through their contact with pupils and members of staff, have the opportunity to receive a lot of positive human interaction. One of the developments that have taken place in the last few decades is an understanding of the importance of good social relationships between members of staff as a key means of ensuring motivation.

The fourth level, esteem, is a teacher's need to be thought well of. It is the need to be considered competent and to have a reputation as a good teacher and a nice person with her colleagues, parents and pupils.

Finally, self-actualization refers to teachers' needs to develop and grow in their jobs. Teachers not only want to be paid, to be secure, to have good social relationships and to be seen as competent at their jobs; they also want the opportunity to develop. They need the opportunity to have new responsibilities, to develop new skills and to have greater control over their lives.

The major implication of the theory is the hierarchical nature of need. If teachers have no job security and their social needs are not taken care of in the classroom or at home, then they will not be motivated by self-esteem or self-actualization needs. The lowest unsatisfied need becomes the most powerful motivator. Satisfying this significant need is what motivates an individual.

Unfortunately for Maslow's ideas, research shows that real life is more complicated than this. Having five levels of need appears arbitrary, as is the view that these must be tackled in a sequential hierarchy. Maslow's five categories have been collapsed into three by Alderfer (1972). These are:

- existence – this corresponds to Maslow's physiological and security needs;
- relatedness – this corresponds to Maslow's social needs;
- growth – this corresponds to Maslow's self-esteem and self-actualization needs (see Figure 6.1).

Alderfer also shows that people have needs in all the three categories at the same time – there is no hierarchy. Alderfer, like Maslow, believes that it is unsatisfied needs that motivate, but he holds that higher-order needs do not become less powerful if they are addressed. Instead, they become more important and powerful. For example, if a teacher is given new responsibility and opportunities to develop in her job then she is likely to want still more responsibility and development, not less.

Alderfer's need theory is simpler and more elegant to work with than Maslow's hierarchy of needs.

Satisfaction and dissatisfaction

A radical variation of need theory is the proposal that satisfaction and dissatisfaction do not stem from the same factors (Herzberg, 1966).

The factors that could cause dissatisfaction at work are similar to Alderfer's 'existence' and 'relatedness' factors. They are normally factors that surround the work rather than the work itself.

Satisfaction and dissatisfaction

Certain factors make teachers dissatisfied at work, but overcoming or removing these factors will not automatically produce satisfaction or an increase in motivation. There is a separate set of factors that must be tackled to produce satisfaction and an increase in teachers' motivation.

Dissatisfaction factors for teachers are:

- pay;
- working conditions;
- quality of headteacher (or head of department);
- relationship with others;
- job security;
- school policy.

So improving teachers' pay may reduce their dissatisfaction, but it will not actually increase their satisfaction, or motivation to teach. This perspective is radically different from that which is common in education. There is an assumption that by improving pay and working conditions motivation can be improved. Certainly these factors are important: they are the key to preventing a dissatisfied teaching force. The distinction is that they are not the key to a satisfied teaching force. It may be that these factors are not motivators specifically in our Western industrial world because they are relatively freely available as conditions of work. Teachers have other expectations about what constitutes a reasonable life.

Satisfaction factors or motivators are more focused on the job itself, and correspond with Alderfer's 'growth' factors. Motivational factors for teachers are:

- feelings of achievement;
- recognition of teaching accomplishments;
- the job itself;
- responsibility;
- the opportunity for promotion;
- personal growth.

If schools are to increase teachers' motivation, it is these factors that have to be addressed.

Herzberg's satisfaction–dissatisfaction theory is intuitively appealing. It is interesting to consider that some factors merely prevent further dissatisfaction while others actually increase motivation. The research, however, does not totally support this distinction, as it appears that both sets of factors can actually have effects on both satisfaction and dissatisfaction. This is because there are individual differences in causes of satisfaction/dissatisfaction. This failure to allow for differences between individuals is a general criticism of all need theories. There is a danger of stereotyping what motivates individuals. Nevertheless, the distinction between satisfiers and dissatisfiers heightens awareness that all factors may not operate in the same way. Specifically, it leads to a focus on the actual job of teaching itself, rather than the conditions of service, as a way of increasing motivation.

All the need theories emphasize that teachers have unmet internal needs. Motivation is the energy that teachers use to fulfil these internal needs.

EXTERNAL FACTORS: REWARD THEORY

In the 1950s, behavioural psychology's emphasis on the importance of reinforcements challenged the need theory of motivation. Skinner proposed that people are motivated not by internal needs but by external rewards; motivation is simply the effective use of rewards, so if teachers are rewarded for their work they will work harder. The rewards that a teacher likes have to be identified and then paired with the desired activity; so teachers can be motivated to plan lessons if they are rewarded for doing so, and if they are not rewarded then they will not be likely to expend much energy on this activity.

There is a range of rewards that can be used to motivate people (see Chapter 1). These range from concrete rewards, such as a pay rise, to social rewards, such as praise from the headteacher. A number of key strategies have been identified for the effective use of rewards (Hamner, 1974). They must:

- *be appropriate*. The size of rewards varies considerably, from being promoted to a small word of praise. If a teacher has put an enormous amount of effort into a task, a small reward will not be seen as appropriate. In fact it may be seen as an insult and will decrease the teacher's motivation. The size or value of the reward must be appropriate to the amount of energy expended.
- *be clear*. Teachers are often unclear what is being rewarded in a school. There should be clear and open communication about what is really important in the school. Is it obtaining good reading results or developing a winning football team? By being clear

about what is of value in the school, teachers can be motivated
to work towards the right goals.

- *be contingent*. If everyone receives the same level of reward
  then no one is motivated. If praise does not follow actual effort
  it becomes habitual and meaningless. Everyone needs praise,
  but it does need to be genuine if it is to increase teachers'
  motivation.
- *provide feedback*. Teachers require information that tells them
  how their teaching is being received and how to improve it, not
  just praise when they are successful. At the moment, many
  teachers get little feedback on the quality of their teaching. Feedback is one of the key benefits of good appraisal systems. Telling
  teachers how they are doing can increase their motivation.

It is important to recognize that withdrawing rewards (see Chapter
1) also affects motivation. If teachers' actions are not rewarded they
will reduce their efforts. For example, if teachers receive no rewards
for marking standard assessment tasks (SATs) they will not be
motivated to complete the task.

Are rewards always external?

One fundamental issue concerning rewards is whether they are
always external things that have to be given to the teacher. Praise,
pay rises and the opportunity to go on the school skiing trip are all
external rewards. Internal rewards, on the other hand, belong to the
individual world of the teacher. They include such things as pleasure
at finishing a piece of work or interest in finding out about how to
teach a particular pupil. They come from satisfaction at having
achieved some internal goal that is important to the teacher. There is
a thin dividing line between internal and external rewards. Praise
from a colleague is an external reward whereas self-praise whereby the
teacher reminds herself of what she has achieved over the last term,
is an internal reward.

The value of the reward to the individual

The distinction between external and internal highlights the fact
that rewards are unique to the individual. A reward will motivate a
teacher only if it is of value to her. So one teacher may value praise
from her head of department whereas another may find it meaningless.
Moreover, the value of certain rewards may change for a teacher as she
grows older. For example, the extra responsibility or promotion that
the newly qualified teacher strove for may not be valued and therefore motivating for the older teacher. It is important for teachers to

recognize that they go through a career cycle. At certain stages, extra pay or the opportunity to attend courses may be very important, but for their colleagues at other stages these may not be motivators.

Reinforcement theory is a help in understanding teachers' motivation. It emphasizes the forces outside the individual that will energize them. Teachers need to recognize the reward systems that motivate them as well as recognizing their responsibility to develop systems that motivate their colleagues – and their pupils.

SOCIAL FACTORS: EQUITY THEORY

Both reinforcement and need theories emphasize the individual teacher. Teachers, however, do not work in isolation, and their social context has an effect on motivation. Equity theory focuses on the social world that the teacher is working in – her macrosystem (Adams, 1965). The basis of equity theory is that teachers are motivated to keep a fair or 'equitable' relationship between themselves and other people. This means that teachers are motivated to change those relationships that are unfair or inequitable.

The theory suggests that teachers make comparisons about whether they are being treated fairly in two main areas:

- the outcomes they get from work – that is, how their work is rewarded;
- the inputs they put into work – that is, the amount of effort that they put into it.

Work outcomes and inputs are compared with other teachers' outcomes and inputs. If they do not appear to be fair, the teacher will be motivated to achieve a better balance (see Figure 6.2). The balance may be achieved by taking actions; that is, by either reducing or increasing the amount of work she does. Or it may be achieved psychologically, by changing her perception of the situation; that is,

	Underpayment (in terms of money or rewards)	Overpayment (in terms of money or rewards)
Psychological	Convince yourself that the other person is working harder	Convince yourself that you are working harder
Behavioural	Reduce own efforts; try to raise outcomes – ask for a pay rise	Work harder – longer hours; try to lower outcomes – do not accept a pay rise!

Figure 6.2 Possible reactions to inequity.

by recognizing that the other teacher is working harder than she is. This is as cognitive dissonance theory would predict (see Chapter 5): the teacher changes to overcome her feelings of unease.

Implications for teachers

Equity theory suggests that each teacher considers what she gets out of her job and the effort that she puts into it. She will consider these two variables in the light of how she perceives other people's (teachers' and non-teachers') input and output. If the teacher feels that what she is putting into the job and what she is getting out are roughly equitable with what other people are putting in and getting out, then she will continue to work in the same way. On the other hand, if she feels there is inequity in terms of either 'underpayment' or 'overpayment', she will adjust her effort. For example, if a teacher feels that she is putting a lot of effort into her work in comparison with other members of staff and that the outcomes for the work are not correspondingly high, in comparison with the other members of staff, she will see this as underpayment. She will reduce the effort that she makes – her input. The underpayment can be in terms of acknowledgement, praise, promotion or whatever the important outcome is for her. In a similar way, if a newly promoted teacher thinks she is being overpaid in comparison with her colleagues, she may adjust the balance by either convincing herself that she is working harder, or actually working longer hours.

The comparisons teachers make are based on their perception of the situation – facts do not necessarily enter into the comparison, as they may not be available. (How, for example, can a teacher really tell whether a colleague is working hard?) Comparisons are certainly likely to be made with other members of staff in the same school, and are likely to extend to teachers in other schools or other LEAs, and even to members of other professions. Many teachers will remember the disillusionment they felt when the police force's pay was raised in the 1980s. Teachers felt unmotivated because they perceived that the balance between their pay and the effort they put into the job was unequitable when compared with that in the police force.

There is a good deal of research support for equity theory, which shows that by manipulating the input or the output in an experimental situation people's motivations can be increased or decreased. The lesson to be learnt from the theory is that teachers' motivation stems not only from their own needs, but from their perception of how hard colleagues around them are working. The theory stresses the importance of the perception of the social context as the basis for an individual's increase or decrease in motivation.

It will be interesting to see how school governors deal with the problem of equity if they use pay as a reward system. Equity theory would predict that perceived inequity would lead to a loss of motivation. Governors will need to consider how a pay increase for one teacher will affect the motivation of that teacher's colleagues in the school.

Postscript on equity theory

Equity theory helps explain the difficulty of motivating some pupils from particular cultural or social groups, since it would predict that if an individual from a particular cultural or social group perceives inequity (prejudice) in the educational system, in terms of not getting as much out of education as others despite his efforts, then he will deliberately reduce his work effort in order to maintain equity. To increase work effort, he would have first to break the vicious cycle where it seems that other pupils are getting more out from the effort that they put in. The 'lack of motivation' of a pupil from a particular cultural or social group can be easily explained by equity theory as a logical reaction to the perceived inequity within the educational system.

A COMBINED APPROACH: EXPECTANCY THEORY

Expectancy theory combines elements of need, reinforcement and equity theories. It is the most complex of all the theories of motivation that will be dealt with in this chapter. There are a number of variations of expectancy theory, but it is most often associated with Victor Vroom (1964).

Victor Vroom (1932–)

Victor Vroom was born in Canada and attended McGill University. His doctoral dissertation on decision making won the Ford Foundation Dissertation Competition in 1959. He is best known for his theories of organizational psychology, particularly on motivation and on decision making. He has lectured at a number of US universities and is presently Professor of Administrative Sciences at Yale University.

Expectancy theory basically suggests that teachers are motivated to work when they 'expect' that they will be able to achieve the things that they want. The assumption is that teachers are rational about the effort that they will put into work.

Expectancy theory

Motivation is the multiplication of the force of three variables:

Valence × Instrumentality × Expectancy = Motivation.

- *Expectancy* is the belief that a teacher's efforts will result in performance. For example, a teacher believes that if she works harder then the pupils will learn more effectively.
- *Instrumentality* is the belief that a teacher's performance will be rewarded. For example, a teacher believes that if her pupils learn more effectively then she will be promoted.
- *Valence* is the value of the reward to the teacher. In this example, the reward is valuable to the teacher because she is seeking promotion.

Motivation is the result of beliefs in these areas. Because of the multiplicative factor, if one of these beliefs is not held (it has a value of 0) then motivation will also be zero. So, for example, if the reward is of no value to the teacher then she will not be motivated, even if the other two beliefs are held.

Expectancy theory can be used to understand teachers' motivation to complete tasks, such as introducing testing (SATs) into the classroom. Expectancy theory predicts that for teachers to be motivated for this task they need to believe three things:

- that their efforts in introducing the SATs will help them with their teaching – in other words, that the SATs will affect pupils' learning;
- that completing the SATs will be rewarded – that is, that they will get something out of having completed them. This can be praise from the headteacher, acknowledgement by the parents or personal development;
- that the reward will be of value to them. If the perceived reward has no value – for example, if they do not care what the headteacher thinks of them, or they are about to leave the teaching profession – then their motivation will be zero.

Failure to believe in even one of these factors will mean the teacher is not motivated to introduce SATs.

This has immediate implications for the introduction of changes in the educational system. If teachers are to be motivated to implement changes, they must believe in these three variables:

- that implementing the change will have a result (whether that is a change in pupils' reading skills, better communication with parents or a more appropriate curriculum);
- that the effort taken to implement the change will be recognized in some way;
- that the way the effort is recognized will be of value to the teacher.

It can be seen that expectancy theory explains teachers' lack of motivation to support change if, at the most fundamental level, they do not believe that the change will affect pupils' learning.

Motivation v. performance

Motivation is not the only factor that affects how well an activity is carried out. For example, teachers may be well motivated to complete SATs, but their performance – how well they actually complete them – depends as well on at least three other factors:

- *abilities and skills*. Different teachers have different skills which play a part in how well each can do any particular task. A teacher can be highly motivated to introduce SATs but if she has poor teaching skills this will affect how well they are introduced.
- *role perception*. A teacher's completion of SATs will also depend on how others see her. If a particular teacher sees herself as taking a lead on assessment then she is likely to complete SATs more effectively than a teacher who does not see assessment as part of her role.
- *opportunities*. If the teacher does not have the opportunity to complete SATs, then it does not matter how well motivated she is; she will not be good at this particular task.

Expectancy theory has dominated theories of motivation since the 1970s, even though the multiplication assumption has been challenged. A teacher, it is claimed, can still be motivated even if one of the factors is zero. So a teacher will work hard at a task for which she will receive a valued reward even if she recognizes that the task is meaningless. For example, a teacher may spend hours working out a computer system for the school even when she knows the system will never be introduced. In this case the rewards, both external and internal, that the teacher receives overcome the 'meaningless' of the task.

Expectancy theory is very important, as it emphasizes that three factors can be changed to increase motivation. It also highlights the importance of the teacher's individual values and needs, rather than expecting everyone to be motivated in the same way by the same things. The implications of expectancy theory can be seen in the development of motivational systems in schools.

SYSTEMS FOR MOTIVATION IN SCHOOLS

The first implication of the above theories for motivating teachers in schools is a recognition of the complexity of motivation. There is no simple answer to the question of what motivates teachers, let alone that of what motivates a particular teacher. Teachers will be motivated in different situations in different ways; their motivation will depend on their particular needs at the time, what they find rewarding, how they view other teachers, and how they view the results of their efforts in school.

Three strategies have been developed for increasing motivation that reflect the above:

- *job design*, where the job is designed to ensure that the actual work is motivating;
- *incentive schemes*, where the job is coupled with reinforcements that meet the teacher's needs;
- *goal setting*, where the above two are combined and teachers develop a clear picture of their goals and then receive reinforcement for their attainment.

Job design

The basic idea of job design is to increase motivation by designing the job so that it is interesting and attractive to the teacher. This can be done by looking at the whole job of the teacher, or at specific aspects of it – for example, marking homework or listening to pupils read.

Though improving job design is a common feature of many business organizations, it is seldom used in education. This may be because teaching is considered so intrinsically interesting! Certainly teaching already has many of the features that are considered essential to a well-designed job, such as variety, challenge, responsibility and social interaction. On the other hand, given the shortage of teachers, in many subject areas, and the exodus from teaching in the 1980s and the early 1990s, it is worth considering whether job design could increase motivation. One possibility would be to rationalize the use of non-contact time; if teachers were given sufficient time to prepare and mark pupils' work, this would have major benefits for teacher motivation.

A particular strategy for job design is job rotation, which gives teachers the opportunity for development without having to move schools. Rotating classes is one means of achieving this – in some primary schools teachers have the opportunity to change the year group they teach in successive years. Being given responsibility for different areas of school activities is another means.

A national survey in the USA of workers (not teachers) indicates

119

the important features of their jobs as good pay, the availability of needed resources, having sufficient authority, having friendly and cooperative co-workers, and having interesting work. These are similar to the satisfaction–dissatisfaction factors found by Herzberg. Many teachers feel that the first three are not features of their job at the moment, and it is dispiriting to realize that the increase in competition both within and between schools is likely to erode the presence of friendly and cooperative co-workers. 'Interesting work' may remain the only important feature for teachers.

A particularly strong motivator in the Western industrial countries in the 1990s is most people's wish to obtain some control over their own working life. People no longer wish to be tied to a particular institution, or even profession, but wish to be able to develop with their changing skills and interests. Teachers, and particularly head-teachers, need to consider how teaching jobs can be designed so that teachers can develop core transferable skills, thus allowing them to change careers during their working life.

Incentive schemes

Reinforcement theory shows how rewards can be used to motivate people. Incentive schemes are built on reinforcement principles. The individual is offered a choice from a menu of incentives or reinforcers for successfully completing her work. In many organizations, a cafeteria-style list of reinforcement options is available as incentives, ranging from lease car facilities and longer holidays to pay rises and time for additional training. As education moves into a more openly competitive system, this sort of incentive scheme may be necessary to attract and motivate teachers.

There is little attempt in education to use incentive schemes overtly; at the moment, such systems are often hidden within the school's culture. Teachers have to discover on what basis praise and promotion occur in their school, often from incomplete if not distorted information. For example, new teachers may be told that hard work will gain them an incentive allowance; the reality, however, may be that supporting the head publicly is a more effective strategy.

Incentive systems are likely to be more formally applied in schools when appraisal schemes are introduced. But for incentive systems to be effective, headteachers and governors have to create much greater flexibility in their schools. This would allow them to use incentives as motivators for effective teaching.

If such an incentive scheme is to be introduced, it needs to be borne in mind that teachers work for both external and internal incentives. The internal incentives are addressed by the strategy of job design, since teachers can be motivated by the job itself as well as by external incentives. In real life, it is difficult to separate internal from external motivation. Teachers can be motivated by their jobs and at the same time be reinforced for completing them, so there is often an interactive element between internal and external factors.

Incentive schemes also recognize that teachers differ widely in their choice of reinforcements. Some teachers may want greater choice over the classes they teach, others may want to work shorter or longer hours – after all, overtime is common in most other organizations! Incentive schemes do motivate people, but their introduction into education would require a radical rethink of the organization of schools, as well as the relationship between members of staff.

Goal setting

One key strategy to increase motivation that is incorporated in most professional development and appraisal systems is goal setting. This integrates elements of both job design and incentive schemes as a means of developing motivation. Essentially it consists of teachers setting goals – tasks that they wish to achieve within a set period of time – a process which encourages them to look at their jobs and then to set new goals that they wish to attain. Achieving these can then be reinforced both internally and externally.

Goals describe a desired future state. For a teacher, they could be:

- to increase Sam's reading skills;
- to increase pupil attendance throughout the term;
- to be timetabled to teach year 8.

Goal setting

Goal setting is an extremely effective way for teachers to increase their motivation. Goals are targets or aims that the teacher wishes to achieve within a certain set period. Goal setting has demonstrated effectiveness in increasing motivation in 90 per cent of the reported research (Locke *et al.*, 1981).

Four key strategies have been identified that make setting goals successful:

- *Set specific goals.* A teacher will work harder if she has clear and specific goals to work for. Goals should be observable and measurable. 'To teach Sam initial letter sounds so that he can use them when reading' is a more specific and therefore appropriate goal than 'To increase Sam's reading skills'.

- *Set difficult but acceptable goals.* Goals need to be set that challenge the teacher. If they are too difficult or too easy, they will decrease rather than increase motivation. So instead of setting a virtually impossible goal of 100 per cent attendance over a term, it is more useful if the goal is a realistic 94 per cent attendance.
- *Set goals jointly.* One of the keys for successful appraisal of teachers is that goals should be set jointly. Discussing goals with a colleague is likely to be a motivator, as there is joint commitment. This can also be seen if teachers are trying to motivate pupils in their class. Pupils are much more likely to accept goals and be motivated by them if they have been involved in setting them, rather than having had them unilaterally imposed by the teacher.
- *Provide feedback.* The importance of feedback has already been stressed – teachers need to know how well they are doing. If there is no feedback, they cannot know how successful they are at achieving their goals and how much more effort they need to expend.

Goal setting can be used by the teacher to increase the motivation of pupils. If this is done, the four key strategies must be kept in mind. It is all too easy to provide unclear, difficult, unilaterally set goals, with no feedback. This is the way to demotivate a pupil rather than to motivate him.

Goal setting is an extremely popular method for motivating people. It is sometimes confused with 'management by objectives' (or MBO). The setting of objectives by management through some kind of appraisal system is common in much of industry, and in the last few years appraisal systems have begun to be introduced into the public sector in health and in education. It is important that appraisal systems in education focus on goal setting rather than MBO. Goal setting emphasizes the collaborative nature of development; teachers are unlikely to be motivated by being told what objectives they have to achieve. Too much of teaching is outside an individual teacher's control to make unilaterally set objectives either achievable or equitable. On the other hand, jointly set goals, which are the essence of teachers' planning for their own development, are a highly successful strategy for increasing motivation. The increased use of 'critical' colleagues (or mentors) who help teachers reflect on their own teaching practice is one key strategy to achieve this.

The effort that teachers put into the classroom can helpfully be seen through the theories described above, but they are not a total explanation of teachers' motivation. An additional perspective is provided by attribution theory, which is dealt with in Chapter 7, and which explains why some teachers feel empowered to teach and some pupils feel empowered to learn.

SUMMARY

This chapter focuses on the concept of motivation and on strategies that can be used to increase teachers' motivation. Three main theories are helpful in explaining what motivates teachers. These theories lay emphasis on different factors. Need theory emphasizes teachers' internal drives – motivation is seen as coming from inside the teacher. On the other hand, reinforcement theory emphasizes forces that pull the teacher from outside. Equity theory highlights the importance of social factors, and in particular how teachers compare the balance between their efforts and outcomes with those of other people. Finally, expectancy theory shows how motivation is tied to a teacher's beliefs about a series of interlocking factors.

Three strategies – job design, incentive schemes and goal setting – are often used in organizations to increase motivation. They are at present rarely used in a systematic way to increase teachers' motivation. One of the challenges for education is to recognize the importance of motivating teachers, as well as motivating pupils.

REFERENCES

Adams, S. (1965) Inequity in social exchanges, in Berkowitz, L. (ed.), *Advances in Experimental Social Psychology*, Vol. 2. New York: Academic Press.

Alderfer, C. (1972) *Existence, Relatedness, and Growth*. New York: Free Press.

Baron, R. (1986) *Behaviour in Organizations*. 2nd edition. London: Allyn & Bacon.

Hamner, W. (1974) Reinforcement and contingency management in organizational settings, in Tosi, H. and Hamner, W. (eds), *Organizational Behavior and Management*. Chicago: St Clair.

Herzberg, F. (1966) *Work and the Nature of Man*. Cleveland: World Publishing Company.

Locke, E., Shaw, K., Saari, L. and Latham, G. (1981) Goal setting and task performance, *Psychological Bulletin* **90**, pp. 125–52.

Maslow, A. (1970) *Motivation and Personality*. 2nd edition. New York: Harper & Row.

Vroom, V. (1964) *Work and Motivation*. New York: Wiley.

RECOMMENDED READING

R. Baron, *Behaviour in Organizations*, 2nd edition (London: Allyn & Bacon, 1986), is a readable introduction to behaviour in organizations. Not specifically aimed at an educational setting, it provides an overview of how psychology can be applied in any organization.

R. Steers and L. Porter, *Motivation and Work Behaviour* (London: McGraw-Hill, 1991), is written for managers, and integrates models of individual motivation with organizational variables. A comprehensive and detailed description of motivation.

CHAPTER 7

Attribution theory

OVERVIEW

Attribution theory is concerned with how people explain other people's actions. It is so called because it focuses on the way people 'attribute' different causes to different actions. Attribution theory is not about ascertaining the 'real' causes of pupils' behaviour but rather the explanation that a teacher gives for that behaviour. A teacher who believes that a pupil's lack of effort in class is caused by personality factors will deal with it in a different way from one who believes that the cause is the pupil's home circumstances.

This chapter concentrates on:

* teachers' explanations for pupils' behaviour;
* attributional error;
* the effects of teachers' attribution on classroom success;
* attribution and pupil effort;
* strategies for changing pupils' attributions.

TEACHERS' EXPLANATIONS FOR PUPILS' BEHAVIOUR

Social psychologists have been concerned for the last forty years with trying to understand how and why people ascribe causes to others' actions. Attribution theory is founded on the work of Heider (1944, 1958). Heider assumes, like Kelly (see Chapter 1), that people need to see the world as predictable and that therefore they act as scientists trying to develop theories to make sense of things.

Fritz Heider (1896–)

Fritz Heider was born in Vienna and received his doctorate from the University of Graz. In 1930 he emigrated to the USA, where he worked at Smith's College, Massachusetts, primarily doing research with deaf pupils. He remained there for 17 years, formulating his ideas for *The Psychology of Interpersonal Relations* (1958). He spent a number of years lecturing before retiring in 1966.

Teachers' attributions of behaviour

Teachers usually attribute behaviour to one of two fundamental causes: the pupil's personality (internal causes), or the situation he is in (external causes). So a pupil's behaviour will be explained by saying 'He's naughty' (an internal cause) or 'He's having a difficult time at home' (an external cause).

In extreme circumstances people's behaviour is attributed to other causes, principally God or the Devil. Usually this occurs when the rational scientist in a person cannot make sense of someone's behaviour.

If teachers act like scientists, what are the cues they look for when trying to understand the causes of behaviour? Kelley (1972) suggests that teachers will make multiple observations of pupils and then try to explain their actions logically in terms of internal or external causes, based on three critical cues (see Figure 7.1):

- consensus – do other pupils act in the same way?
- consistency – does the pupil always act in the same way in this situation?
- distinctiveness – does changing the situation change the pupil's behaviour? That is, does he behave the same way at home or after school?

By analysing these three factors, teachers make decisions about whether the cause of behaviour is internal personality factors or situational factors. These judgements are often made quite unconsciously; this is the normal way of trying to make sense of the world.

If the answers to these three questions about consensus, consistency and distinctiveness are in the negative, teachers are likely to view the

Consensus – do other pupils act in the same way in this situation?	YES	NO
Consistency – does the pupil always act in the same way in this situation?	YES	NO
Distinctiveness – does changing the situation change the behaviour (e.g. at home, after school)?	YES	NO
	Situation	*Internal*

Figure 7.1 Causal attribution grid.

causes of behaviour as an internal, 'personality' problem. If, on the other hand, the three answers are in the affirmative, teachers are likely to attribute the cause of behaviour to the situation. However, teachers are active participants in the process, who weigh up their own perception of the relevance and importance of the three factors. They do not simply decide by adding up the number of 'Yes's and the number of 'No's.

Consider a pupil who loses his temper in class. What questions would the teacher ask herself to explain the pupil's behaviour?

- consensus – do other pupils act in the same way in this situation? The answer may be 'No, he is the only one in the class.'
- consistency – does the pupil always act in the same way in this situation? The answer may be 'No, sometimes he is calm.'
- distinctiveness – does changing the situation change the behaviour? The answer may be 'No, he also loses his temper at home.'

In these circumstances the teacher would probably attribute this pupil's behaviour to internal (personality) factors. Of course life is rarely as straightforward as this example: consider how the explanation of the pupil's behaviour might change if the teacher knew that he never had temper tantrums at home or after school. Teachers also use the same three criteria to explain their colleagues' actions in the staffroom – attributing their actions to internal or external causes.

Kelley's three cues – consensus, consistency and distinctiveness – have stood the test of time. There is now a good deal of research that confirms that people do tend to judge the cause of others' behaviour on the basis of these three factors (Harvery and Weary, 1981). So the first judgement teachers make is whether pupils' actions are caused by the situation they are in or by internal factors.

Inferring personality traits

There is a tendency for teachers, once they have decided that a pupil's behaviour is internally caused, to look for specific personality traits. So teachers may infer that the pupil who loses his temper has a number of different types of traits: aggressive, domineering or egocentric. When teachers are trying to understand internal traits, they focus on cues from three types of behaviour (Jones and Davis, 1965). These are:

- behaviour that is uncommon;
- behaviour that has low social desirability – for example, that goes against the culture or group norms;
- behaviour that the pupil is seen to perform freely and voluntarily.

For example, teachers believe that observing a pupil interacting and sharing a sandwich with a new pupil at lunchtime gives them a lot of cues about the personality of the pupil; this is behaviour that is uncommon, has a low social desirability and is seen to be performed freely. The teacher will use these cues rather than observing the pupil in a controlled teaching situation within the classroom, where he is seen to be influenced by group pressure.

It is important to remember that these are teachers' beliefs about the types of behaviour that tell them more about the pupil's personality, not that these types of behaviour actually do so. Attribution theory is concerned not with reality, but with teachers' beliefs about the causes of behaviour.

ATTRIBUTIONAL ERROR

People commonly fail to understand the causes of other people's behaviour (Farr, 1987), and this is perfectly normal. The first step in a teacher's understanding a pupil's behaviour is to grasp that he may have alternative explanations to the teacher's that are just as rational to him. Farr points out that there are some fairly fundamental illusions in how others are perceived, how others perceive us and in how we perceive ourselves. So far, attribution has been presented as a rational process that is intended to help the teacher make sense of the causes of behaviour. This, though, is a simplification, as there are distortions inherent in the process.

Ichheiser (1943) has identified three fundamental misinterpretations that are made when attributing causes to behaviour, dealt with below as unity of personality, differences between actors and observers, and egocentric attribution.

Unity of personality

There is a tendency to exaggerate the importance of the internal factors when explaining people's actions. This is so common that it is known as the 'fundamental attribution error'. Reference is rarely made to the situation when explaining another person's behaviour, but rather to the person's attitudes or personality.

Teachers do not recognize the different roles that pupils can play. The teacher always sees the pupil in the school context, and tends therefore to see the same behaviour and to explain this behaviour in terms of the pupil's personality. She does not recognize that she is one of the situational factors that affect the pupil's actions. This is one of the causes of the confusion that arises when a parent comes in and describes the pupil's behaviour in a way that is unrecognizable to the class teacher, or vice versa. Each is seeing only one aspect of the pupil and is making an assumption that he or she is seeing the whole pupil. This often becomes strikingly apparent to the teacher if she meets the same pupil on holiday or in another social context; she will often remark on how different the pupil is.

This failure to recognize that a person can act in many different ways depending upon the situation is particularly common in Western culture, where the emphasis is on individuality and self-determinism. People are considered to have some control over their actions and to be able to determine their own lives. This can be contrasted with, for example, Hindu beliefs about the causality of behaviour (Miller, 1984); Hindus believe that situations cause behaviour rather than that behaviour stems from our inner, free-will-based personality. The same Western belief can also be seen in a slightly different way in the press and on television. Here personalities dominate the news and are seen as the keys to understanding the causes of events, rather than situational or social factors.

Differences between actors and observers

Attribution theory makes a crucial distinction between the perspective of the actor in the situation and that of the observer. A teacher observing a pupil in a colleague's class is an observer; if, on the other hand, the teacher is in her own class then she is the actor. The actor and the observer have different perspectives and therefore explain behaviour differently. Research has shown that actors are much more likely to attribute their actions to the situation they are in than is an observer viewing them in the situation (Jones and Nisbett, 1972). The observer tends to explain behaviour in terms of the internal personality of the actor.

This has been dramatically illustrated by Milgram (1965). In possibly the most famous social psychology experiment of all time, he showed

129

that people were quite willing to give dangerously large electric shocks to others if they were told by an experimenter that it was in the interests of science. Before this experiment, it was claimed that people committed atrocities only if there was something wrong with their personality. The experiments showed quite clearly that this 'inhuman' behaviour of giving dangerously large electric shocks could not be explained by reference to deviant personalities. People simply explained their action by reference to the situation – obeying 'orders'.

So the teacher observing a colleague's difficulties in teaching a particular pupil will explain it by attributing it to internal events – 'She hasn't a firm personality.' The teacher actually teaching the class will explain it by factors external to her – 'It's the most difficult class in the school.' However, this distinction between actor and observer can be further complicated by the egocentric position described below.

Egocentric attribution

During the 1960s and early 1970s, attribution was seen as being dependent simply on the analysis of the cues seen by the observer. Jones and Nisbett (1972) showed that the way people view events is in line with the aim of improving their own self-concept. This is known as egocentric attribution, and is similar to the way people develop attitudes to protect their self-concept (see Chapter 5). So another factor when explaining an event is whether it is viewed as a success or a failure.

 There is a tendency to take credit for the successes that happen (that is, to give internal causes) but to ascribe failures to the situation. For example, cricketers often attribute their success at scoring runs to their own skills and explain their early dismissals by good bowling by the other team – they scored runs because they were good and they were dismissed because of the quality of the bowling, not because they batted badly. This has immediate relevance for the teacher. If pupils do badly on a task, student teachers blame the pupils (Johnson *et al.*, 1964), denying their own responsibility for the pupils' failures. If, on the other hand, the pupils improve on the task, the teachers see this as due to their skills as teachers.

More recently, however, Bar-Tal (1982) has reviewed the research in this area and suggests that it is not consistent. If teachers believe that they will not have contact with the pupils in the future, then they are likely in an egocentric way to take credit for any success and assign responsibility for any failure to the pupils. However, teachers are not totally dominated by this egocentric attribute, and if the pupils are well known to them then they acknowledge that it is the pupils' abilities and efforts that determine their success rather than their own teaching.

In Western culture, the whole concept of success and failure is tied into the concept of self-determinism; that is, the belief that people are able to determine their own future. People are held, in Western society, to be responsible for their own success and failure. This is so ingrained that even during the 1930s Depression in the USA people still felt they were responsible for their lack of success, rather than recognizing that it was the situation that they were in.

Attributional error

The three misrepresentations of unity of personality, actor v. observer, and egocentricity explain how a teacher's attribution of any action or event changes according to the circumstances. Teachers' attributions are not constant (see Figure 7.2).

	Failure	Success
Actor	Situation	Internal
Observer	Internal	Situation

Figure 7.2 Explanations of behaviour.

If a teacher is in the position of an actor and she has some success, she is likely to attribute this to an internal cause – her personality or ability. So if the teacher does well in an exam, she will probably attribute this to her ability and effort. If, however, she does badly in an exam, she is likely to explain it by the situation – the wrong questions coming up or not enough time to revise. If the teacher is observing a colleague, she is more likely to explain her colleague's failure in exams to internal causes – the colleague was not clever enough. If, however, the colleague is successful, she is likely to attribute the success to the situation – the right questions came up. This is especially likely if her colleague's success might be seen as a threat to her own self-concept.

EFFECTS OF TEACHERS' ATTRIBUTION ON CLASSROOM SUCCESS

Teachers' attributions of success and failure are beliefs that stem from an attempt to make sense of the world. Despite being only beliefs, they do have a direct and immediate effect on pupils' progress, through the process of the self-fulfilling prophecy. This stems directly from attribution theory. The classic work in this area is Rosenthal and Jacobson's book, *Pygmalion in the Classroom* (1968). The central tenet is that teachers, who are of high socioeconomic status, expect pupils of low socioeconomic status to fail at school – so they do.

Rosenthal and Jacobson wanted to see whether teachers' expectations about pupils' future performance actually affected the pupils' progress. A Californian school, 'Oak School', was the focus of their study. The pupils were assessed using a test of general ability. The teachers were told that the test would identify the 20 per cent of the pupils who would 'bloom' over the next academic year. Following the test, the teachers were told the names of this group – who had in fact been picked at random. A year later Rosenthal and Jacobson retested the pupils. The results showed that the 'bloomers' had made significant gains over the other pupils on the ability tests. The younger pupils, the 6–8-year-olds, had made the greatest gains. 'Bloomers' were also judged by their teachers to be more happy, interesting and appealing than the other pupils. It should be noted that the 'bloomers' did not improve significantly on all the measures that Rosenthal and Jacobson used.

This research has had enormous impact, as it shows that teachers' expectations actually affect pupils' progress. The importance of teachers' expectations has been recently endorsed, almost twenty-five years later, by the Alexander Report (DES, 1992). This once again highlights the fact that standards in schools will not rise until all teachers expect more of their pupils. Teachers' expectations of progress are at the heart of effective teaching.

There have been a number of attempts to replicate the original study. These have not shown the same dramatic results, though each of these has been seen to have methodological flaws (as does the original study). The explanation given for the pupils' improvement is that the teachers' higher expectations lead them to alter their interactions with the pupils. The change of teacher behaviour is then seen to change the pupils' expectations of themselves, and therefore their own behaviour.

There have been a number of research studies to see whether teachers' expectations actually do change their teaching practice. Brophy and Good (1986) report that teachers' expectations of pupils affect their behaviour to them. Teachers are more likely to praise successful pupils for correct answers to questions, to criticize the less successful pupils for giving them wrong answers. Teachers are much more likely to give feedback to responses from successful students than to responses from unsuccessful students.

There is a clear link between teachers' expectations of their ideal pupil and the pupils' achievement (Rist, 1970). Rist studied one nursery teacher over an extended period of time. The teacher grouped the pupils into three sets within the class, claiming the groups were of fast, medium and slow learners. Rist, however, believed that she actually grouped the pupils according to her ideal pupil construct. For example, the top table contained pupils who were well behaved, clean and well dressed, rather than those with the greatest attainments. Rist showed that by the end of the year the teacher was teaching only the top table, and that the other two groups were virtually ignored. In succeeding years, pupils on the bottom two tables found it almost impossible to catch up with the top table.

Teachers' expectations of success and failure are based on their perception of the ideal pupil. Pupils are taught differentially because of this expectation and this leads, as Rosenthal and Jacobson showed, to different levels of attainment.

Teacher expectation and pupil attainment

Teachers' expectations have a significant influence on pupils' attainments. There are four crucial ways that teachers can create positive expectations:

- climate – the creation of a warm interpersonal atmosphere;
- feedback – the extent to which pupils receive high differential praise or reinforcement for their work and behaviour;
- input – the extent to which teachers give pupils more and more difficult tasks;
- responding – the extent to which pupils are given greater opportunities for responding (Rosenthal, 1973).

A meta-analysis of 135 relevant studies showed that climate and input are the two most powerful ways that teachers can influence pupils' expectations and attainments (Harris and Rosenthal, 1985).

The research does not totally support the belief that the teacher's expectations is the determining factor of pupils' progress. What it does show is that teachers' expectations can affect the quantity and quality of their teaching for an individual pupil. Chapter 5 shows how attitude change does not inevitably lead to behaviour change, as other factors are involved. In the same way, a change in teachers' expectations, which are similar to an attitude, does not automatically lead to a change in teaching for a particular pupil.

The other factor is, of course, the pupil. Whether a change in the teacher's expectations affects the pupil depends partly upon the pupil's attributions of success, or lack of success, in the classroom. The pupil's perspective is examined in the next section.

ATTRIBUTION AND PUPIL EFFORT

Of particular interest is the way pupils' attribution of success and failure influence the effort that they will put into their work. Weiner (1979) has adapted Vroom's expectancy theory of motivation (see Chapter 6). Pupils' motivation to engage in any task depends upon the expectation that their effort will result in success and that this success is of value to them. If either of these is not true, the pupils will have no motivation. It is the pupil's expectation – the belief that effort will result in success – that is of particular interest to attribution theory. This is seen as running along three dimensions:

- *internal v. external*. This is the fundamental difference in ways of seeing the cause of success. Pupils may believe that their success at mathematics is due to their ability, an internal cause, or their teacher, an external cause.
- *stable v. unstable*. A stable cause is seen as one that is relatively unchanging over time. So pupils who believe their success at mathematics is due to their ability are likely to see this as stable, whereas their teacher may change over time.
- *controllable v. uncontrollable*. Some factors are seen by pupils to be within their control while others are not. Control is not the same as the internal dimension. Pupils may think that they are not in control of some internal factors, such as ability, whereas others, such as effort, are in their control.

Pupils judge the causes, their explanations for success and failure, along these dimensions. There are a number of possible explanations that pupils give for their success and failure at school. The most commonly cited are effort and ability, but there are a number of other prominent ones, including the difficulty of the work, mood, luck, and the influence of the teachers (see Figure 7.3). The pupil will only be motivated if he judges that his success on a task is internal, unstable and controllable.

Figure 7.3 shows that pupils will be most motivated if they attribute their success or failure to effort or mood. Effort is considered by many pupils as a key to their success. High-achieving pupils attribute their success (and failure) to their efforts – an internal factor that they see they have some control over. Low achievers, on the other hand, attribute their success to luck and their failure to low ability – factors that they feel are either stable or they have no control over. Low achievers deny the importance of their own efforts (Rogers, 1982). This fits in with the tendency to attribute success to internal characteristics and failure to external characteristics, as it serves as a mechanism to protect the self-concept. It is important to note that there may also be differences between boys and girls in their attributions that may in the long term help explain some of

Pupils' explanations of success and failure	Internal/external	Stable/unstable	Controllable/ uncontrollable
Effort	Internal	Unstable	Controllable
Ability	Internal	Stable	Uncontrollable
Task difficulty	External	Stable	Uncontrollable
Mood	Internal	Unstable	Controllable
Luck	External	Unstable	Uncontrollable
Teacher's influence	External	Stable	Uncontrollable

Figure 7.3 Attribution and pupil effort.

the inequalities in performance in schools.

Pupils' motivation in class will depend on how they attribute their previous success or failure. If pupils attribute their past failures to internal, unstable, controllable causes, such as mood, then they are likely to try harder in the future. If, on the other hand, they attribute their past failures to internal, stable, uncontrollable causes, such as ability, then they are unlikely to be motivated in the future.

Past experiences affect present attributions of success or failure. If a pupil's achievement is consistent with previous achievements, it will be attributed to a stable cause; if it is inconsistent with previous experiences, it will be attributed to an external cause, such as luck. The problem for many pupils is that they feel unable to do better in school – they have learnt to be helpless.

Past experiences: learnt helplessness

Learnt helplessness is a very interesting phenomenon that helps to explain the efforts that pupils will put into tasks. The concept was developed by Seligman (1975).

Pupils learn from their past experiences whether to feel helpless or empowered. The theory suggests that pupils will initially try to resolve a difficult or unpleasant situation. If they are unable to resolve the situation they will, after a period of time, give up trying – they have learnt to be helpless. Following such experiences, even when the pupils are placed in situations where they could be successful they will not make an effort.

This is likely to have happened to many pupils who are experiencing learning difficulties in class. People who have been given unsolvable problems in the past make no attempt to solve a new set of solvable problems (Hiroto and Seligman, 1975). In contrast, people who have been given solvable problems in the past quickly learn how to solve

135

Martin Seligman (1942–)

Martin Seligman was born in Albany, New York. He reports that his intellectual life started when he failed to make the basketball team at age 13! In 1967 he obtained a PhD at the University of Pennsylvania. He was interested in what happened to dogs when faced with inescapable trauma. He proposed that they learnt to be helpless. Since then he has lectured in a number of universities and has reformulated his learnt helplessness model with John Teasdale, a British psychologist. Helplessness is now seen to relate to an attributional style that interprets the cause of bad events as internal and stable.

---

the new problem. Pupils' helplessness in one situation generalizes to other situations; so a pupil who cannot do maths problems may also believe that he cannot do science problems.

Attribution is the mediator of learnt helplessness (Abramson *et al.*, (1978). If pupils believe that there is no connection between their actions and success, they will believe that success is out of their control, possibly as a consequence of their low ability. Such a belief develops over time and is encouraged by what those around them say. Consider a pupil who is told by his parents and teachers that he does not have the ability to be successful in a certain area. This will lead to a passive acceptance of failure and a lack of effort – learnt helplessness. Pupils who attribute their failure in the classroom to lack of ability give up trying when faced with complex tasks (Weiner, 1979).

Learnt helplessness is not just a pupil phenomenon; it applies to teachers as well. A teacher who sees herself as unsuccessful in helping pupils progress, or in controlling the class, is just as likely to give up trying as a pupil with equivalent beliefs about himself. The way teachers explain pupils' progress in the classroom has a major bearing on their teaching. So pupils with learning difficulties face a double problem: a lack of belief on their own part that their efforts will make a difference, and a lack of belief on their teacher's part that there is anything that she can do. Teachers need to believe that they can affect both the pupils' levels of attainment and their own behaviour if they are to help pupils develop.

STRATEGIES FOR CHANGING PUPILS' ATTRIBUTIONS

There are a number of strategies that teachers can use to change pupils' attributions. This is a critical area for effective teachers to address if they are to ensure pupils' progress in their classrooms. Pupils' attributions are affected by their own perception of the goals of classroom work (Dweck, 1986). Classroom goals can be divided into two distinct categories:

- learning goals – where the pupils' aims are to increase their competence, or to learn something;
- performance goals – where the pupils' aims are to gain positive rather than negative feedback about their performance.

The effective teacher focuses the pupils on learning rather than on performance goals. Pupils who believe ability is stable focus on performance goals and are likely to attribute failure on a task to their ability. The result of this is that when faced with a difficult task they will reduce their efforts. On the other hand, pupils who believe that ability is unstable will focus on learning goals and increase their effort when confronted with a difficult task.

Teachers can affect the goals that the pupils focus on by the way they structure the activities. If pupils are put in competitive situations – 'Let's see who can finish this first' – they will focus on performance goals – 'Was I the best?'. However, if the task is framed as an individual challenge where the aim is to increase competence – 'Let's see how many you can solve today' – then they will focus on the learning goals.

Though praise and feedback are very important to pupils, a further

---

Changing pupils' attributions

Teachers can affect the way pupils attribute causes to their success and failure both consciously and unconsciously. Through their use of verbal feedback and praise, they can unconsciously reinforce a pupil's perception that he has no control over his achievements in the classroom. They can, however, also consciously retrain pupils' attributions. Pupils can be helped by the teacher to see that school difficulties are due to unstable rather than stable forces. Cecil and Medway's (1986) review of the research concludes that attribution retraining does increase the pupils' motivation and their performance.

complication is that if teachers try to motivate pupils through frequent praise they will orient them to performance goals. These are very fragile motivators, as pupils may fall into a pattern of trying to protect positive feedback by avoiding challenging tasks. Teachers need to ensure that praise is linked to an individual pupil's learning goal.

The basic method for attribution retraining is to present pupils with a series of tasks. After each task, the pupils are given feedback on the task to demonstrate that it is their effort that made them successful or their lack of effort that made them unsuccessful, rather than their ability. Following such training, pupils are much more likely to persist with difficult tasks (Dweck, 1975).

It must be recognized that it is extremely difficult to change long-standing negative attributions – learnt helplessness. By helping pupils see achievement as related to effort, the teacher can help motivate them. However, this also forces pupils into a paradox: if they are failing on a task and are encouraged by the teacher to try harder, and they do but continue to fail, then they are confronted with the proposition that it is due not to their effort but to their ability. It may well be in these circumstances that the pupil will opt out.

A substantial proportion of pupils do opt out of education, either mentally or physically. This is one of the reasons why it is so important for teachers to ensure success in the classroom by differentiating the curriculum and their teaching strategies for individual pupils. If pupils learnt from their first years at school that effort equates with achievement, then the learning difficulties and disillusionment seen at many secondary schools would be much less common. The first step on this path is for teachers to realize that they can actually make a difference to pupils' success in the classroom. It is only if teachers attribute success and failure to unstable controllable factors that pupils can do so too.

SUMMARY

Teachers attribute causes to pupils' behaviour and achievement in schools. The causes can be seen as internal (personality) factors, or external (situational) factors. The teachers' perceptions affect their interactions with pupils in the classroom, which affects the pupils' achievements. The way the pupils attribute their own success or failure will influence their efforts.

Teachers' main influence is through their interactions with individual pupils. This has largely been the focus of this chapter. A key aspect of teachers' development of pupils is making certain that they feel that they have some internal control over their own progress.

However, teachers also affect attribution through the organization of their class and the school. The teacher who groups pupils on 'ability' tables gives a message that ability is fixed and that effort or curriculum factors do not affect their progress. The organization of the class-

room gives clear messages about the way teachers attribute success in the classroom.

REFERENCES

Abramson, L., Seligman, M. and Teasdale, J. (1978) Learned helplessness in humans: critique and reformulation, *Journal of Abnormal Psychology* **87**, pp. 49–75.

Bar-Tal, D. (1982) The effects of teachers' behaviour on pupils' attributions: a review, in Antaki, C. and Brewin, C. (eds), *Attributions and Psychological Change: Applications of Attributional Theories to Clinical and Educational Practice*. New York: Academic Press.

Brophy, J. and Good, T. (1986) Teacher behaviour and student achievement, in Wittrock, M. (ed.), *Handbook of Research on Teaching*. 3rd edition. London: Collier Macmillan.

Cecil, M. and Medway, F. (1986) Attribution retraining with low-achieving and learned helpless children, *Techniques: A Journal for Remedial Education and Counselling* **2**, pp. 173–81.

DES (1992) *Curriculum Organisation and Classroom Practice in the Primary Schools.* (The Alexander Report.) London: HMSO.

Dweck, C. (1975) The role of expectations and attributions in the alleviation of learned helplessness, *Journal of Personality and Social Psychology* **31**, pp. 674–85.

Dweck, C. (1986) Motivational processes affecting learning, *American Psychologist* **41**, pp. 1040–8.

Farr, R. (1987) Misunderstandings in human relations: a social psychologist perspective, *Educational Management and Administration* **15**, pp. 129–39.

Harris, M. J. and Rosenthal, R. (1985) Mediation of interpersonal expectancy effects: 31 meta-analyses, *Psychology Bulletin* **97**, pp. 363–86.

Harvery, J.H. and Weary, G. (1981) *Perspectives on Attributional Processes*. Dubuque, IA: Brown.

Heider, F. (1944) Social perception and phenomenal causality, *Psychological Review* **51**, pp. 358–74.

Heider, F. (1958) *The Psychology of Interpersonal Relations*. New York: Wiley.

Hiroto, D. and Seligman, M. (1975) Generality of learned helplessness in man, *Journal of Personality and Social Psychology* **31**, pp. 311–27.

Ichheiser, G. (1943) Misinterpretations of personality in everyday life and the psychologist's frame of reference, *Character and Personality* **12**, pp. 145–60.

Johnson, T.J., Feigenbaum, R. and Weiby, M. (1964) Some determinants and consequences of the teacher's perception of causation, *Journal of Educational Psychology* **55**, pp. 237–46.

Jones, E. and Davis, K. (1965) From acts to dispositions: the attribution process in person perception, in Berkowitz, L. (ed.), *Advances in Experimental Social Psychology*, Vol. 2. New York: Academic Press.

Jones, E. and Nisbett, R. (1972) The actor and the observer: divergent perceptions of the causes of behavior, in Jones, E., Kanouse, D., Kelley, H., Nisbett, R., Valins, S. and Weiner, B. (eds), *Attribution: Perceiving the Causes of Behavior*. Morristown, NJ: General Learning Press.

Kelley, H. (1972) Attribution in social interaction, in Jones, E., Kanouse, D., Kelley, H., Nisbett, R., Valins, S. and Weiner, B. (eds), *Attribution: Perceiving the Causes of Behavior*. Morristown, NJ: General Learning Press.

Milgram, S. (1965) Some conditions of obedience and disobedience to authority, *Human Relations* **18**, pp. 57–76.

Miller, J.G. (1984) Culture and the development of everyday social explanation, *Journal of Personality and Social Psychology* **46**, pp. 961–78.

Rist, R. (1970) Student social class and teacher expectations: the self-fulfilling prophecy in ghetto education, *Harvard Educational Review* **40**, pp. 411–51.

Rogers, C. (1982) *A Social Psychology of Schooling*. London: Routledge & Kegan Paul.

Rosenthal, R. (1973) The mediation of Pygmalion effects: a four-factor theory, *Papua New Guinea Journal of Education* **9**, pp. 1–12.

Rosenthal, R. and Jacobson, L. (1968) *Pygmalion in the Classroom*. New York: Rinehart-Winston.

Seligman, M. (1975) *Helplessness: On Depression Development and Death*. San Francisco: Freeman.

Weiner, B. (1979) A theory of motivation for some classroom experiences, *Journal of Educational Psychology* **71**, pp. 3–25.

RECOMMENDED READING

C. Antaki and C. Brewin (eds), *Attributions and Psychological Change: Applications of Attributional Theories to Clinical and Educational Practice* (New York: Academic Press, 1982), is a series of papers concerned with how attribution theory can help people change. The final section is concerned with education.

R. Farr, Misunderstandings in human relations: a social psychologist perspective, *Educational Management and Administration* **15**, pp. 129–39, is a very readable article that examines the attribution errors that adults make in their everyday lives.

R. Rosenthal and L. Jacobson, *Pygmalion in the Classroom* (New York: Rinehart-Winston, 1968), is the classic piece of research in this extremely influential area.

PART 3

PERSPECTIVES ON THE CLASSROOM

CHAPTER 8

Managing classrooms: the relationship between teachers and pupils

OVERVIEW

This chapter focuses on the relationship between teachers and pupils. This is at the core of effective teaching. From the mid-1980s onwards, there has been increased emphasis on the contents of the curriculum as the key to effective teaching. This view was reinforced by the 1988 Education Reform Act and the concept of the 'teacher-proof curriculum' came into vogue. There is, however, another view of effective teaching which sees curriculum delivery as dependent on effective classroom management. The concept of teachers as classroom managers draws attention to the importance of the relationship between teachers and pupils. Psychological theories drawn from organizational as well as educational psychology provide perspectives on the teacher's role as classroom manager.

The key areas where psychology helps the classroom manager are:

- the teacher's role: concern for task and concern for pupils;
- making management strategies work: power and influence;
- leadership in the classroom;
- making rules;
- the psychological contract.

THE TEACHER'S ROLE: CONCERN FOR TASK AND CONCERN FOR PUPILS

A classroom can be described in organizational terms as a socio-technical system. The technical task (delivering the curriculum)

143

interacts with the social needs of the pupils (and teacher) to form an interdependent system. If teachers simply concentrate on the task side of teaching (delivering the curriculum) while ignoring the social side, they will not maximize the learning within the class.

The aim instead is to achieve joint optimization of both areas. The teacher needs to organize the class so that the pupils' social and psychological needs support the learning process. Teachers have to be concerned about the learning task and for the pupils.

Concern for task v. concern for pupils

The concern for task is about ensuring pupils' progress through the curriculum. The teachers' role is to organize work, ensure that pupils follow procedures, and set tasks at the appropriate level. On the other hand, concern for pupils means responding to their psychological and social needs. This involves building self-confidence and motivation through positive interactions. Concern for task and concern for pupils are two distinct roles for teachers.

Blake and Mouton (1978) drew together the two dimensions of productivity and people into what is known as the '9,9 Managerial Style Grid' (see Figure 8.1). This can be adapted for teachers into task and pupil dimensions. The vertical axis represents a teacher's concerns for pupils. The horizontal axis represents her concern for task. Each axis is divided into 9 units: 1 = lowest degree of concern, and 9 = highest degree of concern.

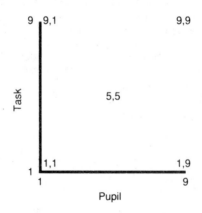

Figure 8.1   Concern for task v. concern for pupil.

The points shown on the grid in Figure 8.1 show the following styles:

- 9,1 = 'task teacher' – high concern for task, low for pupils. Assumption: learning results from efficiently arranging teaching procedures and conditions. Pupils' feelings do not affect their learning.
- 1,9 = 'country club teacher' – high concern for pupils, low for task. Assumption: if teachers are kind to pupils, they will be happy and have a high self-concept. This is the basis for their learning and it does not really matter what task is given.
- 1,1 = 'impoverished teacher' – low concern for pupils and task. Assumption: teachers do not have that much effect on pupils' learning. Neither the right task nor concern for pupils is that important.
- 9,9 = 'class teacher' – high concern for pupils and task. Assumption: high concern for both pupils and task results in enthusiastic pupils and effective learning.
- 5,5 = 'dampened pendulum' – compromises moderate concern for pupils with equally moderate concern for the task. Assumption: the teacher needs to trade getting the task done with pupils' goodwill. This is likely to happen if the teacher has had a particularly difficult class and lost confidence.

Blake and Mouton's grid is used extensively with managers to identify their styles of working. No one always interacts in a particular way but most people have a preferred style. The style that is considered the most effective for managers is the 9,9. Can this be transferred to teachers? What evidence is there that teachers who emulate the 9,9 style are the most effective?

There have been numerous studies on pupils' perception of effective teachers. Seven key features have been identified (Saunders, 1979). These can be divided into the two areas:

Concern for pupils:
1 Tries to understand the point of view of the learner.
2 Shows respect for others.
3 Is concerned for all the pupils.
Concern for task:
4 Is purposeful and in control of herself.
5 Knows what she wants to teach and checks that the pupils are learning.
6 Takes positive action when she discovers they are not making adequate progress.

The seventh factor neatly bridges the two types of focus, pupils and task:

7 Is sensitive to the reactions of the pupils and responds by changing role smoothly and appropriately.

145

Pupils' perceptions of what makes a good teacher endorse the view that teachers need to be concerned about both task and pupils.

This is also supported by research on effective teaching (Rosenshine, 1971). Rosenshine's review of the research indicates that teachers require warmth and enthusiasm as well as being clear on the organization and presentation of activities. Rosenthal (see also Chapter 7) showed that teacher expectation (a concern for pupils) and input (a concern for task) are the two most important factors for effective teaching.

In summary, teachers need to display a high concern both for task and for pupils if they are to be effective. There are a number of effective strategies that teachers can use to achieve this.

Teacher focus: concern for pupils

The most useful strategies for showing a high concern for pupils come from counselling psychologists such as Rogers (see Chapter 4) and Egan (1990). They have identified three crucial skills for building good relationships. These are respect, genuineness and empathy.

Respect

Teachers demonstrate respect for pupils when they show that they are valued, and:

- care about their wellbeing;
- feel that each pupil is worth time and effort;
- remember that each pupil is unique;
- assume the goodwill of the pupil.

Teachers demonstrate these values when they interact with pupils. Consider a pupil who is upset and comes to talk to the teacher. Suppose the teacher's response is, 'What are you doing, boy? I don't have time to sort out your problems. No one else has to come to me!' Such remarks are unlikely to make the pupil feel valued! On the other hand, the teacher who finds the time to talk to pupils and listen to their problems demonstrates in a very simple and practical way her respect for them.

Genuineness

Genuineness is shown by teachers being themselves. This means not playing roles or putting up unnecessary barriers between themselves and the pupils. Teachers show they are genuine when they are:

- open – willing to share their own experiences with the pupils;
- consistent in values and behaviour – not saying one thing and doing another;

- non-defensive even when challenged;
- spontaneous – laughing when something is funny!

The upset pupil will see the teacher as genuine if she admits she may not be able to sort out all the difficulties but she will do what she can.

Empathy

Teachers are empathetic when they show that they understand how pupils feel. A simple statement from the teacher, such as 'You seem upset because you've no one to play with', demonstrates to the pupil that the teacher understands why he is upset. The statement 'You feel . . . because . . .' communicates the teacher's empathy to the pupil.

Empathy is the ability of the teacher to see the world as the pupil sees it. The more the teacher can see the world from the pupil's perspective, the more likely she is to be able to help him.

Teachers show high concern for pupils by using these three skills when teaching. Underpinning them all is Rogers' concept of 'unconditional positive regard' (see Chapter 4). This is the pupils' need to believe that the teacher feels positively towards them. This should be unconditional and not depend on the pupil fitting the teacher's conception of an ideal pupil. A high concern for pupils' psychological and social needs also underpins the teacher's organization of classroom groupings. (Peer interaction is another way that pupils' social needs are met: see Chapter 9.) Showing a high concern for pupils is a key aspect of being an effective teacher.

Teacher focus: concern for task

The second major aspect of the teachers' role is concern for task. Brophy and Good (1986) emphasize that this should be a major aspect of the teachers' role, and that teachers need to allocate most of their available time to curriculum-related activities. The teachers' ability to maximize their time teaching and therefore the pupils' time on the curriculum task is the key organizational issue. In order to achieve this, Brophy and Good identify six key management skills that teachers need. These are:

- good planning and preparation of the classroom;
- variety and appropriate level of difficulty of the tasks;
- momentum of the pacing of lessons;
- smooth transitions throughout the lesson;
- clarity about what options are open at the end of the task;
- clear rules and procedures with consistent application.

Teaching is not simply about applying these six management strategies. There are different situations in teaching – differences between primary and secondary, and urban and rural schools. There are also differences between the demands of different curriculum areas – between PE and history, science and mathematics. Teachers need to be strategic in their approach and able to select and orchestrate the appropriate strategy for a particular context.

MAKING MANAGEMENT STRATEGIES WORK: POWER AND INFLUENCE

All these classroom management strategies assume that the teacher has power, or influence, in the classroom. 'Power' and 'influence' have a variety of meanings, signifying to a greater or lesser extent the ability of the teacher to control the pupils. Power is often used in a pejorative way, while influence is seen as more benign, signifying the personal force that teachers have over pupils.

Throughout the last few decades, there have been frequent attempts by the media to question whether teachers are losing control in schools. This was one of the reasons for the commissioning by the DES of the Elton Report (1989) on discipline in schools. The report did not find any evidence for slipping control, but did provide a series of recommendations for improving pupils' behaviour in schools. This question of teachers' control is of major concern for society. There is an expectation that teachers will be in control of their classes through the exercise of power and influence.

The use of power

There are five basic types of power the teacher can use (French and Raven, 1968). The types employed have implications for teachers' use of management strategies.

Reward power

The behavioural perspective (see Chapter 1) identified rewards as the key variable in understanding and changing behaviour. Head-teachers have reward power over teachers. They can decide who will be promoted and who will teach which classes. Teachers have access to a lot of power through the use of rewards to pupils for appropriate behaviour and work. There is a continuum of rewards that the teacher can use in the classroom (see Chapter 1), ranging from exchangeables to positive feedback from the teacher.

There are a number of reasons why teachers find it difficult to use rewards. First, they are constrained by the situation they are in.

Teachers often feel they have access to minimal resources that they can draw on – certainly not extra pay for pupils! Even such obvious rewards as a choice over activities or learning tasks are limited by the constraints imposed by the actual classroom. The size of classroom and number of pupils often make it difficult to organize rewards.

Another concern that some teachers have is that they equate rewards with bribery. Rewards are in themselves ethically neutral and can be used for either good or evil. If a teacher were to provide a reward to pupils for doing something unethical, then that could be seen as bribery. On the other hand, the teacher who gives a reward to a pupil after he has achieved a legitimate goal can hardly be accused of this. In fact, the opposite argument can be made – that teachers are using their power unethically if they do not use rewards to help pupils. Pupils require a great deal of praise and encouragement, particularly when tackling new and complex tasks, and teachers should use rewards as a positive and useful strategy to help their achievement.

Coercive power

Coercive power is the opposite of reward power – it is the use of punishment. In schools, teachers have access to a range of punishments, such as keeping pupils in at break or behind after school, or making them pick up rubbish from around the school. The general acceptance of the importance of punishment as a means of control is aptly demonstrated by the issue of corporal punishment in schools; when it was abolished, the popular press claimed that teachers would not be able to control classes, and some teachers also felt that the abolition would undermine their ability to control pupils.

The consequences of using coercive power or punishment are outlined in Chapter 1. Coercive power rests primarily on fear – the pupil expects some unpleasant consequence to follow if he steps out of line. The difficulty of using fear as the basis for holding power has been well documented by psychologists (Arvey *et al.*, 1984). Fear is only effective for the particular teacher who is feared; when she is not present, the pupils' behaviour reverts. Fear also negatively affects pupils' learning and their self-esteem. Punishment may be a method of control, but it completely undermines the teachers' other role – that of demonstrating concern for the pupil.

The area of school life where coercive power can be most readily seen is in school bullies, who use it to intimidate and control other pupils. This is unbridled physical power at its worst. A healthy school will take decisive action to ensure that coercive power is not the basis for control in either a formal or an informal way.

Position power

Position power is the legitimate power that certain people have by virtue of their role. A policewoman who asks a motorist to stop his or her car is seen to have the right to do so – and the motorist will almost certainly comply with the request. Similarly, the teacher has power because of her position as teacher. At one extreme, this is enshrined in law – for example, the right of a teacher to act *in loco parentis*. On the other hand, much of a teacher's position power stems from her role in the classroom. The teacher's request to the pupils to take out their books or to start work on a certain page is seen as a legitimate one. What is seen as legitimate – that is, consented to – is defined by the culture of the school; the teachers' position power will vary from school to school and within a school from one teacher to another. The head will have a lot more position power than the new probationary teacher.

Referent power

Referent power is based on the attractive personal characteristics in the teacher. It is the power that charismatic individuals hold, and rests on pupils' wanting to be like the person they admire and therefore wishing to be identified with them. Because they wish to identify with the teacher – to be seen on her side – they comply with the teacher's requests. Referent power is extremely important to teachers, who are often a model for many of the pupils in their class.

Referent power is dynamic in so far as it varies with the age of the pupils. A 6-year-old pupil demonstrates his wish to identify with the teacher by, for example, sitting beside her on a school outing. The teacher is likely to have a good deal of referent power over the 6-year-old. On the other hand, the same pupil at age 14 gains referent power from being identified with his peers – the teacher is likely to have little referent power over him at this age.

Expert power

Expert power is based on the teacher's expert knowledge. Teachers are perceived as having expert knowledge in the areas of the curriculum that they teach. This is helped in secondary schools by teachers specializing in particular areas of the curriculum. With the development of the National Curriculum it may be that primary teachers will also specialize in particular areas, especially in the upper age range.

Teachers' authority when talking about the curriculum is rarely challenged by pupils – unless the teacher invites the pupils to do so. However, sometimes secondary teachers' expert knowledge in other

Figure 8.2 The power–influence continuum.

areas, such as life and the world of work, is questioned. The teacher's infallibility is not taken for granted.

These five sources of power underpin teachers' classroom control. They are not independent, but often linked. So a teacher may use reward and coercive power together – 'If you do what I want, you will be rewarded; if you don't, you will be punished.' In the same way, expert power and referent power are often linked together – a teacher with a very good knowledge of a subject (expert power) will also have referent power if pupils are interested in this area. The pupil will wish to be identified with the teacher.

Negative power

A sixth sort of power – negative power – is easily recognized by teachers. It is the power to disrupt and to stop things happening (Handy, 1985). Teachers may have five sources of power, but that does not mean pupils are powerless. Their negative power does not operate at all times, but in periods of stress or frustration. When pupils' task and social needs are being met, they will not use their negative power; it is when the pupils' needs are not met that they may decide to disrupt, in order to show (to themselves, as well as others) that they still have power and influence within the classroom.

Power v. influence

Many teachers feel slightly uneasy about the use of power, and prefer to see their control as coming from their influence. Influence is often considered to be legitimate while power is seen as a non-legitimate method of control. Influence is gained through expert and referent power. On the other hand, non-legitimate power involves the teacher using reward and coercive power to achieve her own ends. Pupils will go along with this form of power only as long as the teacher holds access to rewards and punishments. Position power falls somewhere between power and influence (see Figure 8.2). It can be seen as a legitimate source of power, but if teachers abuse their positions then their influence becomes non-legitimate, and their right to control is questioned.

Most teachers use a balance of power and influence to manage their classrooms. Ideally they increase their influence by developing their expert and referent power. Nevertheless, if teachers try to use referent or expert power when they do not have it, then there will be anarchy in the classroom. Teachers need to use the right balance of power and influence if they are to manage their classrooms successfully. They need to be seen as the classroom leader.

LEADERSHIP IN THE CLASSROOM

Leadership is one of the factors that has been identified as associated with effective schools. For a school to be effective, the headteacher needs to be an effective leader. Class teachers also need to be effective leaders in their classrooms. There is an expectation that teachers will provide leadership in their classroom by inspiring and influencing the pupils. Leadership is about the influence that teachers have over the pupils, and is based on the concept of referent power. Teachers can be, but are not automatically, leaders – they may have little influence over the class. In most classes, there is at least one pupil who also plays a leadership role and who exerts influence over the other pupils.

There are a number of psychological perspectives on leadership. These seek to explain why some people have this personal influence while others do not. This interest in leadership developed in the 1930s with the growth of fascism in Europe. There was a fascination with trying to understand how one person could have such a great personal influence.

The first approach to leadership was to look for particular personality traits. Various factors, such as intelligence, perseverance and emotional stability, were examined. This 'trait' approach analysed great leaders to decide whether they all had similar characteristics. It has been largely fruitless, and the common factors that have been found are so broad as to be largely irrelevant (Geir, 1969) – factors identified are, for example, intelligence, initiative and self-assurance. This inability to find useful common factors is clearly against many people's expectations. There is still a belief, certainly in Britain, that certain people are born to be leaders; this is seen in the existence of many national institutions in Britain, such as the House of Lords. The research on leadership does not support this belief. It is therefore unlikely that there are specific characteristics in teachers that indicate leadership qualities.

However, it has been found that what effective leaders have in common is the ability to respond to changing circumstances (Kenny and Zaccaro, 1983). This indicates that a teacher's ability to respond to the different needs of different situations is one key characteristic of being an effective leader. It is apparent that the strategies used by teachers to be influential in a small rural primary school may not be so effective in a large urban comprehensive. This is not to say that the teacher cannot be an effective leader in both situations. Rather, it means that the effective leader is able to adapt to changes in the situation.

An effective leader in organizations needs different strategies for different situations. Fiedler (1978) distinguishes between three variables that need to be taken into account by the effective leader. These can be adapted to view how teachers can be effective leaders in the classroom. To understand their positions as leaders, teachers need to analyse the following variables:

- power – the power they have because of their position, and in particular their access to rewards and punishments;
- task structure – the clarity they have about what the pupils are expected to do;
- relationships – the strength of the relationship between the pupils and the teacher.

Fiedler's theory shows that teachers are ideally placed as leaders. They have a good deal of power through their control of rewards, and by clarifying the task and showing concern for pupils, teachers are able to show real leadership in their classroom.

Leadership and individual pupils

Research shows that leaders form distinctly different interactions with different individuals (Dansereau *et al.*, 1975). This indicates the importance of the individual relationship that teachers have with each pupil. This relationship is built on the teacher's giving the pupil greater flexibility in choice of tasks, more open communication and more responsibility. The pupil responds by offering greater commitment to the class.

The relationship between leaders and their team members can be improved if leaders actively listen and ensure that there is an exchange of expectations between them (Scandura and Graen, 1984). What is particularly interesting about this research from the teacher's point of view is that the greatest improvement occurs with the team member who has the poorest relationship with the leader. For the teacher having difficulties with a particular pupil, this is especially encouraging.

> ### Teacher leadership
>
> Leadership and the ability to influence are not, then, a simple characteristic that some teachers have and some do not. There is an interaction between three factors: power, task structure and relationships. By using power fairly, by structuring and clarifying the task, and by building good relationships, teachers increase their ability to influence and therefore lead the class.

MAKING RULES

One of the key tasks for the effective teacher is to create a classroom where pupils are able to work in an orderly and stable environment. Through the negotiation of rules, the teacher builds a shared understanding of how the class will operate. The rules specify the agreed acceptable forms of behaviour – 'We all listen when someone is speaking.' They are the criteria on which the classroom will operate. If these rules are broken, the use of power to enforce them becomes more acceptable. Rules free behaviour as well as constraining it. Pupils who know the classroom rules have greater control over their behaviour than a pupil who is trying to operate in a situation where it is not clear what is acceptable.

The three criteria for rules are relevance, meaningfulness and positiveness (Cohen and Manion, 1983).

Relevance

Rules need to be relevant to the needs of the pupils and teachers. This means that they need to fit a particular class being taught in a particular way. There is no point in having rules that bear no relationship to the situation that the pupils find themselves in. The criterion of relevance is often at the heart of disputes about uniform or hairstyles, as many pupils cannot see the relevance of such rules to their work. If rules are to be relevant there may need to be flexibility within them so that they can be adapted from one lesson to another or from one part of the school year to the next.

Meaningfulness

Rules need to be meaningful in so far as they are seen to derive logically from the nature of the task and are not arbitrary. If a rule bears no relationship to the need of the pupils, there are likely to be difficulties in enforcing it. For example, a rule that specifies that there should be no talking in class is likely to be broken if pupils are working on the same topic area and can see that sharing information would be both interesting and helpful.

Positiveness

Rules should be stated as positive statements for pupils to work towards. All too often, rules are things that should not be done rather than things that should be done. A rule that states that pupils can use the reading corner when they have finished their writing is more helpful than one forbidding pupils to enter the reading corner at all other times.

Negotiating rules

Rules can be made by the teacher on her own, or she can involve the entire class (Glasser, 1969). The essential distinction is whether the teacher has an autocratic or a participative style of decision making. With the participative approach, the whole class is involved in discussing rules and deciding on their implementation; with an autocratic approach, the teacher decides for herself. Each approach has certain advantages and disadvantages (see Figure 8.3).

There is no best way for teachers to make decisions – different situations call for decisions to be made in different ways. Most of the

	Participative	Autocratic
Advantages	Enhances satisfaction	Teacher decides
	Increases commitment of the class	Helpful in high-pressure situations
	Strongly preferred by most people	Speeds decision-making process
	Can increase compliance to decision	
Disadvantages	Raises doubts about teacher's authority	Can reduce pupils' satisfaction
	Slows the decision-making process	Fails to utilize the skills and knowledge of the pupils
		Can reduce compliance to decision

Figure 8.3 Decision making.

decisions in the classroom are made by the teacher; nevertheless, for rule making a participative approach has some decided advantages. It ensures a greater commitment by the pupils, who are more likely to see the rules as relevant and meaningful. It is easier for the teacher to use power to enforce rules decided on participatively without damaging relationships with the class. Using a participatory approach, rules need to be established quickly so that the pupils have a framework that they can work within.

It is most helpful to think of rule making as a cumulative strategy (Doyle, 1979). At the beginning of the school year, teachers should implement a number of routines and familiar procedures in the classroom. These can be familiar routines from the previous year. Because these are familiar, the teacher can concentrate on monitoring inappropriate behaviour by the pupils. As the pupils learn these first rules, the teacher can introduce more procedures, to deal with inappropriate behaviour, and these then also become routine. The teacher can progressively concentrate on more specific aspects of classroom management and teaching. The point is that teachers cannot concentrate on everything at once. Until they establish rules and procedures in the classroom that are routine, the time for effective teaching will be seriously eroded.

Enforcement of rules

The enforcement of rules is a clear example of the differences between espoused theory and theory in practice. The teacher will have certain espoused rules, such as 'no talking in class' or 'no moving around', but there are also rules in practice – that is, what actually happens. Pupils are quite aware of the gap between the espoused rules – what the teacher says should happen – and what actually happens. They will work to understand the size of the gap, so that they can predict the teacher's behaviour. One of the clear things that teachers need to do is to narrow the gap. If there are classroom rules then the teachers need to enforce them.

There are a number of factors in the effective enforcement of rules. Most fundamentally, pupils have to be aware of the consequences of not following rules. These consequences have to be logical and fair, and easy enough for the busy teacher to carry out. There is no point in having rules that are unenforceable because the teacher does not have the time or resources to carry through the consequences. Rules need to be enforced immediately; so if a rule is that homework has to be handed in on a set day, the teacher must enforce the rule immediately it is broken, rather than changing the rule.

The key factor is that teachers need to be consistent in their enforcement of rules both across time and across pupils. To manage classrooms, teachers must apply rules consistently over time. Inconsistency, with rules created and then ignored, creates confusion and undermines the teacher's credibility. The teacher needs also to apply the rule consistently to everyone in the class. One sure way for teachers to ensure poor relationships with pupils is to apply rules unfairly. This does not mean being insensitive to particular circumstances – the pupil who breaks his finger can have the homework rule relaxed! What it does mean is not being consistently inconsistent; for example, by picking on a pupil or group of pupils.

Misbehaviour

It is now recognized that effective teachers are not those who manage misbehaviour better but rather those who manage the class so that misbehaviour does not occur in the first place (Kounin, 1970).

Rules are important for classroom management, but they must be used as part of a proactive, not a retroactive, strategy. Rules are necessary to create a framework in which the teacher and pupils can work – they are not simply a method of punishing undesirable behaviour.

THE PSYCHOLOGICAL CONTRACT

The psychological contract is a concept developed by Schein (1988) to explain the unwritten set of expectations or rules that develop between a manager and the workers in an organization. Workers are likely to have a written, formal contract detailing basic conditions of service, but they also have an unwritten, psychological contract. This is the expectation that they have of the organization (represented by the manager) and that the manager has of them. It is an unspoken agreement between two parties. It is likely to include expectations on the part of the workers that they will be treated fairly, and on the part of the manager that the workers will not cheat the company, or run it down in public. Teachers have this sort of psychological contract with their headteacher.

In a similar way there are contracts between the teacher and the pupils. The formal contract is to do with the formal school rules and procedures, and includes attendance and subjects that are studies. This formal contract is the basis for classroom management. However, the unspoken, psychological contract is also important for understanding relationships within the classroom. Pupils have expections about the teacher's two roles – managing the task or work that the pupil is expected to do, and managing the social interactions in the classroom. They are likely to have work expectations that include being given interesting work that is within their capabilities; but they are also likely to have other expectations to do with the amount of work completed, and the right to ask the teacher questions if they are having difficulties. Similarly, pupils will have unspoken expectations about social interactions. These may include expectations that they can at times talk to each other, as well as the right to a reasonably quiet working atmosphere. At another level, there will be an expectation that the teacher will intervene if there are difficulties with their peers; for example, if they are being bullied.

This is not a written or formal contract between the pupils and the teacher, but the unspoken expectations of what is reasonable. Similarly, the teacher will have expectations about the pupils. These may include expectations that the pupil will work hard, and not question the task that is presented. Most fundamentally, teachers have expectations that their authority will not be challenged.

The psychological contract

The importance of the psychological contract is that both teachers and pupils have unspoken expectations about how the other should behave. As long as these two sets of expectations mesh, then the class will function effectively, with both teachers and pupils acknowledging the others' roles. However, it is when the psychological contract is broken that management problems arise in the classroom.

If, however, the pupils expect the teachers to request one page of writing in a lesson but the teacher suddenly demands three, then the psychological contract is dented. Similarly, if the teacher requests the pupils to sit in their seats and they do not, then once again the psychological contract is dented. This contract can be fairly robust, but sufficient dents will eventually lead to its being broken. Once this happens, the relationships which hold the classroom together are lost.

The psychological contract is not between a class and the teacher but rather between individual pupils and their teacher. Each of the pupils will have his individual expectations of the teacher – as she will have of each of them. With some pupils it will be a very strong contract, but with others it may be broken or damaged. A broken psychological contract can often be recognized from the emotional strain between a pupil and a teacher. It can be seen in a surly or offhand relationship, with either the pupil or the teacher showing fits of petulance with the other person.

The psychological contract is not fixed between pupil and teacher; rather it develops in a dynamic manner. Consider the way the contract develops from the first year of secondary school to the time when pupils leave. The relationship between pupils and the teacher goes through a whole series of changes. It goes from a general eagerness to please in the first year through non-conformity and trying to redefine the psychological contract in year 8 and 9, to a recognition of the particular teacher's humanity by the time they come to leave. Though this is a generalization, most teachers can recognize the developmental aspect of the psychological contract.

The psychological contract is a very helpful perspective in understanding classroom managment. It emphasizes the fact that informal as well as formal rules are important. It also highlights the point that it is when expectations are damaged that individual relationships are also harmed. By recognizing the importance of the unspoken, pyschological contracts, teachers can provide more sensitive leadership in the classroom.

SUMMARY

In this chapter, the teacher is seen as a classroom manager. Psychological perspectives from management and organizational psychology are used to examine the teacher's role as manager. Two key roles have been identified: a concern for pupils and a concern for the task. To undertake these roles, the teacher needs to use power and influence. The ability to influence others is one of the key functions of effective leadership, which depends in turn on a concern for task and a concern for the pupils.

Attempts to teach may be welcomed, ignored or sabotaged, according to the opportunities or threats that the teacher provides for the pupils. What develops between the teacher and pupil is a negotiated social order. This social order, this contract, is dynamic. Class management and organization are essentially a negotiated structure for the way the process of teaching can take place. It is not something that the teacher or the pupil can decide on independently of each other, but a collaborative process between the two.

REFERENCES

Arvey, R., Davis, G. and Nelson, M. (1984) Use of discipline in organizations: a field study, *Journal of Applied Psychology* **69**, pp. 448–60.

Blake, R. and Mouton, J. (1978) *The New Managerial Grid*. Houston: Gulf.

Brophy, J. and Good, T. (1986) Teacher behaviour and student achievement, in Wittrock, M. (ed.), *Handbook of Research on Teaching*. 3rd edition. London: Macmillan.

Cohen, L. and Manion, L. (1983) *A Guide to Teaching Practice*. 2nd edition. London: Methuen.

Dansereau, F., Graen, G. and Haga, B. (1975) A vertical dyad linkage approach to leadership within formal organizations: a longitudinal investigation of the role making process, *Organizational Behavior and Human Performance* 13, pp. 45–78.

Doyle, W. (1979) Making managerial decisions in classrooms, in Duke, D. (ed.), *Classroom Management*. Yearbook of the National Society for the Study of Education. Chicago: University of Chicago Press.

Egan, G. (1990) *The Skilled Helper*. 4th edition. Monterey, CA: Brooks-Cole.

DES (1989) *Discipline in Schools*. London: HMSO. (The Elton Report.)

Fiedler, F. (1978) Contingency model and the leadership process, in Berkowitz, L. (ed.), *Advances in Experimental and Social Psychology*, Vol. 11. New York: Academic Press.

French, J. and Raven, B. (1968) The bases of social power, in Cartwright, D. and Zander, A. (eds), *Group Dynamics*. 3rd edition. New York: Harper & Row.

Geir, J. (1969) A trait approach to the study of leadership in small groups, *Journal of Communication* 17, pp. 316–23.

Glasser, W. (1969) *Schools without Failure*. New York: Harper & Row.

Handy, C. (1985) *Understanding Organizations*. London: Penguin.

Kenny, D. and Zaccaro, S. (1983) An estimate of variance due to traits in leadership, *Journal of Applied Psychology* 68, pp. 678–85.

Kounin, J. (1970) *Discipline and Group Management in Classrooms*. New York: Holt, Rinehart & Winston.

Rogers, C. (1983) *Freedom to Learn for the '80s*. New York: Macmillan.

Rosenshine, B. (1971) *Teaching Behaviour and Student Achievement*. London: National Foundation for Educational Research.

Saunders, M. (1979) *Class Control and Behaviour Problems: A Guide for Teachers*. Maidenhead: McGraw-Hill.

Scandura, T. and Graen, G. (1984) Moderating effects of initial leader-member exchange status on the effects of a leadership intervention, *Journal of Applied Psychology* 69, pp. 45–78.

Schein, E. (1988) *Organizational Psychology*. 3rd edition. Englewood Cliffs, NJ: Prentice-Hall.

Trist, E. and Bamforth, K. (1951) Some social and psychological consequences of the long-wall method of coal getting, *Human Relations* 4, pp. 1–38.

RECOMMENDED READING

J. Brophy and T. Good, Teacher behaviour and student achievement, in M. Wittrock (ed.), *Handbook of Research on Teaching*, 3rd edition (London: Macmillan, 1986), gives a detailed analysis of the research that has been undertaken on how teaching affects student achievement. Gives specific advice on the implications for effective teaching.

C. Handy, *Understanding Organizations* (London: Penguin, 1986), is the classic text on understanding people in organizations. Comprehensive yet very readable.

C. Rogers, *Freedom to Learn for the '80s* (New York: Macmillan, 1983), is a very readable book that suggests that teachers' attitudes need to be challenged if they are to relate in a human way to pupils in the classroom. Practical suggestions on how teachers can facilitate their own learning.

E. Schein, *Organizational Psychology*, 3rd edition (Englewood Cliffs, NJ: Prentice-Hall, 1988), is a readable introduction to the psychology of organizations.

CHAPTER 9

Working in groups

OVERVIEW

Classroom organization and management are a group activity, in so far as any class is a group of pupils. The effective teacher will organize individual and whole-class, as well as small-group, teaching. There is increasing recognition that the effective teacher selects the most appropriate organization depending on the nature of the task. These groupings create forces that affect the pupils in them. This process is known as group dynamics. These forces can be negative, as in the group that the teacher has difficulty in controlling, or the group who are constantly arguing with each other. However, group forces can also be very positive. Teachers can feel a positive class ethos with pupils supporting and cooperating with each other. Group forces can either create problems for teachers or be the cohesive force that makes anything possible.

The aim of this chapter is to show that the way teachers organize classes will either encourage or discourage the formation of cohesive, cooperative, positive groups. In particular, it focuses on:

- the development of different types of groups;
- pupils' needs for groups;
- cohesion and competition;
- cooperative working groups;
- the development of groups.

THE DEVELOPMENT OF DIFFERENT TYPES OF GROUPS

In schools there are both formal and informal groups. The whole class is a formal group in so far as the membership of the class is clear and has been formally decided on – if a pupil is asked whether he is a member of the class, he can easily give an answer. To cross from this group into another similar group (that is, another class) requires formal procedures.

The class is large as groups go; groups are normally considered to consist of between three and twelve members. Once there are more members than this, the effect of group dynamics is not as pronounced. This means that there are inherent difficulties of size for teachers trying to develop a cohesive class.

The whole class as a group can be contrasted with the informal groupings within it. A teacher might group together five pupils for half a term to complete a project. Though formally selected, this group has a temporary and transitory life span. Or the teacher might group together all the girls in the class. Though the characteristic – gender – is fixed, the girls may not see themselves as, or behave like, a group at all. Another type of grouping, by the teacher, might be that of all the 'high-flyers' in the class. Many of these groupings are groups only in the eyes of the teacher. The individual pupils may not even be aware of each other's presence, and they will not automatically show any of the characteristics of a group. However, the teacher can turn these groupings of pupils into groups and thereby unlock the power of group dynamics.

There are also many informal groups in a school which are based on pupils' interactions with and attraction for each other. These may be interest groups, such as a group of pupils who like the same sort of music, or activity groups, such as a group of pupils who like going swimming together. There are also in any school dozens of cliques – informal friendship groups – between pupils, and also between staff.

Pupils will be in various groupings within a school. These groupings change and develop over time. Only some of them generate the force of a cohesive group, which can be a powerful influence not only on an individual pupil but on the whole class.

The development of pupil peer groups

Though every pupil is an individual, there are similarities between the different types of groups in schools. When pupils start school at the age of 4 or 5, they engage in cooperative play – hide-and-seek and chasing games – with groups of other pupils. These are usually mixed-gender groups. Between 7 and 10 years of age, pupils begin to prefer playing with peers of their own sex. Loose groups of pupils,

163

particularly boys, begin to develop into 'gangs' at about age 8. A pupil who is a member of a gang has an affiliation and loyalty to the gang which is stronger than that to the earlier cooperative play groups. These gangs often compete with other gangs.

The alternative peer group for the primary-aged pupil is a clique – a small, intimate group of three to four pupils. It does not have the formal structure of a gang and it is usually based on shared values and interests. Membership of both cliques and gangs may be based on where the pupil lives and his social class, but the prime focus for these pre-adolescent groups is often a particular activity or interest.

In contrast, the adolescent pupil is much more concerned with the interpersonal aspects of his peer group. He is interested in, and worried about, his relationships with the group. He is particularly sensitive to feelings of being accepted or rejected by the group. This need for more personal group experiences means that pre-adolescent gangs tend to dissolve into cliques and then 'crowds'.

Dunphy (1963) studied adolescent groups in Australia. He identified the development of two different types. In early adolescence, there are single-sex cliques made up of between four and six cohesive, intimate friends, who are personally compatible and have bonds of mutual admiration and affection. Girls form cliques earlier than boys and operate within a more exclusive framework. Girl cliques may be more exclusive than boys', because it is more difficult for girls to achieve an independent status during adolescence. Boys, in Australia, often achieve their independent status through sport activities. Exclusive cliques are therefore a particularly important way for girls to achieve status.

From about age 13 to 15, these cliques come together to form mixed-sex crowds. These crowds usually have a shared background and interests. Interpersonal feelings are less important than they are within the clique. The crowd allows the adolescent to develop heterosexual skills in a protected environment. From about age 15, these crowds begin to disperse into heterosexual cliques and finally into couples.

Adolescent and post-adolescent gangs remain a feature of certain parts of society, and in particular of deprived urban areas. Pupils in these gangs obtain an identity by challenging the values of the wider society. The gang thus ensures these deprived adolescents a place and status in society which otherwise is denied them.

PUPILS' NEEDS FOR GROUPS

The importance of other people to the individual is highlighted throughout this book. This social and psychological need for people is the reason why groups are so important. They play a key part in the socialization of the pupil. Group interactions expose pupils to the cultural norms, and they learn what is expected by others and how to behave. This is also true of adults: the new teacher learns the norms of the school through the feedback given by her peer group.

Groups: a fundamental need

Groups meet fundamental developmental needs of pupils, in particular the need for existence, relatedness and growth as described by Maslow's and Alderfer's motivation theories (see Chapter 6). These needs are particularly important for adolescents as they develop their own individuality. To do this, they have to make a break from their parents' influence by, paradoxically, accepting peer influence instead. By achieving acceptance in a group, adolescents gain the necessary self-esteem to explore their new identity.

The peer group gives the pupil new frames of reference which allow him to reject the culture and values of his parents. This is done by the group establishing their own tastes in, for example, music, clothing and style. This shift of allegiance by adolescents from their parents to their peer group is fundamental to their achieving their own identity.

Though adults recognize the need for pupils to establish their own identities, they are also often concerned about the peers pupils form groups with. There are a number of factors that affect this (Napier and Gershenfeld, 1989):

- *cultural similarities*. Pupils from a particular cultural background are likely to group together in schools. This gives them a shared understanding of each other.
- *common interests*. Pupils form groups with others who have common interests, such as a particular hobby or taste in music. The common interest gives a meaning to their interaction.
- *physical proximity*. Pupils form groups with others when placed together and allowed to interact frequently. Pupils working at a table together will begin to form a group.
- *common goals*. Groups form if members have common goals. Sports teams provide one of the few common goals in schools. The achievement of common work goals is one of the key features of cooperative learning.

Teachers have some control over the last three factors and are in a position to influence the membership and development of groups in their class. A cohesive group is a strong force. This need not necessarily be in the teacher's interest, as one way in which a group of pupils achieves cohesion is by being in competition with adults and other pupils.

COHESION AND COMPETITION

The classic psychological research in this area is the 'Robber's Cave' experiment of Sherif *et al.* (1961). They examined the development of conflict and cooperation at Robber's Cave, a boys' summer camp in the USA. The boys at the camp were divided into two groups. Through a series of activities, the psychologists developed in each group a high degree of cohesion and loyalty. At the same time, they used competitive events to develop conflict between the two groups. Unfortunately for them, the conflict began to get out of hand, and initially when they attempted to reduce hostility between the two groups they were unsuccessful. Eventually, they managed to produce cooperation through the introduction of superordinate goals that required the two groups to work together to face an outside force. In this case, it was the development of a superteam to play another camp at baseball, and the development of a joint task force to tackle firefighting.

Sherif *et al.*'s study captures the imagination, as it is a real situation that teachers can easily recognize. One can imagine the researchers desperately trying to stop gang warfare, their reputation as psychologists destroyed for ever! What they demonstrated is that it is easy to establish a cohesive, loyal group (with boys). Such a group takes on a dynamic life of its own that is an extremely powerful force. However, the loyalty to the group manifests itself in hostility to outsiders.

A cohesive group in the class may well have alternative goals to the teacher's, and therefore an increase in cohesiveness does not automatically mean an increase in positive relationships, let alone work productivity. Very cohesive groups have very strong in-group feelings. They feel extremely positive and loyal to each other, but reject outsiders. This can be seen in groups of football supporters, where their loyalty to each other is weighed against a hatred for members of other groups. It can be seen in teenage cliques, where the excluded pupil is treated with scorn and hatred. It can also be seen in rivalry between classes in the same year, which may spill over into fighting at breaktimes.

Cohesion and competition in schools

The organization of secondary schools, particularly though not necessarily through the division of year groups into streams and the allocation of teachers to particular classes, creates subgroups of pupils who reject the entire educational process, including their peers (Hargreaves, 1966). Adolescent pupils develop their self-identity through becoming members of groups who have similar status and values. Pupils tend to identify and form groups with peers from the same stream. So an academic pupil is likely to form a group with academic peers, and pupils in the bottom stream are likely to form a group from within the same stream. For this group, by definition, school is unrewarding. To identify themselves with it would confirm their own failure. So they become deviant, rejecting the school and its values. By the time they reach age 14 or 15, their relationship with not only the teachers but also the other pupils is negative and hostile. Pupils who live in the same street and were friends at primary school may not, because of the secondary school's organization, even be on speaking terms.

The peer group will have an important influence on the pupil. Pupils whom the teacher sees as conforming to the culture of the school may be seen by their adolescent peers as deviant. On the other hand, the pupils whom the teacher sees as deviant may in fact be popular and have high status with their peers. This is particularly important for pupils of low academic ability, who have obtained their high informal status by their rejection of the teacher's culture. Such pupils do not work hard or respond well to teachers' praise, as this would threaten the status that their peer group gives them.

Subgroup alienation

Hargreaves (1966) has persistently argued that the development of alienated subgroups within schools through a rejection of academic aims needs to be prevented. Pupils whose subgroup have rejected education are not motivated. They see no point in working hard because they see no tangible benefit from doing so. Neither are teachers motivated to teach lower-stream pupils, as the educational system rewards teachers, and schools, for exam success.

Ausubel *et al.*'s (1977) view is even more pessimistic than Hargreaves'. The game of inclusion and exclusion of pupils into adolescent groups is very powerful. Adolescent pupils use not only academic ability but also religion and ethnic and cultural background to exclude some pupils from their group. Ausubel believes that this is because of the decreasing tolerance of the adult world for people of a lower status. In the adult world, 'playing is for keeps', and notions of

167

equality are completely rejected. As pupils become older, they are forced to realize that ability or a winning personality will not open the right doors if they come from the wrong side of the economic or social tracks.

COOPERATIVE WORKING GROUPS

One way of mitigating these negative, hostile and competitive forces is to develop cooperative, rather than competitive, working relationships in schools. The development of cooperative interactions is not just important for the development of social relationships, it is also important for development of cooperative learning.

David and Richard Johnson

David and Richard Johnson are brothers who were brought up in Indiana and enjoyed the competitive rivalry of siblings. David gained his PhD from Columbia University as a social psychologist. Richard taught in elementary schools and then became involved in part-time teacher education at the University of California. They presently both teach at the University of Minnesota, promoting their shared interest in group work and cooperative learning in classrooms.

Three types of interpersonal work relationship can be developed in the classroom (Johnson and Johnson, 1987). Their development depends on how the teacher organizes the class. These three types of relationship are:

- cooperative;
- competitive;
- individualistic.

Cooperative learning, where there is positive interdependence between the pupils, is more useful to them than competitive and individualistic learning. A cooperative organization of the classroom promotes positive relationships between pupils, whereby they are encouraged to help each other. Communication is open and information is shared between pupils. Cooperation also implies that pupils give help and assistance to each other on tasks, and that there is an acceptance of each other's strengths and weaknesses.

In contrast, a competitive organization of the classroom results in oppositional interaction between pupils, who try to discourage and hinder each other's work. Communication is poor or distorted, and pupils try to hide information from each other. Competitive goals mean that pupils have a vested interest in trying to obstruct other pupils' learning.

Finally, an individualistic organization encourages students to work alone without any interchange with their peers.

The individualistic and competitive model

Organizing pupils into groups is common practice in most primary schools. It is not as typical in secondary schools, apart from some subjects such as science. Working in groups was recommended by the highly influential Plowden Report (DES, 1967), and by the 1980s almost all primary classrooms used groupings (Galton et al., 1980). However, even when pupils are grouped together, around a table for example, there is often an absence of cooperative group work. In Galton et al.'s sample of 48 classrooms, 90 per cent of the teachers never used cooperative group work. They used grouping to organize their class, but rarely in fact interacted with these groupings. Only 7.5 per cent of all teacher–pupil interactions were with a group as such. The evidence suggests that, having placed pupils in groups, teachers put little time or effort into teaching them as a group or even trying to maximize conditions for successful group learning. Tann (1981) followed up this work and found that the interactions between pupils were largely social in content. There was very little evidence of task-oriented interaction. The pupils talked to each other but worked separately at tasks as individuals. The classroom was organized in groups but the style of learning was individualistic. The conclusion from this is that education in Britain, as in the USA, is largely individualistic.

It is also largely competitive. In the 1980s and 1990s, there has been and is a general reinforcement of a competitive culture, largely characterized by the Darwinian notion of the survival of the fittest. Competition is seen to be the means to achieve quality in education. It is believed that teachers will achieve most if they are placed in a competitive situation with performance-related pay, that schools will increase their effectiveness through the publication of assessment results, and that pupils will achieve most if there is competition between them. Education becomes a grading process – pupil against pupil, teacher against teacher, school against school. The fierce fire of competition will pick out the winners – and the losers. Competition is crystallized in the exam system, which ensures that the majority of the school population feel a failure at age 18. Because the power-brokers in education have generally passed A levels themselves, they see little wrong with the system. Competition is designed to categorize people as winners or losers. Since exam results are fairly

169

stable across classes, as a pupil moves up the school he may have five or six years' experience of being consistently a loser.

Pupils find means of coping with the pressure of this competition. In America, nine out of ten pupils admit to cheating on tests or copying assignments or homework (Johnson and Johnson, 1987). Headteachers are beginning to cheat too. A headteacher in Maryland was recently dismissed for giving his pupils extra time to finish tests. The extra time artificially boosted the pupils' scores, thus making the head look more successful. Another headteacher resigned when he was exposed as having pre-tested his pupils, thus ensuring that they did extremely well at the formal achievement testing.

The competitive culture that is being encouraged between schools under the local management of schools will surely bring the same pressures to bear on teachers, headteachers and governors in Britain. To think this is a problem peculiar to the USA is naive. The increased competitiveness between schools and teachers will increase secrecy, misinformation and cheating in education.

The lack of emphasis on cooperation in education also affects the pupils' perception of life after school. Is life a competitive dog-eat-dog world where success is at least partly determined by ensuring that you do not give your peers any help? In fact, giving them disinformation may be one way of ensuring your own success. This development of an attitude to life is a key part of the hidden curriculum. It probably has a greater effect on young people's work habits than much of the actual contents of the National Curriculum.

Cooperative learning and pupil achievement

Cooperative learning involves groups of two to six pupils working together on a particular task. Many teachers value cooperative learning as an aid to social development and as a model for more effective working relationships in adult work. Nevertheless, there is often a belief that a competitive working relationship is more effective in actually raising the pupils' level of achievement. One of the reasons for this is that the extensive research in this area can be interpreted in a number of ways. However, a major meta-analysis of 122 studies carried out by Johnson and Johnson (1987) demonstrated the benefits of cooperative learning. They found that cooperative learning experiences tend to promote higher achievements than do competitive and individualistic learning experiences. This is true at all age levels and in all subject areas. They also found that cooperative learning experiences produced higher achievement across a range of tasks, including verbal and spatial problem solving and remembering information.

There are logical cognitive and motivational reasons why cooperative learning promotes higher academic achievement. From a cognitive point of view, working together inevitably produces more ideas and knowledge about an issue than pupils' working on their own. The range of ideas means that there will be tension between different pupils' views. This tension between ideas produces a challenge to the cognitive structures – the schemata – that the pupils hold. This challenge produces a greater depth of understanding of the task and therefore a greater retention of the material. The repetition of the information through the group discussion also ensures that it is better remembered than by pupils working on their own. At a motivational level, working cooperatively in groups encourages peer feedback and support. Pupils develop a liking for each other through interaction and the achievement of the task. These relationships and this group cohesiveness increase the motivation of individuals, who feel responsibility to the group and encourage each other to succeed. In a cooperative learning situation, the individual pupil is not left to fail on his own.

To stress the importance of cooperative learning is not to deny the value of individualistic learning. There are times when the latter is more appropriate, particularly when pupils need to learn specific facts or acquire specific skills. However, even in these circumstances cooperative learning aids the remembering of knowledge and increases pupils' motivation.

Cooperative learning strategies

Cooperative learning occurs when the task is structured so that the learning goal is expected to be achieved by all pupils with help and assistance from their peers. There is positive interdependence between the pupils. There are four basic cooperative learning strategies (Elliott and Shapiro, 1990):

- student team learning;
- jigsaw;
- learning together;
- group investigations.

Student team learning involves a group of pupils working together to learn new material before they are assessed. Group members help each other to learn and correct each other's work. Marks are given for how much individual pupils have learned during the lesson.

Jigsaw was one of the first cooperative learning strategies to be developed. The class is divided into a number of groups. Each group member is given a different set of information to understand. Pupils who are studying the same information in different groups meet together to form an expert group. When they return to their own group, they explain to the rest of the group members their set of information, supplemented by the knowledge and understanding gained from working in the expert group. The whole class is then assessed to see how much has been learned.

Learning together revolves around the group obtaining only one copy of the material to be studied and then having to complete a single report. This ensures they have to work together to complete the task.

Group investigation requires the group to decide what its members are going to learn, how they are going to learn it and how they are going to communicate back to the class what they have learned. It is a very open, problem-solving type of strategy, which is nearer to discovery learning (see Chapter 10) than cooperative group learning.

All these strategies allow the teacher to use the forces inherent in small groups to foster learning. The task is structured so that a feeling of interdependence develops – 'We are all in this together.' This can be encouraged by asking pupils to produce a single written or verbal report, which means that they have to work together to produce an answer; and by structuring any assessment so that the points the group gets is the total from each of its members. It is therefore in individual pupils' interest to help each other in order to get a good mark for the whole group.

Despite the demonstrated benefits of collaborative learning, it is infrequently used in the classroom. One of the main reasons for this is that it appears difficult to organize. Certainly, material needs to be planned and assessment systems prepared that allow pupils' progress to be assessed together. The teacher also has to be quite sophisticated at managing classroom groups. However, these difficulties are outweighed by the long-term benefits to both pupils and teachers.

Teachers organizing their classes in this way find it is easiest to start with a group of two or three. It is only when both pupils and teacher become more used to cooperative learning that the size should be increased to six or seven.

Process skills

The teacher has to decide on two types of objectives for a cooperative lesson. There are the academic objectives of the lesson – what is to be learned – which are described in Chapter 11. There are also the process objectives of the lesson – learning the skills of working together.

Teachers can organize cooperative lessons as the means to achieve the task. Cooperative learning will not be achieved unless the pupils have the appropriate skills to work together. There are a number of key interpersonal skills pupils need, such as effective communication and negotiation skills, as well as the respect and genuineness that lead to trust between pupils.

Some psychologists believe it is important for the pupils simply to concentrate on the goals of the task – the learning outcome (Slavin,

1983). Others, including Johnson and Johnson, follow the group dynamic literature, and suggest that the pupils also need to be able to analyse what is happening in their cooperative working group – group processing. This consists of the pupils' observing the way they are working together and then developing and building on their strengths. The aim of group processing is to give pupils a feeling of self-efficacy and empowerment, so that they can improve the way they are working together. One of the keys for group processing is understanding how groups develop.

THE DEVELOPMENT OF GROUPS

Groups go through certain stages of development (Tuckman, 1965). These stages are not fixed and rigid, but they do provide a useful framework for teachers to view the development of groups. Understanding the stages of group development can help the teacher organize cooperative learning. It can also help pupils understand the process of working in groups.

Four principal stages can be identified (Schein, 1987):

- forming;
- storming;
- norming;
- performing.

These can be depicted as the four quarters of a clock (see Figure 9.1). Pupils can learn to recognize the stage they feel their group is at. There is no set length of time that a group will stay at any stage; that will depend on a range of factors, including how often they

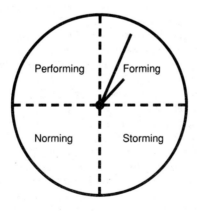

Figure 9.1 Stages of group development.

173

work together, the type of cooperative learning strategy used, and the age and experiences of the pupils. Though there is a general movement through the stage, the group can also move back as well as forwards.

Stage 1: Forming – becoming oriented in a new group

When new groups form, the first stage is characterized by the pupils being very concerned about themselves and their position in the group. This can be described as self-oriented behaviour. The members need to answer certain questions for themselves. In a class, these would include:

- What role am I going to play in this group? (*identity*)
- Will I be able to influence others, including the teacher? (*influence*)
- Will the group include my own needs? (*needs*)
- Will I be liked and accepted by the group, and by the teacher? (*acceptance*)

Pupils will want to know what is expected of them, what procedures there are and how the group is going to function. Pupils will expect the teacher to explain the goals of the various activities and any rules that they have to follow. It will be the teacher who signals the start and end of activities and organizes the groups within the class.

Stage 2: Storming – resolving unmet needs

The pupils' preoccupation with having these self-oriented questions answered leads to typical tensions. Pupils will try to overcome these by acting in a number of ways.

The first is to be hostile and aggressive to the rest of the group as a means of establishing power. Pupils will try to influence the other pupils and challenge the leadership of the teacher. The second is to look for peers to form alliances with. The pupil looks for acceptance by cloning other pupils' likes and attitudes. Obviously, making friends should be encouraged, but this type of alliance is not a friendship between two equals; rather, it is one pupil being emotionally dependent on the other. The pupil may become the class clown in order to gain acceptance; or, as we have seen, the adolescent pupil can easily become attached to a subculture, the function of which is to challenge the influence of the teacher. The third strategy is to withdraw from group interaction. The pupil will not volunteer for activities and will start to become socially distanced and isolated from the group.

Teachers need to understand that these tensions are a natural response to the group's dynamics. By sensitive and positive handling of the roles and the relationships in the group, they can help the pupils move to the next stage of group development. Before we move on, however, it is important to remember that a group is not really 'new'. The pupils may have worked together in previous years, or at least have been in the same class. This means that at the beginning of a working group there may be old agendas still running, or partly running. Part of the strategy for the teacher is to recognize these previous agendas and to see how much she needs to build on the formal and informal groupings from the previous year, and how much she deliberately wants to create new groups by arranging tasks and seating in different ways. The teacher does not have a clean slate at the beginning of the year.

Stage 3: Norming – 'the way we do things around here'

As the group develops, norms are formed. Norms are normal or common ways of doing things – 'the way we do things around here'. They are the behaviour of the group that expresses its values.

Norms can be seen at a number of different levels, ranging from clear rules (see Chapter 8) to implicit agreement about the way the pupils should behave. In every group there are implicit rules. They may not be readily on display, but they are there just below the surface and are the means by which the group knows what to do. They have not been agreed either formally or informally within the group. Such an implicit rule might be to share the coloured pencils.

Problems happen in groups when these implicit rules get broken – a pupil refuses to share his coloured pencils with the others. It is then that the group exerts influence over the individual pupil to conform to the norms. Pupils will differ in how much they conform to, or deviate from, the norms of the group. The group will put strong pressure on its members to conform, and will reject a pupil who deviates too much. He may try to create a deviant subgroup in the class. The level of acceptance of the group norms is one of the keys to understanding deviant behaviour in class.

There are a number of strategies the teacher can use to create group norms (Feldman, 1984), which are described below.

Precedents set over time

What happens when a group starts up usually becomes established as the norm. This is why it is important for the teacher to negotiate rules and procedures quickly. It needs to be quickly established where pupils will sit in the group, when they can talk, and generally how formal or informal the group is.

175

Carry-overs from other situations

Pupils carry over from other situations norms about how they should behave. Thus at the beginning of a year pupils will carry over from previous groups expectations about how they should behave. The teacher does not have a blank sheet to start with, but should be aware of the norms from previous years.

Explicit statement by a teacher or another pupil

A new pupil in a group will quickly learn how things are done by both watching and listening to the teacher and the influential pupils. These people will try to tell the pupil what the group norms are; whether they are this in practice leads to the next point.

Critical events in the group's history

The pupils' and teacher's reaction to critical events will establish new norms for the group. For example, when the group sends a card or a book to a pupil who is in hospital, it establishes a norm. Similarly, the way the teacher handles a difficult situation will establish a group norm. For example, if the parents of a pupil who swears at the teacher are sent for, this then becomes the norm for swearing in the group.

The establishment of norms is what gives the group its cohesiveness and feeling of being a group. Without norms, the group does not have any identity – there is nothing about it that makes the pupils feel that belonging to it is special.

Stage 4: Performing

'Performing' means a commitment by the pupils to getting the task done. They are happy to help each other and to work together cooperatively. Pupils understand and accept the differences between members of the group and focus their energies on the work rather than on tensions with interpersonal relationships. This is the stage in development that the teacher wants every group to reach.

To reach this stage, it is necessary to keep a group together long enough for it to go through the stages of development, even if this means at times its members are not working well together. It is important that the pupils work out their own solutions to some of the problems of interpersonal relationships and gain success in having a productive working group by the end of the year.

Teachers can help group processing in a number of ways. Most importantly, they can understand the process themselves. By understanding the different stages, teachers can recognize how the group is progressing and react and intervene appropriately. They can also explain to pupils how groups develop. By helping pupils understand group dynamics, they can give pupils a sense of self-efficacy rather than helplessness. The level of explanation can be tailored to the age of the pupils, but even young pupils will benefit from a simplified explanation. By explaining to pupils how groups work, the teacher also legitimizes the pupils' talking about the process. Not only can pupils discuss the task they are tackling, they can also discuss how they are working together. By ensuring pupils learn how to understand the process, teachers can make every cooperative learning task into a lesson in learning how to collaborate too.

Finally, it is important to recognize the cognitive importance of working in groups. The key cognitive element is the development of the ability to take another pupil's perspective. If a pupil simply sees relationships from his own perspective, then social interaction will depend on what advantages can be got out of a relationship – a good friend is someone who gives the pupil something. Selman (1980), influenced by Piaget's work on cognitive development, describes five levels of social understanding that the pupil goes through, and relates them to stages in understanding groups. It is only gradually that pupils understand that different members of a group can have different needs but that members can still coexist and work together.

This cognitive ability to take perspectives depends on social interactions. So pupils need to work in groups if they are to develop the ability to take perspectives. There is reciprocal determinism between cognitive development and working together: pupils' thinking affects their ability to work in groups, and working in groups affects the development of their thinking.

SUMMARY

This chapter describes the importance of groups for the effective organization of the classroom. Pupils form a variety of different types of groups. These can have, in the teacher's eyes, a positive or negative influence on them. The more cohesive the group, the greater the influence. One way of achieving cohesive groupings that has a positive influence is through strategies for cooperative learning.

Cooperative learning emphasizes the mutual interdependence between pupils rather than an individualistic or competitive culture. To achieve cooperative learning, teachers and pupils have to understand group processes – how groups operate. Understanding how groups form and develop empowers both pupils and teachers, giving them control over the forces of group dynamics.

REFERENCES

Ausubel, D., Montemayor, R. and Svajian, P. (1977) *Theory and Problems of Adolescent Development.* New York: Grune & Stratton.

DES (1967) *Children and their Primary Schools.* (The Plowden Report.) London: HMSO.

Dunphy, D. (1963) The social structure of urban adolescent peer groups, *Sociometry* **26**, pp. 230–46.

Elliott, S. and Shapiro, E. (1990) Intervention, techniques and programs for academic performance problems, in Gutkin, T. and Reynolds, C. (eds), *The Handbook of School Psychology.* New York: Wiley.

Feldman, D.C. (1984) The development and enforcement of group norms, *Academy of Management Review* **9**, pp. 47–53.

Galton, M., Simon, B. and Croll, P. (1980) *Inside the Primary Classroom.* London: Routledge & Kegan Paul.

Hargreaves, D. (1966) *Social Relations in a Secondary School.* London: Routledge & Kegan Paul.

Johnson, D. and Johnson, R. (1987) *Learning Together and Alone.* Englewood Cliffs, NJ: Prentice-Hall.

Napier, R. and Gershenfeld, M. (1989) *Groups: Theory and Experience.* 4th edition. Boston, MA: Houghton Mifflin.

Schein, E. (1987) *Process Consultation.* Reading, MA: Addison-Wesley.

Selman, R. (1980) *The Growth of Interpersonal Understanding.* New York: Academic Press.

Sharan, S. and Sharan, Y. (1976) *Small-Group Teaching.* Englewood Cliffs, NJ: Educational Technology.

Sherif, M., Harvey, O., White, B., Hood, W. and Sherif, C. (1961) *Intergroup Conflict and Cooperation: The Robber's Cave Experiment.* Norman: University of Oklahoma.

Slavin, R. (1983) *Cooperative Learning.* New York: Longman.

Tann, S. (1981) Grouping and group work, in Simon, B. and Willcocks, J. (eds), *Research and Practice in the Primary Classroom.* London: Routledge & Kegan Paul.

Tuckman, B. (1965) Developmental sequence in small groups, *Psychological Bulletin* **63**, pp. 384–99.

RECOMMENDED READING

D. Ausubel, R. Montemayor and P. Svajian, *Theory and Problems of Adolescent Development* (New York: Grune & Stratton, 1977), is a detailed guide to the social development of adolescents. Helpful analysis of the impact of the adolescents' peer culture.

D. Johnson and R. Johnson, *Learning Together and Alone* (Englewood Cliffs, NJ: Prentice-Hall, 1987), provides a detailed guide to cooperative, competitive and individualistic learning. Full of practical suggestions – especially on how to set up cooperative learning.

E. Schein, *Process Consultation* (Reading, MA: Addison-Wesley, 1987), is a very readable introduction to what happens in groups. Primarily aimed at understanding adult groups, but the processes apply to pupils as well.

CHAPTER 10

Teaching strategies

OVERVIEW

There has been considerable debate throughout the twentieth century about the most effective teaching strategies. This debate continues into the 1990s, and has been given extra impetus by politicians' interest. Over the years, it has focused on key issues for effective teaching, and in particular on whether formal or informal approaches are the most effective. Many educationists believe that a polarized, win-or-lose choice between teaching methods is unhelpful. Effective teaching is selecting the right strategy at the right time.

Teachers use formal and informal strategies to organize their teaching and to maximize pupils' learning. Teaching strategies are a sequence of planned activities, arranged, organized and managed by the teacher and designed to ensure pupils learn.

This chapter focuses on the psychological theories that underpin the teaching strategies that teachers use. In particular, it concentrates on:

- cognitive teaching strategies;
- behavioural teaching strategies;
- meaningful reception learning;
- the expositive–discovery dimension;
- selecting the appropriate strategy.

COGNITIVE TEACHING STRATEGIES

The basic behavioural and cognitive psychological perspectives for understanding learning are introduced in Part 1. The behavioural perspective emphasizes the importance of the external environment and the teacher when viewing learning – the expositive approach. The cognitive perspective emphasizes the internal mental processes that the pupils uses to respond to the teaching situation – the discovery approach.

The discovery approach was developed by Jerome Bruner (1960, 1966). It has had a major influence on primary teaching in Britain, particularly on the teaching of mathematics. Bruner emphasizes that the focus of teaching should be on developing the internal thought processes of the pupils – their cognitive representations of the world. Learning is seen as an active process whereby the pupil constructs models of the world. These conceptual models are based on the pupils' culture and adapted to the pupils' use – 'instrumental conceptualism'; that is, pupils conceptualize things in ways that are of instrumental use to them. In this way Bruner, like Kelly (see Chapter 1), sees pupils as constructing their own world in a way that is useful and makes sense to them.

Jerome Bruner (1915–)

Jerome Bruner was born in New York and has been a professor of psychology at Harvard, where he founded the Center for Cognitive Studies. He also taught in Britain, at Oxford, from 1971 to 1979. His work is particularly influenced by Piaget and he has tried to show how children use their environment to develop their thinking. He believes that it is impossible to explain many psychological processes and that the best one can do is to describe them.

Pupils' conceptualization develops through their manipulation of objects and materials. By manipulating objects, regularities are established between them and the cognitive structures that the pupil already has. In other words, a match takes place between what the pupil is doing in the outside world and some frameworks, templates or representations that he already has, cognitively, in his head. This model for the development of thinking stems from Piaget (see Chapter 3) and can also be seen in the network models of memory developed by Anderson (see Chapter 2).

This manipulation of things in order to develop cognitive structures is termed 'discovery learning'. This involves an internal recognition and then reorganization of previously known ideas in order to fit better the regularities that the pupil has experienced through activity. It involves asking questions about new information and then working out provisional ways of making sense of it.

Pupils' representations of the world develop through three progressively more complex levels. Different teaching activities are appropriate for each of the three levels:

- *Enactive level.* The pupil represents through action. He needs to manipulate objects and materials directly, and the teacher provides concrete objects for him – for example, he fits templates of triangles into a form board.
- *Iconic level.* The pupil represents objects through mental images rather than directly manipulating them. The teacher provides tools, such as pens, pencils, crayons and paper, so that the pupil can represent images – for example, he draws a triangle from memory.
- *Symbolic level.* The pupil has symbols to manipulate rather than mental images or objects. The teacher introduces language so that the pupil can store concepts – for example, when told to draw an isosceles triangle, the pupil can do so. This stage is characterized by the pupil's ability to use language to represent the world.

Pupils have three major means of representing experience: action, imagery and language. The three modes can be used separately or together. In learning a skill such as addition, a pupil uses all three levels: the enactive level might involve finger counting; the iconic level might involve visualizing blocks that can be grouped as tens; finally, the symbolic level would be using written numerals.

The enactive level is particularly important for young pupils and is the basis for much of the 'play' that goes on in infant schools. As the pupil becomes older, language is the principal means of thought. The pupils use language as the prime method of symbolic representation. Language allows pupils to consider what might be and what might exist as well as their actual experiences. Language is the principal method for reflective thinking.

The importance of discovery learning

Bruner sees the purpose of teaching as the development of thinking rather than acquiring knowledge in terms of facts. Pupils cannot learn all the facts and information that are presently available. What is important is that they develop structures to understand, integrate and transfer knowledge.

Bruner describes how discovery learning (what he called 'hypothetical' learning) helps pupils learn knowledge in such a way that they will use it in new situations to solve problems. This highlights the need for pupils to learn how to explore alternatives rather than be taught solutions. The discovery process allows the pupil to take some control over the contents of the lesson and to discover new ideas and concepts. This can be contrasted with expositive teaching, where the teacher controls the process. The benefit for the pupils of discovery learning is that, as they have discovered the knowledge for themselves, they are more likely to organize it in a meaningful way and thus remember it better.

Bruner has had an enormous influence on the teaching strategies used in British primary and nursery schools. The use of activity and 'play' as the vital first step to cognitive development stems largely from his perspective. Teaching that starts at the symbolic level, without the pupil developing an enactive or iconic representation, simply results in rote learning. Instead, knowledge can be introduced at a simple level in every curriculum area. The teacher can then gradually increase the pupils' knowledge and understanding through the development of more complex representations. By allowing the pupils to discover the connection between areas of knowledge, teachers produce active learners who can make sense of the complexities of the world.

BEHAVIOURAL TEACHING STRATEGIES

Behavioural psychologists have long been interested in making teaching more effective. One of Skinner's (see Chapter 1) fundamental beliefs was that psychology is the means for placing education on an efficient basis (Skinner, 1974). In contrast to the cognitive perspective, the behaviourist's focus in education is on the teacher. To understand learning, teachers need to focus on what they do, and in particular on how they present the task (the input) and reinforce the pupil after learning (the output). Learning occurs if there is a change in what the pupil can do - after teaching, the pupil can spell 'elephant' when before he could not. Teachers should not be concerned about what happens inside the pupil's head - whether he has a good long- or short-term memory - but rather with how they have structured their teaching so that the pupil can now spell 'elephant'.

Teaching (or 'instruction', as it is known as in behavioural literature) is seen as structuring a situation so that learning is maximized. In particular, behavioural psychology has emphasized the need for clarity about three aspects of teaching:

- what teachers are teaching;
- how they are evaluating progress;
- how they are teaching.

Teaching to objectives

Behavioural psychology highlights the importance of teachers being clear about what the focus or aim of the task is, and to have clear objectives about what they want to teach.

Mager's work in this area is of particular interest. His book, *Preparing Instructional Objectives* (1962), demonstrates the actual process by which programmed instruction works, as well as teaching the reader about objectives. He establishes the importance of stating objectives in clear and precise terms. An objective is a description of what a pupil is expected to be able to do after he has been taught. Objectives have three components:

- *performance* – what the pupil is able to do;
- *conditions* – the important circumstances under which the performance happens;
- *criterion* – the quality or level of performance that is considered acceptable.

An example of an objective is: 'Given a list of thirty chemical elements, the pupil will be able to write the valences of at least 20'. The performance is 'will be able to write'; the condition is 'given a list of thirty chemical elements'; and the criterion is 'at least 20'.

Setting objectives ensures clarity about what teachers are trying to teach. It means teachers can judge whether learning has occurred. The teachers know what they are trying to teach; they can then judge whether they have been successful.

Mastery learning

Setting clear objectives is one of the foundations of mastery learning (Bloom, 1956). By carefully planning and organizing objectives, teachers can specify the levels of success or criteria that most, if not all, pupils can be expected to master. Time is taken out of the learning equation by allowing a pupil unlimited time to 'master' a set unit of work. This opens up the possibility that the achievement of an objective is open to all pupils.

Mastery learning works by breaking up the subject to be taught into small learning units of approximately two-week blocks. Each of these blocks has key objectives that need to be learnt in order to master the subject area. The teacher teaches each unit using small-group teaching methods.Through diagnostic assessment, she checks that each pupil has mastered each objective and that any difficulties are ascertained.

If a pupil has difficulty with a certain objective, he is then given supplementary teaching in this area until he has mastered it. There is considerable evidence that mastery learning is an efficient way of teaching pupils (Block, 1971).

The mastery model is the basis for competency-based education. This aims to make pupils competent in an area by following mastery learning with modularized individual teaching. This is one of the ways of achieving differentiation of teaching to ensure that all pupils progress on the National Curriculum.

The behavioural approach in education

Setting objectives and mastery learning both emphasize the importance of teachers being clear about what they want to teach. The specification of clear objectives, the 'what to teach', is epitomized in the National Curriculum. It has also become increasingly popular in other areas of education: setting objectives for both teacher appraisal and school development plans is becoming increasingly common practice. The popularity of performance indicators and quality standards has come directly from the perceived value of setting clear behavioural objectives.

Programmed instruction

Programmed instruction was one of the first strategies designed to achieve some clarity about how teachers were teaching. It is a process that uses written materials and, in the last few decades, computer technology to allow pupils to work directly with the materials. The teacher's role is to set up the programme; the pupil then follows it, which usually means a short section of reading followed by a multiple-choice question. Depending on the pupil's answer, he is then instructed to turn to another page in the book, where he either has additional reading, explanation on the same topic if he got it wrong, or a new piece of information if he answered correctly.

The significance of the method is that it allows teachers clarity about what they are teaching – the information contained in the programme – and about the teaching process. The pupil also receives reinforcement through the direct feedback he obtains on how he is progressing. Pupils work at their own pace and have control over their own learning. The appeal of programmed instruction is that it offers a means to individualize learning. In fact, all that is usually individualized is the rate at which pupils travel through the materials.

The actual path and the end-point are always fixed. Nevertheless, programmed instruction does give one way of obtaining some clarity about the teaching process.

Programmed instruction is infrequently used in schools, largely because of the limitations of the actual programmes that have been designed. In the 1990s, the development of interactive computer systems should allow programmed instruction to become a viable strategy in education.

Direct instruction

Following on from the introduction of clear objectives and programmed instruction, there developed a desire for greater clarity on strategies for how to teach pupils directly. Becker and Engelmann (1977), working at the University of Oregon, developed direct instruction as part of Project Follow-Through, the extension of the Head Start programme (see Chapter 3) in the USA. The Head Start programme had initially failed to demonstrate the advantages of early intervention with disadvantaged children. Project Follow-Through was designed to select and evaluate different promising educational programmes.

The evaluation showed that pupils made the greatest progress in basic skills – reading and mathematics – when taught over four years on Becker and Englemann's direct instruction programme, called DISTAR. Pupils on this programme caught up with the national average; no other educational programme showed this amount of gain. What is this method of teaching and why is it not more widely used?

Direct instruction is a method of teaching pupils basic skills. It assumes that learning basic skills such as reading and writing is essential to pupils' educational progress, and that if pupils do not have these basic skills they need to be directly taught. It also assumes that all pupils can be taught and that a lack of basic skills is due to a failure in teaching, and cannot be excused by saying a pupil is not developmentally ready, or has low ability, or comes from a disadvantaged background. Engelmann asserts (1977) that 90 per cent of learning failure is due to instruction rather than any cognitive or processing difficulties that the pupil has.

The focus in direct instruction is not on the pupil but on how the teacher teaches. If pupils have failed to learn basic skills, they have to be taught in order to 'catch up' with their peers – they have to be taught more in less time (Solity and Bull, 1987). The key to teaching more in less time is teaching the pupil how to generalize. When learning how to read or write each piece of information cannot be taught separately; pupils taught letter sounds have to learn how to generalize this information so that they can read unfamiliar words on their own.

So the focus for teaching in order to 'catch up' is the specific pieces of information or skills that the pupils can then generalize to new tasks.

The best-known direct instruction programme is still DISTAR (Direct Instructional System for Teaching and Remediation). It contains nine programmes: three each in reading, arithmetic and language. The focus is on how the teacher is teaching, and each lesson is taught in a very precise way through the use of a script, which the teacher is expected to follow.

The importance of DISTAR and the other direct instruction programmes (Engelmann, 1978; Dixon and Engelmann, 1979) is that they demonstrate the impact of teaching on learning, rather than the pupils' abilities or cognitive processes.

Some teachers feel alienated by direct instruction, as it highlights the controlling aspects of the teaching process. The script also constrains the role of the teacher. These feelings relate to the teacher's attributions of the causes of the lack of pupils' progress. Direct instruction is a highly effective way of teaching pupils basic skills, and teachers can use the teaching strategies it promotes as an integral part of regular classroom teaching.

Teaching to objectives, programmed instruction and direct instruction are all based on behavioural psychology:

- There is a focus on the conditions, both the antecedents and consequences, rather than on the processes in the pupil's head. Learning occurs when pupils respond in a different way to the stimulus material; behaviour has changed.
- Rewards such as praise and tokens are used to reinforce progress.
- There is a focus on what teachers actually do, with a close analysis of exactly what is happening in the teaching process.

Though both behavioural and cognitive perspectives on teaching have their exclusive advocates, many psychologists find elements of both helpful. These 'neo-behavioural' perspectives are best exemplified by Gagne's description of guided discovery.

Guided discovery

For Gagne (1970), the purpose of psychology is to observe the conditions under which learning occurs and then to describe these conditions in objective terms. Gagne distinguishes between the external and the internal conditions necessary for learning. Internal conditions are the processes inside the pupil and include such states as motivation, attention, and the recall of previously learnt information. He assumes an information-processing model of the mind to help understand the processes of learning (see Chapter 2). The external conditions are the arrangements for teaching that the teacher sets up. They include the grouping of the pupil, the actual task and the instructions that the teacher gives. So to understand how learning occurs, both the pupil's internal conditions and the teaching arrangements must be taken into account.

Robert Gagne (1916–)

Robert Gagne is a leading American educational psychologist. He received his doctorate from Brown University in 1940. His interest is in how teaching can be made most effective. He has worked as a research psychologist at a number of military establishments as well as universities. His concept of 'conditions of learning' is a major theoretical underpinning of approaches to learning.

Gagne categorizes five types of learning. The most important is the highest level – problem solving.

Problem solving

Problem solving is dependent on using rules. A rule can be considered as a chain or combination of two or more concepts, and is different from a fact in so far as a pupil can apply it in all relevant situations once it is known. Mathematics contains useful examples of rule learning: to understand $3 \times 3 + 6 = 15$, the pupil has to understand a set of rules about multiplication and addition.

Though rules can be directly taught, problem solving cannot. For problem solving, pupils need to generate the higher-order rules for themselves through the use of guided discovery by the teacher. The teacher sets up the problem and the pupils test the hypotheses they have generated using various strategies. Learning occurs when the pupils develop new rules to solve problems for themselves. By combining rules into new higher-order rules pupils are able to solve novel problems – thus developing their thinking.

MEANINGFUL RECEPTION LEARNING

David Ausubel (1968) does not believe that problem solving is that important, as it is not the type of learning that actually occurs in the classroom, especially with older pupils. He believes that the focus of teaching is not learning new rules, but rather the acquisition of knowledge.

David Ausubel (1918-)

David Ausubel trained in medicine and psychiatry at Columbia University. He has conducted extensive research, particularly in child and adolescent personality development. He was a Fulbright research scholar in New Zealand before returning to the USA and lecturing at the Graduate School of the City University of New York. Here he ran the PhD programme in educational psychology.

Most of the time, successful learning is achieved through a process of teaching that leads to 'meaningful reception learning'. This occurs when new material is linked with pre-existing knowledge and concepts, and is contrasted with 'rote learning', which does not link new information to old structures and is therefore not made meaningful. For example, pupils will learn the scientific formula for copper by rote if they have no existing knowledge of scientific formulae. If, however, they have a structure of existing knowledge – the Periodic Table – then the scientific formula for copper can be learnt in a meaningful way.

The focus for meaningful reception learning is the way the tasks are organized and presented – the entire content of what is to be learned is presented to the pupil in the final form. Thus in chemistry lessons, the Periodic Table is presented to pupils in its final form; they do not have to discover it for themselves. Ausubel argues that most teaching is organized along these lines. Material containing ideas, concepts and generalizations can be remembered meaningfully without either learning by rote or having to go through a discovery process. Pupils do not have to discover principles or information independently in order to be able to understand and use them.

One of the problems is that material that is meaningful is often presented in such a way that pupils will only learn it by rote. This may be because they have learnt that only verbatim answers are accepted by teachers; or it may be because a high level of failure has left the pupils with such chronic anxiety that they do not think that they can learn meaningfully – they think that the only method of learning is by rote. The Periodic Table is meaningful and does not have to be learnt by rote but all too often pupils will see it as a rote-learning task.

> ### *Meaningful reception learning*
>
> Learning occurs when information coming from the teacher is actively anchored in the pupils' existing knowledge and concepts. Teaching consists of transmitting well-established facts, concepts and information which come from an academic discipline.

There is a similar emphasis on teaching rather than pupils' cognitive processes in both meaningful reception learning and the behavioural approach. Where they differ is in the emphasis in meaningful reception learning on the structure and interconnections that the pupil forms between the areas of knowledge that are essential to learning specific objectives. Meaningful reception learning happens in most schools – areas of knowledge or concepts are identified in, or between, different subject areas and then taught within a structure that makes sense to the pupil. The teaching is directed at pupils' understanding the relationship between the new information and their previous knowledge.

THE EXPOSITIVE–DISCOVERY DIMENSION

The different strategies for teaching are often seen on an expositive-discovery dimension (Romiszowski, 1981). Each of the two extremes of this dimension has a number of key features:

> ### *Alexander Romiszowski (1939–)*
>
> Alexander Romiszowski received his doctorate from the University of Technology at Loughborough. He has worked extensively both in Britain and elsewhere on instructional design in education and training establishments. He has worked with international bodies such as UNESCO, the ILO and the Council of Europe as an educational troubleshooter. His book, *Designing Instructional Systems*, though not classroom focused, is one of the most comprehensive books on planning strategies for teaching that is presently available. He is currently teaching in the School of Education at Syracuse University, New York.

Expositive strategy:
- The teacher presents information, in the form of either a verbal explanation or a practical demonstration.
- The teacher checks for understanding and assimilation. The information is repeated or rephrased as necessary.
- The teacher provides opportunities for practice. These are usually concerned with applying the general principle to a range of examples. This work is checked to ensure the pupil has learned the principle. The practice items are modified to ensure they are at the correct level.
- The teacher provides opportunities for the newly learnt information to be applied to real-life situations and problems.

Discovery strategy:
- The teacher presents opportunities for pupils to act and to observe the consequences of their actions.
- The teacher checks that the pupil understands the cause–effect relationships. This is done by questioning or by observing the actions of the pupils. Further opportunities to act are presented if this cause–effect relationship is not clear.
- The teacher checks, through questioning, whether the pupil understands the general principle underlying the activity. She presents further cases until the general principle is understood.
- The teacher presents opportunities for the newly learnt information to be applied to real-life situations and problems.

Between these two positions there is a continuum of methods for teaching (see Figure 10.1). Different strategies are used by skilled teachers to fit the task that they want the pupils to learn.

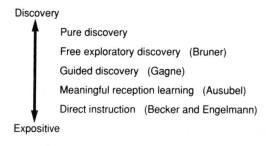

Figure 10.1 The expositive–discovery dimension.

At the pure discovery end of the continuum, there is learning that is not dependent on direct teaching. The teacher's role here is to organize and manage the pupils' experiences. An example is a class of pupils who are given the opportunity to explore a zoo independently.

The teacher does not give the pupils specific questions to answer; instead the pupils are encouraged to develop knowledge in the areas that are of interest to them, which are dependent on their prior knowledge.

The next strategy is Bruner's exploratory discovery. The broad learning goals are set and the pupils are asked to explore a particular concept in order to develop their learning processes. For example, the pupils at the zoo are asked to discover how they can tell which animals eat meat and which eat grass.

Further along the continuum is Gagne's 'guided discovery' approach. Here the objectives are fixed and the pupils are guided to generate the higher-order rules for themselves. In the example above, the pupils are asked to decide on means of grouping and categorizing the animals.

The next strategy is Ausubel's meaningful reception learning. Here the teacher gives, in the final form, information to be learned. In our example, the teacher wants the pupils to be able to name the family groups of the animals, so she gives them a chart to fill in detailing the animal groups.

The final strategy, right at the expositive end, is direct instruction. In our example, the teacher wants the pupils to be able to spell the names of each of the family groups, so she uses direct instruction to ensure that each pupil can spell the names.

Once broken down in this way, the gradual shift from discovery to expository teaching is apparent. Effective teaching moves up and down the continuum, selecting the appropriate strategy for the particular objectives of the lesson.

SELECTING THE APPROPRIATE STRATEGY

From a psychological perspective, the key issue is not about the distinction between subject areas or topics within the National Curriculum, but rather about how specific objectives can be most effectively taught within a lesson. Teaching objectives can be divided into three areas:

- knowledge;
- skills;
- attitudes.

Education is not very explicit about the teaching of attitudes (see Chapter 5). Teachers do shape attitudes, consciously and unconsciously, but there is considerable hostility to acknowledging this aspect of education.

There is also an ambiguous attitude to the teaching of skills. Reading, writing and mathematics are seen as fundamental skills and have been given a high political priority in the last few years. As pupils become older, however, there is a clear shift in emphasis: Design and Technology – one area of the National Curriculum that is skill based – certainly does not open the same gates into higher education as 'academic' subjects.

Examinations, at the highest level for university places, depend entirely on assessing pupils' knowledge, and the prime focus for most teaching is the development of knowledge. Knowledge is divided, in Chapter 2, into declarative and procedural, to which Romiszowski (1981) adds two further types:

- declarative – knowing about facts, events or people;
- procedural – knowing what to do in a given situation;
- concepts – knowing how to recognize and distinguish groups of phenomena, or being able to define things;
- principles – knowing how to link together concepts or facts in specific ways, thus enabling an explanation or prediction of events.

The first step for teachers is to clarify the purpose of the lesson. Is the purpose of the lesson the learning of knowledge or the learning of skills? If it is the former, what sort of knowledge? Unless there is clarity about what the pupil has to learn, it is impossible to decide on the appropriate teaching strategy.

The match between the type of knowledge and the style of teaching

The different types of knowledge give a framework for deciding on the most appropriate teaching strategy.

Declarative

The simplest way of teaching facts is through a direct expository strategy. Facts exist on their own, though clearly facts are better remembered if they are put into a meaningful structure.

Procedures

Procedures are defined as a category of facts that answer the question 'How do I do this?'. Most pupils are taught to do mathematics by following procedures. An expositive strategy is the most effective way to learn procedures; the pupils are given a model that allows them to follow the way the procedure operates.

Concepts

Two types of concepts can be distinguished: concrete and defined. Concrete concepts, such as the colour 'red' or 'horse', can be best learnt through a discovery strategy. Pupils need the opportunity to sort many types of coloured shapes and objects in order to learn the concept of red. Defined concepts, such as 'colour' or 'mammal', can only be learnt once some concrete concepts are known; that is, 'red', 'green', 'blue' or 'horse', 'dog', 'cat'. Defined concepts can be learnt by a discovery teaching strategy, but this is a long and time-consuming business. On the other hand, defined concepts can be easily taught using an expositive strategy – simply telling the pupils what a mammal is.

Principles

Though principles can be taught through an expository method, there is evidence that if they are learnt through the discovery method there is much more transfer to new learning situations (Romiszowski, 1981).

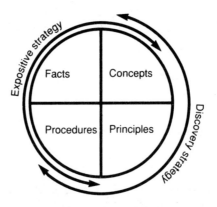

Figure 10.2 Strategies for teaching knowledge.

Figure 10.2 provides a framework for teachers to select an initial strategy. However, the different types of knowledge can be taught using different strategies. For example, if teaching spelling rules – procedural knowledge – two strategies are available. The first is the expository (from rule to example). The teacher first of all gives the rule, such as 'i before e except after c'. She then gives an example, such as 'field'. This rule/example method is often preferred, as generally it takes less time. The second strategy is through guided discovery (from example to rule). In this case the teacher writes up a number of 'ie' and 'ei' words and asks the pupils to generate rules that the spelling

follows. With the help of some 'guidance', through teacher questioning, the pupils are helped to 'discover' the rules for themselves. The
guided discovery approach may be of more use when long-term recall
or transfer to other learning tasks is required, but it takes excessive
time, given the demands of the National Curriculum.

Effective teaching strategies

Mayer (1987) has summarized the research evaluating the
effectiveness of the different teaching strategies:

- Pure discovery methods require an excessive amount of
  learning time. There is little evidence that information is
  remembered for longer or that knowledge transfers to other
  tasks. Pupils do become actively involved in the tasks,
  which increases motivation. However, there is no guaran-
  tee they will learn a particular rule or concept, and the
  teacher may end up having to teach this in a different way
  anyway.
- Guided discovery leads to better long-term retention and
  transfer than the expositive methods. It ensures that pupils
  come into contact with the rules to be learnt and that they
  are actively involved in the learning process.
- Expositive methods usually need less learning time than
  guided discovery. Initial learning is as good as with
  guided discovery, but long-term retention and transfer
  are inferior – the rules are learned but they may not be
  remembered.

One of the key factors when selecting an appropriate teaching
strategy is a recognition that the discovery method is time-consuming.
There needs to be a justification for the extra time spent when using it.

Sequences of teaching strategies

Any particular objective is best taught through a sequence of teaching
strategies. The framework above indicates the best starting point, but
there needs to be a sequence of activities based on a combination of
the described strategies.

Learning knowledge needs to be considered in a dynamic way.
The divisions between the four types of knowledge is not static;
Neeves and Anderson (1981), building on the Network ATC model (see
Chapter 2), propose that declarative knowledge is often turned into

procedures and that these procedures are then integrated. This ensures that knowledge develops in order to undertake a complex activity. The three steps in development are:

- *encoding*. Facts are initially simply encoded within the pupil's memory. This knowledge has to be actively searched for when it is to be used. It takes the pupil time to use the knowledge that is simply encoded; so a pupil learning to spell basic words, such as 'cat' and 'house', will have to think actively through each sound.
- *proceduralization*. Encoded facts can be transformed into procedures. Procedural knowledge can be acted upon without actively thinking about it; so as the pupil gains skills in spelling, he can spell 'cat' and 'house' quickly and fluently without thinking about each letter.
- *composition*. Procedures can be integrated and combined. Learning does not end when the pupil is fluent with a particular procedure; instead, the pupil can integrate it with others – he learns not only how to spell 'cat' and 'house' but also how to write these words quickly and fluently.

Neeves and Anderson's dynamic model means that if an expositive strategy is used to teach facts, initially, then the teacher needs to ensure that these facts are turned into procedures. If pupils are to use the factual knowledge fluently and skilfully, the teacher needs a sequence of teaching strategies that move the pupils through the three steps – to combine expositive and discovery strategies into a planned cycle of teaching.

SUMMARY

This chapter describes the range of teaching strategies that have been developed. These strategies are seen along an expositive-discovery dimension. The expositive end ties in with a behavioural perspective, which argues that the focus of teaching should be the teacher. What is required is clarity about the teaching process, about how the task is presented, and about the evaluation of the pupils' progress. The discovery end ties in with a cognitive perspective that highlights how the pupils' thinking develops when confronted with problems. The teacher's role is to provide experiences that develops the pupils' capacity for thinking.

Both perspectives are helpful in recognizing that it is teaching that leads to learning. What is important to remember is the limitations of both approaches, and that dogmatic adherence to one or the other is definitely out of place. Teaching is most effective when the teacher is clear about what the objectives of the lesson are, and then selects a sequence of strategies to ensure that the pupils learn effectively.

REFERENCES

Ausubel, D. (1968) *Educational Psychology: A Cognitive View*. New York: Holt, Rinehart & Winston.

Becker, W. and Engelmann, S. (1977) *The Oregon Direct Instruction Model: Comparative Results in Project Follow-Through. A Summary of Nine Years' Work*. Follow-Through Project. Eugene: University of Oregon.

Block, J. (1971) *Mastery Learning: Theory and Practice*. New York: Holt, Rinehart & Winston.

Bloom, B. (1956) *Taxonomy of Educational Objectives: Cognitive Domain*. London: Longman.

Bruner, J. (1960) *The Process of Education*. Cambridge, MA: Harvard University Press.

Bruner, J. (1966) *Toward a Theory of Instruction*. Cambridge, MA: Harvard University Press.

Dixon, R. and Engelmann, S. (1979) *Corrective Spelling through Morphographs*. Chicago: Science Research Associates.

Engelmann, S. (1977) Sequencing of cognitive and academic tasks, in Kneedler, R. and Tarver, S. (eds), *Changing Perspectives in Special Education*. Westerville, OH: Merrill.

Engelmann, S. (1978) *Corrective Reading Programme*. Chicago: Science Research Associates.

Gagne, R. (1970) *The Conditions of Learning*. 2nd edition. New York: Holt, Rinehart & Winston.

Mager, R. (1962) *Preparing Instructional Objectives*. Belmont, CA: Fearon.

Mayer, R. (1987) *Educational Psychology: A Cognitive Approach*. Boston, MA: Little, Brown.

Neeves, D. and Anderson, J. (1981) Knowledge compilation: mechanisms for the automatization of cognitive skills, in Anderson, J. (ed.), *Cognitive Skills and Their Acquisition*. Hillsdale, NJ: Erlbaum.

Romiszowski, A. (1981) *Designing Instructional Systems*. London: Kogan Page.

Skinner, B. (1974) *About Behaviour*. New York: Knopf.

Solity, J. and Bull, S. (1987) *Special Needs: Bridging the Curriculum Gap*. Milton Keynes: Open University Press.

RECOMMENDED READING

J. Bruner, *Toward a Theory of Instruction* (Cambridge, MA: Harvard University Press, 1966), provides a theoretical overview of Bruner's beliefs about teaching strategies. Highly thought-provoking.

R. Gagne, *The Conditions of Learning*, 2nd edition (New York: Holt,

Rinehart & Winston, 1970), describes the eight types of learning outcomes and the teaching strategies that each demands. A complex book.

R. Mager, *Preparing Instructional Objectives* (Fearon, 1962), was written as a programmed text and is a clear, practical introduction to writing teaching objectives.

A. Romiszowski, *Designing Instructional Systems* (London: Kogan Page, 1981), provides an invaluable, clear, yet complex guide to designing and writing a curriculum. Highly recommended.

CHAPTER 11

Pupils' learning strategies

OVERVIEW

The three major components that affect the learning process are the teacher, the pupil and the task. Effective teachers analyse both the task (as described in Chapter 10) and the pupils' learning strategies before they decide on a teaching strategy. Teachers have their own particular knowledge, skills and attitudes about how to teach; but pupils also have knowledge, skills and attitudes about how to learn. The nature of the task affects both the teacher's strategy for teaching and the pupil's strategy for learning.

This may seem logical, but it is also difficult to implement in a busy classroom. Galton and Simon (1980) found that only 9 per cent of the time in primary classrooms is focused on teaching at the appropriate level. Much of the time is spent in teaching the whole class. This allows very little time for teaching individual pupils, when the teacher can directly match her teaching to the pupil's learning strategy. Effective teachers promote learning through developing teaching strategies that take account of the task and the pupil; these teaching strategies are dynamic and flexible and depend on the inter-relationship between the three components.

Chapter 10 gives a basis for organizing this dynamic strategy in terms of the teacher and the task. The third component, the pupil's learning strategy, is dealt with in this chapter. In particular, it focuses on:

- understanding learning strategies;
- cognitive strategies: regulating the thinking processes;
- metacognitive strategies: planning and organizing the thinking processes;
- teaching metacognitive strategies.

UNDERSTANDING LEARNING STRATEGIES

In Part 2, motivation, attitudes and attribution were examined mainly from the teacher's perspective. These factors also affect the way pupils learn, and need to be taken into account when planning teaching strategies. The focus in this final chapter is, however, on a fourth factor – pupils' cognitive learning strategies. These are key mediating variables between a teacher's teaching strategies and whether the pupil learns.

Cognitive learning strategies are, in one sense, not new in the body of psychology, as witnessed by the whole debate on intelligence outlined in Chapter 2. What is new is a dynamic and constructional view of pupils' cognitive learning strategies not as fixed capacities of the brain, but rather as learnt strategies that the pupil brings to tackling a task. So, for example, a pupil's learning depends on his organization of his own memory, his knowledge of problem-solving techniques, and his understanding of an area of knowledge. Pupils are not just passive receivers of teaching, but make sense of the task through their past learning.

The description of thinking in Chapter 2 is of the way information is processed. There has to be a control system through which the pupil operates these cognitive processes. The mind is not just a machine waiting to be started up; instead, it is an executive decision-making system by which the pupil actively processes information. Understanding the pupil's executive control is the key to understanding learning strategies. What is attended to, what is perceived and how, and the way that knowledge is stored all depend on the information or task itself, but also on what the pupil does with the information.

One of the key strategic skills that experts develop is that of regulating and monitoring their own learning. Studies of children and adults who are experts in a particular field show that they undertake this monitoring by rapidly checking their work, judging its difficulty, and assessing their progress. They are also able to predict the outcome of their activities (Glaser, 1990). These self-monitoring, self-regulating skills are cyclical in nature. Pupils who have these skills acquire knowledge easily; because they acquire knowledge easily, they have the time and capacity to self-monitor and self-regulate, thus being able to acquire more knowledge. Teachers are faced with a chicken-and-egg dilemma – should they focus on teaching pupils how to monitor and regulate their learning so that they can acquire knowledge more easily, or should they focus on teaching knowledge, which is a precursor to developing monitoring skills? This dilemma is summed up by Resnick (1989, p. 2): 'Is it possible to teach reasoning without knowledge or knowledge without reasoning? If not, if the two are inextricably linked, how is it possible to break the cycle in which the knowledge-rich become still richer and the knowledge-poor remain poor?'

Cognitive learning strategies

Pupils who have limited knowledge when they arrive at school, or when they transfer to secondary school, have *ipso facto* shown that they do not have the strategies to acquire knowledge quickly. However, these strategies are dependent on their present knowledge. They are therefore in a vicious circle, where their lack of present knowledge limits their acquisition of more knowledge. One of the promises of cognitive learning strategies is to give pupils a way to break out of this cycle.

It is helpful to divide pupils' cognitive learning strategies into two areas, although the distinction between the two is not rigid:

- cognitive strategies – regulation of thinking processes;
- metacognitive strategies – planning and organizing strategies.

The cognitive and metacognitive aspects can be seen as the two 'cogs' of pupils' learning strategies (see Figure 11.1).

Underlying the cognitive learning strategies are the cognitive processes outlined in Chapter 2. It is emphasized that these are not structures in the brain but dynamic, interactive processes. At the next level, pupils can be seen to regulate the processes, though not necessarily in a planned way. The next, metacognitive level assumes

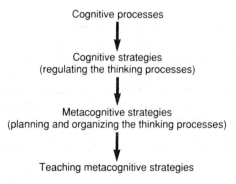

Figure 11.1 The 'cogs' of cognitive learning strategies.

that pupils have methods for planning and organizing. At the final level, teachers have means for teaching the methods for planning and organizing strategies. These 'cogs' in the learning process will be examined in the rest of the chapter.

COGNITIVE STRATEGIES: REGULATING THE THINKING PROCESSES

Pupils can regulate their cognitive processes in a number of areas (adapted from Mayer, 1987):

- *Paying attention* – the pupil actively selects some of the incoming information to pay attention to.
- *Making sense of new information* – the pupil actively makes sense of the information and transforms it in the working memory.
- *Building internal connections* – the pupil actively builds, organizes and structures internal connections that hold the information together.
- *Building external connections* – the pupil actively retrieves information from the long-term memory. This prior knowledge can then be connected to the incoming information so that the latter is remembered.

Whether a teaching strategy is successful will depend on how the pupil processes the task. If he does not pay attention, learning cannot occur; if he pays attention but the information is not meaningful, he can learn only by rote. It is only if internal connections are made that the new information can be transformed so that it can be used in new situations. Finally, only if there is a process by which the pupil can retrieve information will it be useful at a later date.

Paying attention to incoming information

Pupils can attend to only a very limited number of the demands that compete for their attention in the classroom. They can give their attention to what the teacher is saying, to what is written on the paper in front of them, or to what their peers are doing. They can also attend to their own thoughts: previous or forthcoming events, dinner, the game after school, or whether they are going to be laughed at because they cannot do the work. The focus of the pupils' attention determines what information is processed. They actively decide what to attend to.

Time on task

Attention is often thought of as the time that pupils spend on task (Bennett, 1979). Studies by Peterson and her colleagues (1982, 1984) show that the time that pupils spend on task is unrelated to the pupils' own reports on how they are attending. More crucially, they found that the pupils' own reports on attention are more accurate indicators of their learning.

Pupils have different work habits and different patterns of attending. Appearing 'on task' is not necessarily the same as actually attending to the lesson. The pupil who has his head down and appears to be reading may in fact be thinking about the disco that he is going to that evening, while the pupil staring out of the window may in fact be trying to integrate what the teacher is saying with his previous knowledge.

Attention is selective

Treisman and Geffen's (1967) classic research, though very laboratory-oriented, clearly illustrates the selective nature of attention. Adults were given headphones to wear, and different stories were played through each headphone. They were asked to attend, by repeating aloud, to one of the stories while at the same time listening for key words from either story. Nearly 90 per cent of the key words in the ear attended to were identified, while in the other ear only 8 per cent of the key words were heard. The implications of the research are clear: pupils have difficulty in attending to more than one thing at a time.

Attention, however, is not an all-or-nothing phenomenon: a pupil with good literacy skills can copy off the board while at the same time listening to the teacher. Attention can be split between a number of events under some circumstances.

The complexity of the task

One of the factors that influences attention is the complexity of the task that is being attended to. The more complex the task, the greater the effort that must be put into the attention; and the task may be so complex that it uses the pupil's entire capacity for attention (Rivlin and Gravelle, 1985). Complexity is not, however, a fixed, inherent characteristic of the task, but depends on a pupil's skills. A pupil who is a fluent reader need devote only a small amount of his attention to the mechanics of a reading task; his attention can instead focus on the meaning of the text. On the other hand, a pupil who is just beginning to learn to read will need to devote a great deal of attention to the mechanics of the text – the decoding of the words. He will have very little attention left for the meaning of the material. The task is the same; both pupils are asked to read the same books. But in another way the task for the two pupils is not the same. The complexity of the task varies between the two pupils and therefore their attention is used in different ways.

Selection

A pupil's ability to select the important information to attend to is a key strategy for effective learning. Selective or discriminatory attention has been shown to underlie pupils' rates of learning. A distinguishing characteristic of gifted pupils is that they focus their attention on relevant rather than irrelevant information. Children with learning difficulties have been identified in a number of studies as not knowing what the important parts of the task are (Torgeson, 1977). So they fail to learn because they do not know which parts of the task to attend to.

Paying attention

Pupils have to focus on a specific task within a 'noisy' environment, but also, within the task, they have to select specific information that is relevant – meaningful – for them. The information that is relevant is specific to the particular pupil and relates to his prior knowledge. Teachers can only really find out whether pupils are attending by ascertaining what they are learning. Staring at the teacher is not necessarily the sign of an attentive pupil!

Pupils need to know when and where to pay attention in the classroom, and also what to pay attention to. The more complex teachers make this challenge, the more difficulties pupils will have in attending.

Making sense of new information

Attention is clearly in itself not sufficient for processing information. An 11-year-old pupil placed in a physics class with 18-year-olds could attend to the lesson yet not learn anything – the lesson could not be processed because it would have no meaning for the pupil. If a pupil is to understand new knowledge, it has to make connections with previous knowledge.

Orientation to the information

The way pupils' orientation underpins their understanding of new information is nicely illustrated by the research of Pichert and Anderson (1977). Three groups of pupils were asked to read a story about two boys who did not attend school. Contained within the story was a detailed description of a house and its contents. One group was asked to read the story from the perspective of a burglar, the second was asked to read the story from the perspective of a potential house buyer, and the third was not given a context within which to read it. There were significant differences between the parts of the story that were remembered. As might be expected, the 'burglar' group remembered how to enter and get out of the house as well as the location of the valuables, the 'buyer' group remembered the condition of the house, and the third group remembered the narrative story. What is remembered depends on the orientation and expectations of the pupil. A pupil's orientation to a visit to the Tower of London or to the history curriculum will be a decisive factor in what he learns from the visit.

Pupils have to make sense of new information by activating a framework to understand it. The teacher can help the pupil's orientation and expectation by focusing him on the goals of the activity.

Maintenance rehearsal strategies

To understand new material, pupils have to hold it in the working memory or store. One strategy for consciously doing this is to rehearse it. As pupils go through primary school, they are increasingly likely to use rehearsal strategies; younger infants have rehearsal strategies available, but rarely use them (Flavell, 1970). Older pupils can be seen moving their lips during learning, indicating that they are rehearsing the material. Pupils need to be taught how to use these strategies.

This type of rehearsal, where pupils repeat information to keep it alive in their working memory, is called maintenance rehearsal. If information is not rehearsed, it will rapidly decay, as it makes no connections with the long-term memory. An example in adult life is looking up a telephone number and then rehearsing it before dialling. Unfortunately, teachers will sometimes use this type of rehearsal as a method of rote learning of meaningful information; but it is highly inefficient for this purpose in the long term. Described below are other, more elaborate rehearsal strategies whereby the pupil can build internal connections for meaningful information.

205

Building internal connections

The complexity of organizing

Pupils need to decide on the level of complexity at which they will process new information. For example, a pupil who is taking notes on a lesson about Australia can process the information in a number of different ways. If he simply writes down the key words as the teacher puts them up on the board, he is working at a simplistic level; he is not making connections between this information and other knowledge that he has. On the other hand, a pupil who is making connections between this material on Australia and previous lessons on the Pacific basin is processing the information at a different level. The more elaborate, or complex, the pupil's processing of the information, the more likely he is to remember it.

The teacher can facilitate memorization by giving different examples of the same problem and making interconnections between it and the pupil's knowledge. The more the pupil tries to make meaningful the new information, the more likely he is to remember it.

Encoding specificity

Encoding specificity means that cues for remembering information are always part of the original memory. Teachers need to ensure that if information is to be remembered, then cues to its retrieval must be part of the information when it is first learnt. In other words, the context in which the material is learnt will give the pupil cues to remembering it. If pupils are expected to remember information about a historical event, placing it within a present-day context will ensure that cues from the present environment are available as an aid to memory.

Elaborative rehearsal strategies

As well as organizing and encoding material in order to make it easier to recall, pupils also need to rehearse it. There are a number of specific rehearsal strategies that are under pupils' control. These have been shown to have a clear benefit for remembering information. Though a maintenance rehearsal strategy such as repeating dates over and over will help a pupil memorize them, they are much more easily remembered if the pupil places them in a meaningful and elaborate structure. Using visual imagery (see Chapter 2) is particularly useful.

Another type of elaborative rehearsal strategy encourages the pupils to generate internal connections (Weinstein and Mayer, 1986). The pupil is asked to generate connections actively between parts of a passage or written information by writing headlines and summaries and by underlining the main points. By saying, writing or pointing to parts of the material, the pupil selects and rehearses the specific information that he wants to remember.

Mnemonics

Mnemonics are visual or auditory 'hooks' designed to help pupils remember information. They operate by pairing the new information with something that is easily remembered – the 'hook' – which gives an easy way for the information to be encoded. Different types of mnemonics are particularly suited to remembering different things.

One type is based on visual imagery. The pupil 'hooks' the things that he wants to remember by thinking of them linked together in an imaginative way. If he had to remember the equipment that he needs for a science experiment, for example, he could visualize it in the form of an ostrich; the Bunsen burner as the body, with two test tubes sticking out for legs and the pipette tube as the beak. The incongruous visual image makes the items easier to remember.

First-letter mnemonics are also very popular. Many pupils have used the mnemonic 'Every Good Boy Deserves a Favour' to help them remember the lines of the treble clef. Similarly, the mnemonic 'Richard Of York Gained Battles In Vain' makes it easy to remember the colours of the rainbow.

One of the best-researched and most effective mnemonics is the key-word method. It was originally used to help learn a second language, but it has since developed other uses. There are two stages to using it. In the first stage, the pupil focuses on one auditory part of the word he wants to remember – for example, if he wanted to remember the meaning of the word 'horoscope', he could focus on 'horo', which sounds like 'hours'. At the second stage, he would picture to himself hours on a clock face divided into the twelve signs of the zodiac. He should easily be able to imagine the large clock face and how it copes with time and uncertainty. The next time the pupil was confronted with the word 'horoscope', he would remember its meaning through the clock image.

The key-word method is not confined to remembering the meaning of words; it can also be used to remember other information.

Building external connections

Remembering depends not only on storing information but also on retrieval processes. The memory must contain executive search strategies for retrieving information.

One of the key features of the memory store is that it is organized (see Chapter 2). Pupils will try to organize information to give it structure, as it is more readily recalled like that than when it is unorganized. One clear strategy for the teacher to facilitate this is to present information in a structured way. This is the idea behind Ausubel's 'advance organizer' (see Chapter 10 for more on Ausubel), which anchors new material in previously learnt material. The teacher presents at the beginning of a lesson the key aspects of the information that is to be taught. This can be in the form of key-words, short paragraphs, diagrams or drawings. This advance organizer activates the pupils' cognitive schemata and provides a bridge between the new material and their present knowledge. Pupils who lack a basic knowledge of a topic area find their learning significantly increased if the teacher provides advance organizers (Mayer, 1979).

Advance organizers are effective only if the pupil actively uses them. The most effective are in the form of a paragraph that prefaces the material to be learnt (Dinnel and Glover, 1985). This should contain concrete examples or an analogy for the material to be learnt, and should relate the information to the pupils' present knowledge.

Selecting the appropriate strategy

There is no one best cognitive learning strategy that pupils need to use. Different strategies serve different cognitive purposes, and pupils need to use different strategies for different tasks. One may be best for remembering concepts, another for dates, and another for increasing vocabulary usage. Different strategies are most effective at different times.

In secondary schools, a significant proportion of pupils' learning comes from reading texts, whether for English, History, Geography, Science or other subjects. Pupils are required to do three distinct things with the texts that they read: Understand, Remember and Apply (URA). Levin (1986) suggests that different strategies are most useful for each of these different tasks. He entitles his model 'You're A (URA) Good Strategy User'.

Understanding strategies

Understanding is an information-processing component, based on making sense of new information by building internal connections. It can be improved by contextual analysis, whereby pupils are taught to use internal and external contextual cues to infer the meaning of unfamiliar words. By relating unfamiliar words to concepts that they already know, they improve their understanding. This strategy does not, though, help their remembering or applying.

Remembering strategies

Remembering can be improved through the use of mnemonics, which may also improve a pupil's ability to use and interpret vocabulary. So using a remembering strategy can also improve the pupil's application. Mnemonics do not, though, help understanding.

Applying through understanding strategies

The use of concrete analogies and models as critical components of advance organizers is one strategy that enhances both understanding and applying. When complex, unfamiliar concepts are metaphorically linked to familiar concepts, pupils are better able to process and apply relevant information.

This sort of analysis is just beginning to develop. Pupils need to use a series of strategies, depending on what they want to learn. Combining a concrete organizer with a mnemonic strategy will improve understanding, remembering and applying.

Some pupils learn to use cognitive strategies effectively. These are the pupils who have no difficulty understanding, remembering and applying new information. Many pupils do not, however, recognize that they control these processes, and consequently learning becomes a hit-and-miss affair. Pupils need to recognize that they have executive control over their own learning – they need to develop their own metacognitive strategies.

METACOGNITIVE STRATEGIES: PLANNING AND ORGANIZING THE THINKING PROCESSES

Of all the cognitive learning strategies, metacognition has received the most attention in the search to understand pupils' learning. Metacognition is thinking about thinking. It is being aware of one's own thinking processes and being able to plan and organize cognitive strategies. The more pupils are able to think about the strategies that they use, the more control they have over their own learning. A pupil who knows what captures his attention, whether that is a worry about home life, or a teacher's enthusiasm about biology, is one step nearer to having control over his own learning. A pupil who knows the importance of re-reading his chemistry notes and rewriting them so that they are meaningful is at a great advantage when it comes to remembering them.

A pupil's metacognitive knowledge is also useful for ascertaining any learning difficulties. If a pupil is able to describe the cognitive processes that he goes through when reading a sentence, it can

guide the teacher to the reasons why he is having difficulties with
the text.

Pupils' metacognitive strategies can be ascertained by asking them
for their thoughts during a lesson. Winne and Marx (1982) found that
there is a considerable mismatch between the teaching strategies that
teachers think are useful and the cognitive processes these trigger off
for the pupils:

- Pupils usually focus on the immediate task in front of them.
  Teachers are therefore often unsuccessful in getting pupils to
  attend to new material.
- The more instructions the teacher gives, the more likely it is that
  the pupils will become confused about what they are supposed to
  be doing, even if the task is easy.
- If the pupil has a clear strategy for doing the task, he can use this
  even if the contents are difficult.
- If the teacher's instructions are not clear, the pupils will still try
  to make sense of them. For example, if it is not made clear, pupils
  will try to guess whether the teacher wants them to understand
  or remember a piece of text.

The research shows that pupils use metacognitive strategies even
when the teacher is not facilitating their use. Pupils may, however, be
using most of their strategies to try to understand the teacher's instructions, rather than having them free to use on higher-level planning
and organizing their learning of the material.

Higher-level planning strategies

Self-control strategies

One of the earliest attempts at using metacognitive strategies was
to teach pupils how to plan to tackle a task through self-control
(Meichenbaum and Asarnow, 1979). The pupil is taught a series
of self-statements that he can use to guide his thinking. A typical
sequence is:

- problem identification, which involves defining and self-
  interrogation skills ('What is it I have to do?');
- focusing attention, which involves response guidance to self-
  inquiry ('Now, carefully stop and repeat the instructions');
- self-reinforcement, which involves goal setting and self-
  evaluation ('Good, I've finished the whole page');
- coping skills, which involve error-correction strategies ('That's
  OK . . . when I make an error I can go back and change it').

This is a self-control process for planning. Pupils can use this metacognitive strategy in a variety of situations, across a range of tasks and
people.

Metacognitive learning strategies

The metacognitive strategies that pupils use are key factors for effective learning, and teaching them to pupils is one of the key strategies for effective teachers. There are two aims for teaching:

- teaching pupils specific knowledge, skills and attitudes;
- teaching pupils how to learn.

Successful pupils are those who have learned how to select strategies. Unsuccessful pupils have no strategies for learning and therefore no way to break out of the vicious circle of failure unless the teacher helps them. Teachers need teaching strategies to teach learning strategies to pupils.

Comprehension monitoring strategy

Metacognitive strategies can also be used in specific situations. A metacognitive strategy has been designed for improving comprehension (Palinscar and Brown, 1989) by using four basic strategic activities when reading:

- questioning ('Can this strategy be used with psychology books?');
- clarifying ('I need to check how this ties in with cognitive schemata');
- summarizing ('So there are a number of specific examples of cognitive strategies');
- predicting ('I need to understand how these can be taught').

These four strategies are used by pupils who have good comprehension, but not by pupils with poor comprehension. Pupils can be taught to use these strategies when they are reading texts.

The four strategies work at two levels: they improve comprehension, and they also allow the pupil to monitor his understanding. If, for example, the pupil cannot summarize the text, it alerts him to the fact that he does not comprehend it. The strategies therefore have an internal feedback loop which ensures the pupils understand the text.

Problem-solving strategy for mathematics

A different set of metacognitive strategies is available for solving mathematical tasks (Peterson *et al.*, 1982, 1984). These are:

- checking answers;
- applying information;

- going back and reworking problems;
- re-reading directions;
- relating new information to prior knowledge;
- asking for help;
- motivating oneself.

Pupils who use these strategies are more successful at mathematical tasks than pupils who do not.

TEACHING METACOGNITIVE STRATEGIES

In the last decade, there have been a number of programmes designed to teach metacognitive learning strategies. The most interesting of these is reciprocal teaching. This pulls together a number of key points that have been made in this book.

Reciprocal teaching is based on Vygotsky's theories for the development of thinking (see Chapter 3). For Vygotsky, thinking depends on speech and is developed and maintained by interpersonal experiences. So teaching, as the basis for interpersonal experiences in the classroom, is of fundamental importance to the development of thinking. Learning involves at least two people, the teacher and the pupil, and it is naive to look at either in a vacuum. Vygotsky describes learning as the transfer of responsibility from the teacher to the pupil for reaching a particular goal. 'Responsibility' is to be understood not in any moral sense of the word but rather in terms of the active participants in the process. The teacher actively starts the process, but unless the pupil takes it up in an active way, then learning will not occur.

Zone of proximal development

The venue for this transfer of responsibility Vygotsky calls the zone of proximal development (ZPD). The lower limit of the zone is the level of skills reached by the pupil when working independently. The upper limit is the level of skills the pupil can currently reach with the help of the teacher. It is useful to think of the ZPD as the 'scaffolding' system that the pupil can use to build his learning. This scaffolding is an area of learning potential. As such it gives a completely new perspective on the concept of ability or intelligence, as the ZPD does not belong to the pupil. Since learning is interpersonal and depends on the teacher and the pupil, so the ZPD is interpersonal and is 'shared' between them. It depends on the skills of both.

The scaffolding is specific to a particular area of learning; for example, an area of mathematics. The scaffolding for a particular area is identified and mapped out through the dynamic interaction between the teacher and the pupil. The teacher selects a particular goal and finds how much or what parts of it the pupil knows or can do unaided.

She then, through prompts and demonstrations, tries to ascertain how much the pupil can achieve with her assistance. The more he can do with her help, the greater the ZPD in that area. So the size of the scaffolding is relative not only to the task but also to the skills of the teacher, as well as those of the pupil.

Teaching should start at the top of the scaffolding – that is, where the teacher takes most responsibility and is most involved with the pupil. Through giving the maximum amount of help, demonstrating and prompting, the teacher draws the pupil into the task. As he learns to achieve this goal unaided, the responsibility for learning gradually shifts to the pupil, who takes greater and greater responsibility for the task until he can do it without any help from the teacher. At this point, the teacher's responsibility is to explore the boundaries of a new ZPD – to build the scaffold upwards, once again starting teaching at the point where the pupil needs the most help, to move him up towards the new goal. The teacher's job is to provide an expert scaffolding that the pupil can climb up.

Reciprocal teaching

This reciprocal teaching takes place not only between the teacher and the pupil but also between the pupil and his peers. This is a development of cooperative learning (see Chapter 9). If pupils work together, each contributes his knowledge and each gains from the contribution of others more skilled. Cooperating on a complex task makes it more manageable without actually simplifying it.

An excellent example of such a cooperative reciprocal teaching programme is Palinscar and Brown's (1984) teaching of reading comprehension. They were interested in discovering whether Vygotsky's methods of reciprocal teaching could be applied to teaching reading comprehension. They focused on seventh-grade pupils who had poor reading skills – reading ages over 2.5 years behind the norm. The pupils were taught specific reading skills and also a set of metacognitive learning strategies for monitoring their reading. These are as previously described: questioning, clarifying, summarizing and predicting.

Palinscar and Brown used a reciprocal teaching method specifically based on Vygotsky, with the teacher using prompting, demonstrating and modelling techniques to move the pupil towards the goal. There are three major components of the teaching strategy:

- instruction and practice of metacognitive learning strategies in the course of reading a text;
- provision, initially by the teacher, of an expert model of these metacognitive strategies;
- a cooperative setting for learning – pupils took turns in leading the group. This approach supports Vygotsky's belief that teaching

is a shared, reciprocal process. The group extends the breadth of thinking by exposing the pupil to alternative points of view that challenge and clarify the learning process.

The procedure is simple: The teacher initially provides expert guidance, then the pupils in the group take turns in leading a discussion on a particular text. The leader starts the discussion by asking a question on the main contents of the text, then ends by summarizing it. If there is disagreement about the contents, the group members re-read and discuss the areas of difference. They ask questions and use summary statements until they reach agreement.

Pupils who have been taught to use these metacognitive learning strategies using reciprocal teaching show remarkable progress. In Palinscar and Brown's (1984) research they made an average gain of 15 months in their comprehension skills after 3 months of teaching.

It is interesting to note that though reciprocal teaching and direct instruction originate from very different psychological perspectives, there are similarities between the two approaches. Both use an expert model and gradually transfer the responsibility for learning from the teacher to the pupil. The two approaches differ in so far as direct instruction's goal is the mastery of specific areas of knowledge or skills, whereas reciprocal teaching emphasizes the learning of process skills.

Reciprocal teaching

The reciprocal teaching perspective answers some of the difficulties inherent in the view that teaching is something that teachers do to pupils. It reaffirms that it is the teacher's interaction with the pupil that is the crucial aspect of teaching. Not only does the task have to be analysed for the appropriate teaching strategies, but also the pupil's learning strategies have to be understood.

This has important implications for teachers. There has been a tendency in the last few years to believe that teaching can be made 'teacher-proof'. There often appears to be a belief that someone who is knowledgeable about a subject area – the curriculum – can quickly learn how to teach it. This trend has overemphasized the importance of the curriculum as the basis for effective teaching. The implication of reciprocal teaching is that teaching is much more complex than that: teachers have to interact with the pupils in order to understand their cognitive learning strategies if they are to teach the curriculum.

SUMMARY

The key to effective teaching is to develop flexible 'contingency' strategies for teaching based on the particular situation. A contingency strategy emphasizes that there are no simple generalizations that can be made about pupils' learning. If, however, the teacher can spell out enough about the people in the situation – both herself and the pupils – the task that they are faced with and the organization of the classroom and school, then she can begin to make propositions about how learning can be facilitated. Such propositions might be along the lines of: 'If I, a skilled reading teacher, am given a settled class with a number of pupils with no functional reading skills, my initial strategy should be to improve basic reading skills, through direct instruction, in order to improve their access to the curriculum.' A change in any of the factors above is likely to affect the effectiveness of the strategy. What a contingency strategy emphasizes is that there are no simple answers to the complexity of the real world of the classroom.

The recognition that successful learning depends on the development of pupils' learning strategies, as well as an analysis of the task and the teaching strategies, is a valuable if complex perspective. The swing from the use of within-pupil variables to explain educational progress in the first half of the century, to the search for teaching and curriculum strategies in the last few decades, is gradually beginning to settle into a more appropriate, interactive perspective.

There is a recognition that successful learning depends on the interaction between the teacher and the pupil. Teaching strategies cannot be prescribed in a vacuum; nor are pupils simply good at modern languages or mathematics (let alone the old concept of simply stupid or clever); instead, it is recognized that the strategies that pupils bring to learning can be developed. Pupils' learning cannot simply be focused in their heads, but rather is an interactive transfer of responsibility between the teacher and each pupil.

For Vygotsky, there was no difference between 'teaching' and 'learning'. In Russian a single word, 'obuchenie', means both. Once again, the constraints in thinking about education are based on the limits and structure of language. Maybe some new words that encapsulate the concept of interaction between the pupil and the teacher, as based on their own but also shared worlds, would help clarify what education is really about.

REFERENCES

Barnes, B. and Clawson, E. (1975) Do advance organizers facilitate learning? Recommendations for further research based on analysis of 32 studies, *Review of Educational Research* **45**, pp. 637-59.

Bennett, N. (1979) Recent research on teaching: a dream, a belief, and a model, in Bennett, N. and McNamara, D., *Focus on Teaching*. Harlow: Longman.

Brown, A. and Palinscar, A. (1989) Guided, cooperative learning and individual knowledge acquisition, in Resnick, L. (ed.), *Knowing, Learning and Instruction*. Hillsdale, NJ: Erlbaum.

Dinnel, D. and Glover, J. (1985) Advance organisers: encoding manipulations, *Journal of Educational Psychology* 77, pp. 514–21.

Flavell, J. (1970) Developmental studies of mediated memory, in Reeves, H. and Lipsitt, P. (eds), *Advances in Child Development and Behaviour*, Vol. 5. New York: Academic Press.

Galton, M. and Simon, B. (1980) *Progress and Performance in the Primary Classroom*. London: Routledge & Kegan Paul.

Glaser, R. (1990) The reemergence of learning theory within instructional research, *American Psychologist* 45, pp. 29–39.

Levin, J. (1986) Educational applications of mnemonic pictures: possibilities beyond your wildest imagination, in Sheikh, A. (ed.), *Imagery in the Educational Process*. Farmingdale, NY: Baywood.

Mayer, R. (1979) Twenty years of research on advance organisers: assimilation theory is still the best predictor of results, *Instructional Science* 8, pp. 133–67.

Mayer, R. (1987) *Educational Psychology: A Cognitive Approach*. Boston, MA: Little, Brown.

Meichenbaum, D. and Asarnow, J. (1979) Cognitive–Behaviour modification and metacognitive development: implications for the classroom, in Kendall, P. and Hollon, S. (eds), *Cognitive-Behavioural Interventions: Theory, Research and Procedures*. New York: Academic Press.

Palinscar, A. and Brown, A. (1984) Reciprocal teaching of comprehension-fostering and comprehension-monitoring activities, *Cognition and Instruction* 1, pp. 117–75.

Peterson, P., Swing, S., Braverman, M. and Buss, R. (1982) Student aptitudes and their reports of cognitive processes during direct instruction, *Journal of Educational Psychology* 74, pp. 535–47.

Peterson, P., Swing, S., Stark, K. and Wass, G. (1984) Students' cognition and time on task during mathematics instruction, *American Educational Research Journal* 21, pp. 487–515.

Pichert, J. and Anderson, R. (1977) Taking different perspectives on a story, *Journal of Educational Psychology* 69, pp. 309–15.

Resnick, L. (1989) *Knowing, Learning and Instruction*. Hillsdale, NJ: Erlbaum.

Rivlin, R. and Gravelle, K. (1985) *Deciphering the Senses: The Expanding World of Human Perception*. New York: Simon & Schuster.

Torgeson, J. (1977) Memorization processes in reading-disabled children, *Journal of Educational Psychology* 69, pp. 571–8.

Treisman, A. and Geffen, G. (1967) Selective attention: perception or response?, *Quarterly Journal of Experimental Psychology* **19**, pp. 1–17.

Weinstein, C. and Mayer, R. (1986) The teaching of learning strategies, in Wittrock, M. (ed.), *The Handbook of Research on Teaching*. 3rd edition. New York: Macmillan.

Winne, P. and Marx, R. (1982) Students' and teachers' views of thinking processes involved in classroom learning, *Elementary School Journal* **82**, pp. 493–518.

Wittrock, M. (1986) Students' thought processes, in Wittrock, M. (ed.), *The Handbook of Research on Teaching*. 3rd edition. New York: Macmillan.

RECOMMENDED READING

J. Glover, R. Ronning and R. Brunning, *Cognitive Psychology for Teachers* (New York: Macmillan, 1990), is an excellent introduction to cognitive psychology for teachers, and particularly to the regulation of cognitive processes and their implications.

R. Mayer, *Educational Psychology: A Cognitive Approach* (Boston, MA: Little, Brown, 1987), gives a detailed guide to cognitive psychology in education, and in particular in the teaching process.

L. Resnick (ed.), *Knowing, Learning and Instruction* (Hillsdale, NJ: Erlbaum, 1989), contains a selection of important papers on reciprocal teaching and metacognitive learning.

NAME INDEX

Note: Page numbers in **bold** type refer to figures and page numbers in *italic* type refer to brief biographical notes about the individual concerned.

Abramson, L. 136
Adams, S. 114
Adorno, T. 93
Ajzen, I. 99
Alderfer, C. **109**, 110, 111, 165
Anderson, J. *36*, 36–8, 45, 53, 181, 195–6
Anderson, R. 205
Argyris, C. 2
Arvey, R. 149
Asarnow, J. 210
Atkinson, R. 31
Ausubel, D. 167–8, 188–90, *189*, 192, 208

Bandura, A. 24–6, *25*, 95
Barnett, W. (Berruta-Clement et al.) 56
Barrett, K. (Campos et al.) 77
Baron, R. 107–8
Bar-Tal, D. 130
Beck, A. 20
Becker, W. 186

Bennett, N. 203
Bernstein, B. 62
Berruta-Clement, J. 56
Binet, A. 38–9, 48
Blake, R. 144–5
Block, J. 185
Bloom, B. 184
Boldsmith, H. (Campos et al.) 77
Bowlby, J. 48, 73, *75*, 75–6, 81
Braverman, M. (Peterson et al.) 203, 211
Brehm, S. 102
Bronfenbrenner, U. 48, 78–80, **79**, 82
Brophy, J. 132, 147
Brown, A. 211, 213–14
Bruner, J. 56, *181*, 181–3, 192
Bull, S. 187
Burns, R. 14
Burt, C. 40
Buss, R. (Peterson et al.) 203, 211

Cacioppo, J. T. 96–8

Campos, J. 77
Cattell, R. 68–71, *69*
Cecil, M. 137
Cicchetti, D. 81
Clarke, A. 77
Clarke, A. 77
Clifford, M. 90
Cohen, L. 154
Coopersmith, S. 66–7
Croll, P. (Galton *et al.*) 169

Dale, J. 56
Dansereau, F. 153
Darley, B. 91–2
Davis, G. (Arvey *et al.*) 149
Davis, K. 128
Department of Education and Science 169
Dinnel, D. 208
Dixon, R. 187
Doyle, W. 156
Dunphy, D. 164
Dweck, C. 137–8

Egan, G. 146
Eiser, R. 88, 101
Elliot, S. 171–2
Ellis, A. 20
Engelmann, S. 186, 187
Epstein, A. (Berruta-Clement *et al.*) 56

Farr, R. 128
Feigenbaum, R. (Johnson *et al.*) 130
Feldman, D. C. 175–6
Festinger, L. 100
Fiedler, F. 153
Fishbein, M. 99
Flavell, J. 54, 205
Forness, S. 14
French, J. 148–51

Frenkel-Brunswick, E. (Adorno *et al.*) 93
Freud, S. 48, 71–5, *72*, 81
Furth, H. 56

Gagne, R. 187–8, *188*, 192
Galton, M. 169
Geffen, G. 203
Geir, J. 152
Gershenfeld, M. 165–6
Glaser, R. 200
Glasser, W. 155
Glover, J. 208
Good, T. 132, 147
Graen, G. 153
Gravelle, K. 203
Green, A. 97
Gross, P. 91–2
Guildford, J. 40

Haga, B. (Dansereau *et al.*) 153
Hamner, W. 112–13
Handy, C. 151
Hannah, M. 96
Hargreaves, D. 89, 167
Harper, R. 20
Harris, M. J. R. 133
Harvery, J. H. 127
Harvey, O. (Sherif *et al.*) 166
Heider, F. 125–6, *126*
Heilman, M. 90
Herzberg, F. **109**, 110–12
Hiroto, D. 135
Hood, W. (Sherif *et al.*) 166

Ichheiser, G. 128–31

Jacobson, L. 132–3
Jensen, A. 51
Johnson, D. *168*, 168, 170, 173
Johnson, R. *168*, 168, 170, 173

Subject index

Note: Page numbers in **bold** type refer to figures and page numbers in *italic* type refer to boxed text.

'is learnt' proposition *12*, 12–13, 16
self-oriented 174
teacher attributions of 125–8, *126*, **127**
understanding 9–11, **10**, *10*, **11**
behavioural psychology 9–16, 24, 26, 73
American 58
implications for teachers 16
Russian 58–60
behavioural teaching strategies 183–8, **185**, 196
beliefs **22**, 22–4
Binet–Simon Intelligence Test 38–9
bullying 15, 149

careers perception 61
categorization process 89–91
challenges 80–2
chiasms 70
child development 47–8
early experiences 71–5, 75–8, 77
child-rearing practices 66–7, 73
classroom management 138–9, 143– 61, 168–9
and behaviour antecedents **11**, 11–12, 16
key skills 147
leadership 152–4
making strategies work 148–52
routines 156
cliques 164
coercive power 149
cognitive capacity 40
cognitive development 62–3
Piaget's influence 52–7
application 56–7
development stages 53–5
validity 55–7
cognitive dissonance theory 100–2
cognitive involvement 98

cognitive learning strategies 200–14, **201**, *201*
cognitive strategies **201**, 201, 202–9
metacognitive strategies **201**, 201–2, 209–12
teaching 212–14
selecting appropriate *208*
cognitive psychology 17–20, 24, 26, 28–46
cognitive teaching strategies 180–3, 196
cognitive–behavioural approach 20–6
implications for teachers 23–4
and the unconscious 73
cohesion and competition 166–8
competence
development 80–2, *81*
social 43
competency-based education 185
competition and cohesion 166–8
competitive learning 168–70
componential subtheory of intelligence 44–5
composition 196
comprehension monitoring strategy 211
concepts 194
conceptualism, instrumental 181
concern
for pupils 146–7, 159
for task 147–8, 159
v. pupils 143–8, **144**, *144*
congruity principle 93
constructive alternatism 67–8
constructs 43
pupil 17–20, *18*
teacher 19
contextual subtheory of intelligence 42–3
contingency theory 3, 215
contract, psychological 157–9, *158*

gangs 164
genuineness 146–7
goal setting *121*, 121–3, 137–8
grant-maintained schools 41
group dynamics 162, 163, 174–7
groups
    pupil need for 164–6, *165*
    see also working in groups
guided discovery 187–8, 192, 195

halo effect 90
Head Start programme 50–1, 186
helplessness, learnt 135–6, 138
High/Scope training programme 56
Hindu beliefs 129

ideal pupil 89–90, *90*
    and physical attractiveness 90–1
ignorance 93–4
imaginal memory 59
implicit theories of intelligence 43
incentive schemes 120–1, 123
individualistic learning 169
influence 148, 159
    v. power **151**, 151–2
information
    imaginal 32–3
    making sense of new 204–5
    paying attention to 202–4
    processing 206
    retrieving 207–9
    selection 204
    verbal 32–3
information-processing models
    of intelligence 41–5
    of thinking *29*, 29–32
instrumental conceptualism 181
intelligence
    concept *38*, 38–41, 45
    information-processing models 41–5

signs 43
tests 28–9, 38–9, 40, 44, 50
    criticisms 41
IQ (intelligence quotient) 38, 39, 43
    in Head Start programme 50–1
    see above intelligence: tests

jigsaw learning 171–2
job design 119–20, 123

knowledge
    acquisition components 44
    declarative 33–5
    development 193
    learning 195–6
    procedural 33
    teaching strategies **194**
    type and teaching style 193–5

language 182
    development 55, 63
    theory 60–2, *61*, 67
    and thought 57–62
leadership 153–4, *154*, 159
learning
    difficulties 135
    goals 136–7
    meaningful reception 188–90, *190*, 192
    successful 215
learning strategies 199–217
    learning together 172
    understanding 200–2
    see also cognitive learning strategies
learnt helplessness 135–6, 138
linguistic relativity and determinism theory (Whorf) 60–2, *61*, 67
long-term memory 32–6
love, unconditional 66
'lumpers' 39–40

maintenance rehearsal strategies
205, 206
management by objectives (MBO)
122
mastery learning 184–5
mathematics 188, 211–12
meaningful reception learning 188–90, *190*, 192
memory
imaginal 32–3
long-term 32–6
network model 36–8, 45
verbal 32–3
working of 35–6
mental ages 39
mental operations development
54–5
metacognitive learning strategies
45, 209–12, *211–12*
teaching 212–14
mind, social construction of 58
misbehaviour *157*
mnemonics 207, 209
monitoring skills 200
mothers 77
motivation
concept *107*, 107–8
pupil 134, **135**
teacher 106–24
external factors 112–14
internal factors 108–12
school systems 119–23
social factors 114–16
v. performance 118

National Curriculum (England
and Wales) 48, 117, 150, 185,
192–3
nature/nurture debate 49–52
need theories 108–12, **109**, 123
for groups 164–6, *165*
neo-behavioural perspectives
187–8
network model of memory 36–8,
37, 45

9,9 Managerial Style Grid 144–5

object permanence 53–4
objectives, teaching to 184–5,
192
organismic approach 80

paying attention 202–4, *204*
peer groups 163–4, 165–6, 167
perception 30–1, 35
performance
components 44
goals 137
indicators 185
v. motivation 118
personal construct psychology
17–19, 67, 68–9
implications for teachers 19–20
personality
development 65–83
testing 70–1
traits 68–71, **69**
implications for teachers
70–1
inferred 128
for leadership 152
unity of 129
phenomenological approach (to
self) 67–8, *68*
physical attractiveness 90–1
physiological needs 109
Piagetian theory 52–63
principles for teachers *57*
planning 210
Plowden Report (1967) 169
points system 14
position power 150
power
pupil *151*
teacher 148–51, 153, 159
v. influence **151**, 151–2
prejudice 87, 92–6, *94*, 103
psychological theories 93–5
racial 95–6, 98, 103